SAINTS + SINNERS
2014

NEW FICTION
FROM THE FESTIVAL

edited by

Amie M. Evans and Paul J. Willis

2014

SAINTS + SINNERS 2014:
NEW FICTION FROM THE FESTIVAL

© 2014 BY SAINTS & SINNERS LITERARY FESTIVAL. ALL RIGHTS RESERVED.

ISBN 13: 978-1-62639-159-8

THIS TRADE PAPERBACK ORIGINAL IS PUBLISHED BY
BOLD STROKES BOOKS, INC.
P.O. BOX 249
VALLEY FALLS, NY 12185

FIRST EDITION: MAY 2014

CREDITS
EDITORS: AMIE M. EVANS AND PAUL J. WILLIS
PRODUCTION DESIGN: SUSAN RAMUNDO
COVER DESIGN: SANDY BARTEL

From *The Days of Good Looks: The Prose and Poetry of Cheryl Clarke, 1980 to 2005* by Cheryl Clarke, copyright © 2006. Reprinted by permission of Da Capo Press, a member of the Perseus Books Group.

SAINTS + SINNERS
2014

NEW FICTION
FROM THE FESTIVAL

Acknowledgments

We'd like to thank:

The John B. Harter Charitable Trust for their continued support of the contest and anthology as well as the Festival.

Radclyffe & Bold Strokes Books for their continued support of the Festival.

Sandy Bartel for her fabulous cover design.

Jewelle Gomez for serving as this year's final judge.

Everyone who has entered the contest and/or attended the festival over the last 11 years for their help in keeping the written LGBT word alive.

Greg Herren and Wendy Stone for supporting us in countless ways during our endless projects.

Dedicated to the memory of Michel G. Delhaise for his support and devotion to the arts and his community.

Contents

INTRODUCTION

"So...don't be taken in your sleep now. /Call your assailant's name now./...Leave signs of struggle. /Leave signs of triumph. /And leave signs."

—Cheryl Clarke

Those lines are from the poem "Living as a Lesbian Underground: A Futuristic Fantasy" which was published by Perseus Books Group in *The Days of Good Looks: The Prose and Poetry of Cheryl Clarke, 1980 to 2005*, a collection of Cheryl Clarke's poetry, in 2006. The admonition to 'leave signs' calls to mind the instructions provided for escaping slaves to aid others making their way to freedom. It's also a call to action for any group seeking to survive the domination of a colonizing culture.

At the time Clarke's poem was published seeing the word 'lesbian' in a book title was a rare occurrence (still true) and the number of queer writers—especially lesbian writers—found on bookstore shelves (remember them) was still relatively small. More than twenty years later queer writers are everywhere, at least on the internet, if not in print; and it's a relief to know that so many writers heeded her advice. The pieces included here in this anthology are the signs we leave for each other to help us find our way to full and free lives. They are the footprints, the bent twigs, the strips of fabric hidden in tree branches for us to savor, knowing others have come before us.

Of course the stories we write are an urgent, personal expression of some idea or emotion we're driven to express; but they are also signals as visible as the Batman sign projected in the sky. From the stories we learn how others have survived and even better, surpassed the impediments that lay in the paths of queer people like unearthed boulders that have rolled down a steep mountain to block a narrow, cliff-side path.

The emergence of Saints and Sinners in New Orleans as the signature conference for queer writers is one of the most valuable events in queer literary history and goes a long way toward helping overcome those impediments that might block our paths. Saints and Sinners is a welcoming path for all of us who at some time doubt ourselves as writers, or wonder who'll be interested in our work, or long to connect with other queer writers. Gathering queer writers together in one of this country's most seductive and sensuous cities provides a vital spark to our writing community. The event draws on the deep and complex history of New Orleans to strengthen our connections with the city and with each other. And the stories in this collection reflect that complexity and connection we feel with each other. I still want to see more people of color coming to the festival and submitting work for the anthology (something I hope to help with next year). That said I was excited to sit down with the collection and read the 'signs'.

The winner of the competition, "Corset," was an easy choice for me. I'm a corset fan myself and as a feminist I've been intrigued with the evolution of that undergarment from a device of torture to one of seduction. More importantly in the story the author, Sally Bellerose, explores how we fight addiction and how we stay in a long-term relationship, using both the humor and the anxiety that are inherent in both situations. Her characters are full and rich; I can sense the years they've spent together…from the proprietor of the Chinese restaurant, to the poker players, to the lovers. The story's twist and how it's used by one of the lovers is an example of the kind of writing we can all aspire to.

The two runners up are more edgy and one represents a speculative fiction sensibility that threads through many of the stories. James Russell's "Voodoo John" is a chilling morality tale that captures a kind of gay ideal and takes it to the outrageous extreme. The essence of New Orleans cloaks the story like an ominous fog which you know is hiding something in plain sight.

"Love Thy Neighbor" by N.S. Beranek offers up an alternative view of family with the sharp reality that has cut many of us. Her story is of a divorced father in a small town maneuvering his responsibility to his daughter and the danger of living with his never-married lover. It is pitch-perfect.

The other stories—from a lesbian retelling of a children's fable to the revelation of living Christmas tree ornaments—are each their own sign. They each open up new queer worlds to us and remind us how far we've come and show us ways of going forward.

We are a hugely varied community; still much of the world sees us as a monolith, either dangerous or at least unknowable. Even queers in isolation often don't know how to move beyond the narrow confines and beliefs of the communities into which they were born. Queers themselves can carry as many prejudices and as much misinformation as others who don't know us.

These stories dismantle that bleak monolith and further the work of the Saints and Sinners Festival which is the home we find our way to when we follow the signs.

—Jewelle Gomez, 2014

Runner-up

VOODOO JOHN
JAMES RUSSELL

Jack didn't believe in flaws. A thing is either whole or broken.

Jack believed in what he could see, and he loved what he saw in this particular floor-to-ceiling mirror. He was in the locker room of the Hotel Monteleone's gym, flexing for himself.

There were no flaws. None. His torso was a capital V. His face was dark, sharp, and toned. His legs had equine muscularity—they looked like they could hurtle the Mississippi.

Wait. Back to the face. No.

Jack handled it carefully, surgically. He took two Q-tips from the complimentary basket of health and beauty aids. He leaned toward the mirror. He pressed the sides, gently. The blackhead came out clean. Jack rinsed it down the sink, making sure it didn't fall onto some other part of him, spreading its foulness.

He surveyed the damage. The pore itself was left gaping. He knew better than to clean it with soap—that would only gunk it up worse. He headed outside to the pool. Chlorine would dry the area, close it up. Then he could moisturize.

Jack dove into the pool. The Hotel Monteleone's rooftop pool was one of his favorite haunts in New Orleans' notorious dead of summer. A good swim and sun-delivered vitamin D was what his broken skin needed. A nap after his swim would ease his mind. Stress clogs pores, creates blemishes. Blemishes create more stress. You have to break the cycle.

As he swam, Jack took in the sights through his goggles. The bottom of the pool was that perfect shade of barely-there blue, sleek as snakes. He went under to touch it. No bumps. No scratches in the lining. He turned on his back. White sunlight tangoed across the surface of the pool. His clockwork muscularity let Jack glide with the ease of a predatory fish.

Flawless.

When his swim was done, Jack walked to his recliner, dripping. The only other person poolside was a kid in a Hotel Monteleone polo, folding towels to look busy. He was a pretty young thing: trim, bright-eyed, and tanned. Probably a Tulane kid working his way through a party summer. Jack caught his glance and smiled. The kid's eyes lit up. He had a Tom Sawyer grin.

Of course he did. Jack didn't say a word. Jack walked to the locker room, knowing the kid would follow.

Time to share his gift.

❖

The physical exchange went smoothly, with Jack, it always did. But then the kid had to mess it up. Some lame joke about not expecting a ring. Jack watched in horror as the kid took a Hotel Monteleone post-it and a pen out of his pocket. He clicked the pen open like a switchblade. He wrote his phone number and e-mail address meticulously on the post-it using the locker room sink as a desk.

He handed it to Jack, like a terrorist handing the flight attendant a bomb threat.

The kid did his grin. This part made Jack feel invaded.

Jack smiled charitably. He put the post-it in his gym bag while the kid was still looking.

"Later," the kid said.

"Goodbye."

Jack showered and changed. He returned to the mirror and got to work with hands and gel, until his hair was carefully arranged to look casually thrown together.

He took the elevator down to the lobby. He treated himself to a whiskey on the rocks at the Carousel Bar. He was thankful the heat was keeping the tourists at a minimum. The only times he ever left town were during Mardi Gras and French Quarter Fest.

Jack finished his drink and left. He walked two blocks. He threw the towel boy's post-it in a public trash bin. He saw it land next to some plastic beads and a disposable hurricane cup.

That was the thing about flaws. Tulane kid was perfect, head-to-toe. And then the unwanted sharing, the desperation it revealed. The flaws he couldn't see ahead of time, the intangible ones, those were Jack's least favorite.

Jack pushed that thought out of mind as he walked Royal. It was nice, not having to navigate a mob, but the afternoon heat was giving his antiperspirant fits. He already felt a trickle down his side. Seeing an ATM, he slowed his pace. This time of day, Jack always checked his trust fund. He waited behind a fat, slurring, red-faced tourist, struggling for her ATM card and balancing a plastic yard glass. She must've wandered from the hetero stretch of Bourbon Street.

"Can I help you with that?" Jack asked.

"Aren't you a doll?" the woman beamed. "Thanks, but I'll manage." Jack smiled. He looked at the tourist's melting drink. He imagined his whiskey buzz trickling out of him, as another sweat drop raced down his side.

He passed the time thinking of phrases for the woman: Bulbous rube. Mountainous hick. Gigantic bumpkin.

She finally finished. He checked his trust. It was there. He had received his regular deposit.

Why not celebrate at the Bourbon Pub? Jack turned the corner at Royal and St. Anne's and picked up his pace.

It was dark and cool inside Bourbon. Jack had arrived just in time. He was dangerously close to sweating from his walk. The regular crowd was there. That was nice. They knew how to worship him.

Bartender Dave greeted him with his standard big hug and kiss. Art Gallery Josh grunted an obligatory "Hi". Someone next to him waved awkwardly.

"White Russian?" Dave asked.

"Why not?" Jack replied.

"Coming from your swim?" Dave eyed Jack's torso.

"Of course he is," Art Gallery Josh groaned. "He only has the one day. He just keeps re-living it while the rest of us go to work."

"It's a perfect day. I swim and drink. I eat and fuck," Jack countered.

"Like an alligator in a whole world of swamp," Josh muttered.

Jack smiled. Josh's contempt was just as gratifying as Dave's affection. Maybe more so.

"Jealous?" Jack asked Josh.

"Completely!"

Bartender Dave laughed and got busy mixing. He brushed Jack's hand with his finger when he brought the drink. Then he winked. Dave flirted with everyone for tips, but Jack knew his tell. He winked like an eighties porn star when he was doing it for real.

Too bad. That move could make a hard dick into a leaky balloon. Dave would've had a good game otherwise. Jack thought about using his moves on Dave sometimes. One of those good guys you could cuddle up to, settle down with, if that was your thing. But there was this weird transaction going on between his eyebrows. Not a unibrow, just this broken bridge of hairs that dotted across. It was like lefty and righty were reaching out for one another.

Dave was fun. He made great drinks. Fantastic conversationalist. But those brows and that wink...a thing is either whole or broken. Jack sipped his drink. That, at least, was flawless.

Art Gallery Josh was chatting up a storm. Unfortunate facial hair. Queeny. Talked with his hands like an Italian grandmother. When he wasn't milking Josh for contempt, Jack ignored him like promotional mail.

But today Josh had a tourist at his hip—the one who'd waved awkwardly when Jack walked in. Now the tourist was sneaking casual peeks in Jack's direction.

Shy type. Always good for a snack. Jack listened, collecting data.

Bill. A schoolteacher. Jack scanned him. Fine head of curls. Hazel eyes. Light-skinned but not sickly. A little uptight. Jack could tell by how he stood next to a perfectly good bar stool, clenching his butt cheeks.

Bill caught Jack's eyes and smirked. Art Gallery Josh spotted Jack's scan.

"You are *not* going home with this one!" he said to Bill. "Jack is the biggest heartbreaker in the quarter!"

Jack grabbed himself. "The biggest," he confirmed. Bill laughed. And blushed. As he sipped his beer, his eyes followed Jack's hand.

"He's a *pig*! You are *not* going home with him."

Jack turned to Bill. "Free tour. Just you and me. I can give you the locals' experience."

Bill smiled. He had dimples.

"Okay."

"Oh for fuck's sake…"

Two drinks later, Bill left with him. But first, a stop at Voodoo John's. Tourists love it, Jack knew. And Jack had a tourist tucked under his arm.

Turned out, Bill couldn't hold his liquor.

There was this old man in a red rocking chair, always sitting just inside the front door of Voodoo John's. A sway-walking Bill almost fell in his lap.

"Mm sorry," Bill said.

The old man never even looked up. Jack was pretty sure he was senile, staring through the shelves of figurines, looking into his own past.

"Just go," Jack said to Bill.

"Kay."

Jack couldn't stand to look at the old man too long. In general, he hated seeing old people—the inevitabilities they reminded him of. But there was something about this one in particular. He mumbled, low and foreboding, incomprehensible. His face wasn't just wrinkled, it looked parched, cracked. He always seemed troubled and dazed, like there was some vital task he'd forgotten.

"Zat Voodoo John?" Bill slurred. The old man's lips quivered, but for now, no noise.

"No," Jack explained. "Actually, I have no idea who Voodoo John is. The guy who runs the place is named Nelson."

Nelson emerged from a beaded curtain behind the register. He was an interesting dude. Creole-looking. Mulatto? No. Bi-racial. That was the polite term. Tight grey 'fro like Nelson Mandela, as if he was named with that look in mind.

"Speak of ze Devil and 'ee shall appear," Nelson said in his best island voodoo accent. He was wearing a red Hawaiian shirt. That was Nelson's flaw: A vacuous absence where his fashion sense ought to be.

"Whoa," Bill said. "Love yer accent."

"He's fucking with me," Jack said. "First time I came in he had me going for an hour, thinking that was his real voice."

"And zen I tell heem..." Nelson dropped the accent "...I'm from the enchanted island of Morristown."

"Where'szat?" Bill asked.

"New Jersey," Jack answered for Nelson.

Bill looked at Jack. "Didn't...you said yer from New York?"

"Jersey is New York's kid brother," Nelson explained, looking at Jack. "We adore you, and you have nothing but contempt for us."

"It's true," Jack conceded. "But it's okay now, we're both honorary Cajuns. You aren't Cajun unless you've lasted a year in the quarter without going to rehab. That and you have a favorite voodoo shop."

"Or you own one," Nelson added.

"Oh," Bill said, swaying. Then a slender skeleton figurine in a tuxedo caught his gaze. He was transfixed.

Jack took Nelson to the side.

"Do you have anything...herbal?"

"Ha! Of course, Jack. There are some forms of magic you believe in." Nelson nodded over toward Bill. "This one? Not really your style, my friend."

"He's cute, in a lost puppy kind of way," Jack explained. "Besides, you know I need my three a day: breakfast, lunch, and dinner."

Nelson shook his head and tsk-tsk-tsked. "Men as meals. You should be ashamed of yourself." Then he laughed. He went behind the beaded curtain to retrieve Jack's order.

"Tourist," Jack called to Bill. "You almost ready to head back to my place for a late lunch?"

Bill's eyes were woozy. "Lunch? Innit it after six o'clock?"

"You're in the quarter. Time moves differently here." He played with Bill's curls. Bill gave him a sheepish smile.

Nelson emerged from behind the beaded curtain, carrying a bright orange bag with a Fleur-de-lis on the side.

"Tha's discreet," Bill laughed. "Lezzgo," he said to Jack.

"Wait outside," Jack said. Bill nodded and went out the door.

Nelson frowned. "That one, not really your style," he repeated.

Jack took the bag and handed a folded wad of bills to Nelson. "It's just a late lunch." Nelson laughed.

"Careful not to break his heart." Nelson held up a doll and rattled it in the air. "Some spells can never be undone."

"Later," Jack said, headed for the door.

"Later, my friend."

Jack woke at dawn with thunder in his skull. There was no noise down on Royal. He wasn't sure what had woken him. Jack sat up. He hated when this happened. It was that awful time when a good buzz is in the middle of souring into a hangover. The human body isn't made to be awake for that.

There was a sunken place in the mattress next to him, where Bill had passed out. He must've woken up sometime in the night to do his walk of shame. That was for the best. Clean split. No sticky attachments.

There was a flutter out on the balcony. One of Jack's plants crashed.

Maybe Bill was out there. Maybe he had decided to sleep it off where there was a view. Then again…

Jack grabbed the aluminum baseball bat under his bed. There were barriers on the balconies, but it wasn't unheard of: a tourist has five too many and decides to climb buildings like some tipsy Spider Man.

Jack burst through his floor-to-ceiling doors, bat in hand.

There was no one on his balcony. Dry dirt and ceramic shards carpeted the wood, but his eyes were drawn to the presence on his antique table.

It was like an elongated lady bug, the size of an adult cat. It fluttered its wings rapidly. The sound was melodious, something he never would've associated with an insect. Its eyes were shining and sad, like a doe's. Its carapace was gold.

Jack placed the bat gently on the balcony. He didn't want to startle the…there was no word. 'Creature' didn't fit at all. 'Bug' was an insult.

It was flawless. Truly. Here was a thing he wouldn't change at all. Jack saw himself reaching out.

The wings fluttered again, carrying it away. Jack watched helplessly as it cleared the top of the bed and breakfast across Royal.

Jack fell gasping on the floor. The sense of overwhelming loss hit him in the gut. He curled up on his side. Shivering, he blacked out.

❖

Jack woke with a start, feeling cheated.

What could he do but stumble through his typical day?

His early afternoon swim was routine. He touched the sleek bottom of the pool. He looked up at the sun. But he couldn't forget the sight of dark and gentle eyes. That perfect, underwater muffle couldn't silence the memory of harmonious wings.

His whiskey at the Carousel Bar had a metallic aftertaste.

His ATM card didn't work. "See a teller," it suggested.

Bartender Dave was at Bourbon Pub.

"Where's Josh?"

"The Gallery," Dave answered, cleaning a glass. "Work."

Jack felt an old shame, on top of the bloated sense of loss that had settled in his gut. He thought about confiding in Dave, this person he had some shared history with.

He laughed out loud.

"What?"

"Nothing."

How could he even begin to explain it without sounding crazy? Jack had to put it out of mind. He looked around the bar, packed for mid-day.

"Crowded," he muttered. Dave laughed at him. "What?"

"It's Saturday. You know, one of those days other people aren't working."

It wasn't like Jack to feel wounded by one of Dave's good-natured ribbings. He felt himself pouting as he swirled his White Russian. He looked around the bar again and thought he saw more than one guy giving him a sideways glance of disapproval.

"Jack? You okay?"

He hadn't even had his breakfast yet.

It was then Jack realized, he'd been taking his dinner boys to Voodoo John's. Nelson was the one person who wouldn't judge him. He was the one man Jack could ask, *Do you know anything about pretty gold beetles and inescapable feelings of loss?*

He left a tip and a bewildered Dave behind. He half-ran to Voodoo John's.

"Do you know anything about pretty gold beetles and inescapable feelings of loss?"

That was exactly how he phrased the question.

Nelson stood on a stool, dusting a high shelf. He didn't even turn to look at Jack. He answered with one word.

"Chibaku."

"What?"

Nelson laid a trio of dream-catchers on the counter. "Chibaku."

"Sounds Chinese."

"Egyptian. Vessels, my friend. A man calls them to store things of value." Dust rained down from the shelf and Jack coughed.

"What's wrong with a safe? P.O. box?" Nelson didn't laugh at Jack's sarcasm, he just kept dusting.

"Chibaku store the intangible," Nelson explained. Jack coughed again. He took a step back. Now Nelson laughed. "You don't clean much."

Jack cleared his throat. "You got me. Not much of a chimney sweep. I played Oliver Twist when I was a kid, if that helps."

"Ha! I can see it. Soot on your cheeks. Just the once."

"They store the intangible," Jack repeated. "But I didn't summon anything. I don't cast spells." He seemed to be telling it to the figurines on the shelves. "I don't even cook."

"Ha! No you don't, Jack. Chibaku are not just used for storage. They are also used for theft. They can be used to siphon away a man's most valued intangibles."

Jack laughed. Nelson turned to look at him. He had a sad, paternal gaze.

"What? C'mon, man. This is me. You sell tchotchkes to buzzed tourists. There's no magic. A man's got a wallet, a dick, and a brain. Everything else? 'Intangibles?' Pure fantasy. Bullshit."

Nelson climbed off the stool and placed his feather duster on the shelf. He went behind the counter, through the beaded curtain. Jack worried. He liked Nelson. He realized he didn't want to offend him.

Nelson returned with a well-worn book with brown leather cover. No title. No listed author. He placed it in Jack's hand.

"Page eight, my friend."

From their tea-dipped hue, Jack was afraid the pages would flake away if touched. But when he felt them between his fingertips, there might've been cables woven in the fiber. Jack turned the unnumbered pages, counting as he went.

On page eight, there was a fantastic pencil-shading of a Chibaku, a wondrous, if flawed, attempt to capture its perfection—right down to the gleam in the unforgettable eyes. Underneath was a list.

"Parsley? Cloves? This is how a curse happens?"

Nelson looked over Jack's shoulder at the ingredients. "I would have a harder time making hash brownies."

Jack sighed. "Who would curse me?" He couldn't help but think of the bar, the gym, and a very long trail of broken hearts.

"Who can say? The point is, I can negate it for you."

"How much?"

"I'm sorry?"

"How much money do you want?" Nelson laughed at him. "What?"

"I thought you didn't believe."

"I don't."

"Then why do you believe you need a counter-curse?" Nelson smiled.

"Just...how much?"

"You won't be able to pay with money. The gold Chibaku represents wealth. Your wealth is leaving you."

Jack thought of the ATM machine. His card hadn't worked.

Bullshit. There was no way. He would go to the bank tomorrow. He would 'See a teller'. He would call his father, if it came to that.

"You don't have to pay in money. I simply want you to recognize the truth of what is happening to you. I want to hear a non-believer express belief. It would gratify me. Tell me you need me, and I will help you."

Jack could just say it. He could just lie. Jack had lied a thousand times before. But there were certain sentences that made him squirm. One of those sentences was, 'I need you.'

"I'll check with my bank tomorrow. I'll check with my father."

"Your wealth is leaving you, my friend."

"We'll see." Jack turned and left, feeling more lost than before.

❖

Jack looked around his apartment, imagining price tags dangling off of everything. He placed the phone on his expensive end table. His apartment was his masterpiece—perfectly arranged antiques, rustic opulence.

How much longer would the phone or the table be his? How long would the room that contained them?

The conversation was over. Certain phrases and sentences his father had pronounced were still tumbling in his skull.

"…not doing you any favors."

"…tired of being an enabler."

"This vacation had to end sometime."

He had tried to explain it to his father. Jack tried to explain that it was impossible at this point, in this economy, to go to any employer with his resume. He had a B.A. in English that was seven years old. Then a two-year gap. Then his M.F.A. Then another two years, empty. Lost in the French Quarter. Lost in idle non-sobriety, celebratory malingering. But what the hell had he been celebrating, other than the fact that he was rich, relatively young, and perfect-looking?

When he looked at his life in years and blurbs, Jack had to admit, it didn't amount to much. And now, his wealth was leaving him. Nelson was right. And it didn't take herbs or Egyptian spirit vessels to make it happen. Just a call from dad that hit him like a blast wave.

"How can I explain the lost years? Prospective employers, they ask about that kind of thing."

"Son, if this is ever going to be your life, that has to be your problem. In thirty days, I'm cutting you off."

He looked out on his deck—a beautiful thing that might no longer be his. Had he really seen what he thought he'd seen? He had been drunk. Maybe he'd been dreaming. But the sense of loss was so visceral.

Enough. Jack stood up and marched to his bathroom. He fixed his hair so it was gym-sloppy. He headed straight for the Hotel Monteleone's weight room. He lifted. He squatted. He ran. He devoured a tourist from West Hollywood in the sauna.

He didn't go to Bourbon Pub. No drinking. He had a light dinner—actual food, not a stranger. He broke out his old laptop, the one that was going to birth the great American novel after grad school. He typed his resume, lean as it was. He checked the time.

It was 8:00 p.m. and he was sober to the bone. He sat at his computer, staring.

He needed the beginnings of a novel. Something that could explain all that lost time, if a prospective employer asked. He would come up with something. He had a month. He could do this.

Jack wrote a sentence. He ate a snack. He wrote a sentence. He had some wine on the balcony. He wrote a sentence. He flipped through the dumb sitcoms. Back to the computer.

By midnight, he'd written three quarters of a page. A promising start. Something. Something that wasn't there before. He could tell his employer he'd taken the time to write, and soon enough, he'd have something to show for his years in the Quarter.

Something. He'd written something.

Something flawed.

The old itch came on strong. He was tempted to delete. He saved it in multiple places, e-mailed attachments to himself. He wouldn't delete. He would not delete this flawed attempt at expression, as he'd done with all the others—everything he'd ever written that wasn't assigned.

Jack put himself to bed. He tossed and turned, hearing the humid revelry out on Royal. He curled into himself, facing the wall, trying not to hear the festivity. He tried lying on his stomach. He finally fell asleep on his back.

It was past four when he heard the music of fluttering wings. His eyes opened. He heard the first of the street cleaning vehicles, the last of the drunken shouts.

The red Chibaku sat on his chest, like a heavy housecat. Its mandibles were inches down from his chin, but Jack felt no fear. It wouldn't bite. He sensed it. Something this perfect needed no meat. There was nothing but peace in its shining eyes.

It couldn't fly away, not in here. The doors to the deck and back stairs were shut and locked. This was still his place. The Chibaku was his and it was safe. It was safe and he had it. He had it. It was his. It would always be his. He could stare at this flawless thing forever.

Then he realized he could see his bookshelf. He could see through the Chibaku.

"No."

The pressure on his chest was getting lighter.

"No."

It was fading.

Jack froze. He hoped he was seeing it wrong—some trick, some practical joke between the light and his eyes.

No. He could read the titles of his dusty old college books on the shelf. He could feel the pressure on his chest lifting.

Jack sat up to grab the red Chibaku. He was in it. It was merely a spectral image now. He was wearing it. All he could do was lie back down and steal one last look into its eyes, as they vanished in the new day's light.

❖

It was past three when he scraped himself out of bed. He shaved. He didn't bother to brush his teeth. He didn't even use mouthwash. He went to the gym, knowing the futility, knowing that tossing endorphins at such a towering sense of loss was like attacking a fighter jet with a slingshot.

He lifted lackadaisically and jogged as if through knee-high sludge. Jack felt no rush until he saw him, Tulane kid from the other day.

"You never called!"

"C'mere." He led Tulane kid by the hand into the locker room. This would be more than launching a stone. This was his surface-to-air missile.

Four minutes later, they emerged.

"It happens to some older guys. No biggie," the kid said. Jack just walked. He went down the elevator, out the door and down the street—he skipped Bourbon Pub and went straight to Voodoo John's. The old man was there. He tried to murmur something at Jack.

"Nelson?" Jack called. He heard the desperation in his own voice. Nelson emerged from the beaded curtain.

"Jack," Nelson frowned. "You saw a red one. It faded. Your youth…"

Jack was shocked. "How could you tell?"

"Your face."

Jack felt his face. Flawless. Nelson went digging under the register and emerged with a corroded piece of glass. Jack looked into it.

There were fine lines traveling south, between his nose and chin. Jack choked back tears.

"I need you."

Nelson held the curtain open.

"Step inside, my friend."

Modest was a kind way to describe Nelson's apartment. Flawed didn't even begin to cover it. No curtains. Strangely-patterned towels in the bathroom clashed mightily against his funky table cloth and couch covers. It was like geometry had tried to swallow a rainbow and barfed it up. There was rust and dust, but it didn't look intentionally antique, just insanitary. If Jack looked too long at any one spot, he felt itchy.

Nelson stirred a pot on his stove and hummed. "You don't like my place."

"No! Of course I like it! It's fine. Just…"

"It's not what you're accustomed to, my friend."

"Yeah." Jack wondered what he might have to grow accustomed to if this didn't work. He'd seen the rent boys down on Canal, flawed as they were. He wasn't old, just old to start that line of work. But according to Nelson, according to his crusty mirror, youth was leaving him. Jack wondered what that meant, beyond what hadn't happened in the locker room. What humiliations lay in wait? Grey hairs and rolls at dawn? Senility for his thirtieth birthday?

"Don't worry, Jack. Just believe." Nelson tapped the spoon, poured something steamy into a blank ceramic coffee cup, and handed it to Jack.

"What is this?"

"Just sip."

Jack took the tiniest sip.

"Chicken soup?"

"Everyone tastes something different. For me, it was gumbo."

"My mom used to make this. Canned, but still. I always liked it." Nelson handed him a spoon. Jack finished it quietly.

"Everything will be better."

"Just like that? Somebody steals my money and my hard-on…"

"Your youth and wealth. Your joyful spirit and the means to enjoy it."

"Fine. My youth," Jack conceded. "The point is, the counter-curse is soup?"

"Magic is ritual and belief. For some reason, plants tend to be involved," Nelson said, shrugging.

"That's it?"

"That's it, my friend. Go home. Go home and believe."

Jack's nightmare made perfect sense to him. Regardless, he was horrified. He was eating men. Not blowing them, detaching his jaw like a boa constrictor and gulping them down, head-to-toe. He ate Bartender Dave and Art Gallery Josh, the old man, and Nelson, Bill, and the Tulane kid. He ate a line of male tourists watching sidewalk jazz. Three a day. Twenty-one a week. Eighty-four in the shortest month.

When he was full, he lay on his couch with a distended belly. The gold Chibaku fluttered in through the window and lay on his stomach. It purred like a cat and he stroked its gleaming carapace.

Then he saw inside his gut. The men had gone Lord of the Flies in there. They wore savage masks and grass skirts. The old man and Nelson were in there too, throwing herbs into a pot, shaking their spears and chanting gibberish.

Jack's belly burst from the inside out, cutting him in half. The savage, gore-matted men danced around his apartment, celebrating their liberation. Jack was left living, quivering on the floor in anguish as only arms, chest, and head. They towered over him and laughed. Tulane kid threw Jack's severed lower half over the balcony. Art Gallery Josh stuck his spear in the Chibaku over and over, until gold blood flowed through the cracks in Jack's floorboards.

Jack woke in a Louisiana sweat.

He heard the wings. It was in the living room. Jack saw his laundry basket in the corner of his bedroom. He grabbed it on the move. He had to try something.

This one was emerald green, and seemed quite content on his coffee table.

"What are you?" Jack asked angrily. "My will to live? My personality? What abstract noun do you fly off with?"

The Chibaku fluttered its wings. Jack jumped, tossing the laundry basket over it. He stared through the little slits on the side, just to make sure it wasn't fading like the red one had. He grabbed the heaviest book he could find and placed it on top.

He made a mad run for Voodoo John's.

❖

Jack barged into the shop. He felt like he was fighting for air.

"Hello, my friend," Nelson said. "You seem distressed. Why don't you sit?" He motioned to the red rocking chair, which was empty.

Jack struggled to remember. "The old man? That's his spot."

"Don't worry, my friend. He doesn't need it anymore." Nelson eased him into the chair. "You worry too much. My uncle used to say the only thing worse than having a job is not having a job." He pointed to his skull. "You live in your head."

"My head," Jack repeated. "I'm so foggy."

"I suppose you've guessed the green Chibaku is wit. Wealth, youth, and wit. The things a man like you values most. How did you put it before? 'A man has his wallet, his brain, and his cock.'"

Jack rocked in the old man's chair. It was soothing. But something was screaming behind bars in his head. Something told him not to relax.

"It was you," Jack said. "It was always you."

Nelson smiled. "Wit has not left you yet, my love."

My love. Not 'my friend'.

"No. I still have the green one. I still have my wit."

Nelson tsk-tsk-tsked. "Did you really think you'd trap a spirit vessel under a laundry basket?" He motioned to the curtain. "I have it in back."

Jack tried to gather his thoughts. "I don't believe you."

Nelson smiled. He turned and walked back through the beaded curtain. Jack thought about running, but he had to see, he had to know.

Nelson returned, holding the green Chibaku in a clear plastic box.

"Why?" Jack's thoughts whirled. His mind felt whiskey-pickled. He dreamed of running, but his head felt heavy, besieged.

"I loved you the moment I saw you," Nelson said. "Tan skin and visibly expensive clothes. Deep brown hair and eyes, like the richest soil. Muscular and moisturized—so hard and polished, you might as well be a shiny thing on my shelf."

Jack's lips moved soundlessly.

"I loved you from the first time I saw you," Nelson repeated. "But I knew you couldn't love me back. You couldn't love at all. Love is need. And you were truly flawless, unable to need. You were arrogant, but that's always the flaw of the flawless. It does nothing for love."

Jack felt warm drool dribble down his chin.

"When I first saw you, you were like a painting. You were a flat form of beauty, pleasing to the eye, but void of life. I'm going to teach you to need. And need will teach you how to love."

Nelson walked behind the counter, through the beaded curtains. Jack was left with a vague sense of being upset. He struggled for a solution to a problem he couldn't define.

Nelson returned with two more clear plastic boxes stacked in his arms. He placed them on the counter near the curtain. The red and gold Chibaku stared at Jack with their doe eyes. Nelson pushed the green one further down the counter, toward Jack's chair. Jack felt himself grow instantaneously sharper.

"You have them," Jack smiled. "You're giving them back because you love me."

"No," Nelson said. Jack felt the corners of his mouth drop. "Don't despair, my love. I'm going to let you have them near you. Some days you'll enjoy portions of your wit." He tapped the side of the green one's cage. "Some days we'll enjoy your wealth." He tapped the top of the gold one's cage. He strolled to the rocking chair and touched Jack's cheek. "Some days we'll enjoy your youth, together." Nelson strode back casually behind the counter, stacking and lifting the boxes, taking all three Chibaku off to some unseen place.

Jack cried. He wept like a child realizing the unfairness of life for the very first time. And then he couldn't remember what he was so upset about, but the feeling lingered.

Nelson stepped back through the curtain. Jack was weeping, hunched over in the chair. Nelson took out his handkerchief and wiped Jack's face.

"Why am I crying?"

"You are feeling something entirely new. You need another person completely, and before him, you are little more than a ball of yearning. For the first time, you are helpless, utterly without power." Jack sniveled and whimpered. Nelson smiled. "This is love, the purest ache."

Jack pressed his face into Nelson's chest. He felt himself spiraling downward, with no idea how to make it stop.

Nelson watched Jack break. He looked down at the blubbering, broken, incoherent creature in the chair, and knew that Jack belonged to him.

"Now, my love, you truly are flawless."

Mum's the Word
Jeff Lindemann

Reverend Bosco Byrd swung around in his office chair, removed his new cassette of Debby Boone warbling "You Light Up My Life," inserted a requiem for pipe organ, and pressed 'play'.

Young Peter Boggs, the freshman ministerial student whom the Reverend had just summoned, grew alarmed for he knew that somber organ music on a weekday afternoon was a bad omen. Word around campus on the small East Texas Bible College had it that whenever the Dean of Biblical Studies was ready to slit a throat, he played his organ music.

"Mr. Boggs. Somethin' jus' ain't quite right 'bout you," he declared in his high-pitched nasal squawk cutting through the bass pipes of the death march.

Peter sat on the edge of his chair. "Whut d' you mean, Rev'rend Byrd?"

With his dark-brown flattop, beady eyes close to his pointy nose, and buffy cheeks, Reverend Byrd, dressed in a blue-gray shirt and brown necktie, resembled a chicken hawk.

The Reverend stretched his head forward, scrutinized the boy as would a feathered predator eying its prey, and pronounced, "You look funny." He pointed a claw-like finger. "Are you one of them dev'lish sinners who feels urges—sinful urges—'round other men?"

Reverend Byrd's pipe organ began to swell.

"Ugh, I don't understand. Whut sinful urges? I got only one urge—an' that's t' be a min'ster an' one day preach the good word in the little church where I done grew up."

Reverend Byrd sharpened his glare. "We're not talkin' 'bout preachin' the good word. Were talkin' 'bout feelin' unusual urges—naughty pref'rences!"

"Ugh, I don't feel no naughty pref'rences 'bout nuthin'.'."

"Hah! You're either dumb as a clod or the biggest liar since the serpent spoke t' Eve, 'Ye shall not surely die.'"

"My Mummy done taught me never t' lie."

"Yer Mummy! Jus' whut kinda fruitcake are you, Mr. Boggs?"

"Call me Peter. My Mummy done named me after St. Peter, keeper of the keys t' the kingdom of heaven."

"Mr. Boggs, don't lecture me—of all people—on St. Peter."

The organ surged.

"You can call me Pete fer short."

"Mr. Boggs!" With a sudden dive off his lofty perch, Reverend Byrd swooped down to nab the boy. "I'm gonna cut the chit-chat an' git right t' the point. Yer teachers report you done mis'ribly failed all yer courses, an' they all agree you ain't got no potential fer the min'stry. Truth is, you jus' ain't cut out fer preachin' the word, so I'm expellin' you. I want you packed an' off campus by Sunday night."

As the dirge decrescendoed, the boy shuffled back to the dormitory and lapsed into a deep sleep.

When Peter awoke, his head ached from the enormity of his expulsion. Reverend Byrd's words 'You look funny' tolled like a death knell. He stripped and stood naked before the full-length mirror on his closet door. Pitiful, he thought, for a boy of eighteen. Distraught at the site, he grabbed a frayed gray terry towel to cover his loins. With his lanky frame and skinny bowlegs, he looked like a pair of pliers wrapped in a strip of duct tape.

Observing his flap-like ears and curly red hair framing a prematurely balding crown above a pasty-white freckled face, Peter believed he resembled a carnival clown. He imagined that with a round red rubber nose, a pair of big floppy feet, and a few stage props, he could juggle his balls and perform tricks at birthday parties.

Peter recalled his own sparsely attended eighth birthday party when he had what some would call a bad clown experience. His mother, whom he affectionately called 'Mummy', had hired an amateur party clown—a college student needing money—to perform magic tricks. The clown got right in the boy's face. Peter could see the slovenly buffoon's beard stubble under the white pancake makeup. His breath smelled bad, too, like strong cough syrup, and his eyes looked red. Then the demonic trickster smacked his lips and slurred, "Hey little birthday boy! I'm Jacko de Clown. Would you like t' see the funny-lookin' monkey I got in my secret box?"

Little Peter nodded.

"Mum's the word. Okay, Chicken Little?"

"Mum's the word."

But when Peter peeked into Jacko's box, there was no monkey—only a mirror. The boy quickly recoiled in tears as the sinister clown laughed heartily.

Since that traumatic experience, Peter dreaded not only clowns, but also mirrors.

Standing in the gray terry towel before the mirror, he quickly recoiled, rummaged through his meager belongings, and donned a pair of blue jeans and a crumpled T-shirt with the words 'No Laughing Matter' printed across the chest.

To the sound of Debby Boone warbling "You Light Up My Life," Peter sat in the Happy Time Coffee Shop and combed through the employment section of the *Jacksonville Herald*. A large blue fly buzzed around him and landed on a boxed ad that pronounced:

Wanted! Night Shift Crew for Packaging Department.
Loco Pollo Chicken Processing Plant.
Apply at Main Office in Deadpecker, Texas.

❖

The bus drove Peter directly from Jacksonville to Nacogdoches, where it rumbled down North Street passed the campus of Stephen F. Austin University and parked briefly at the station across from the old Fredonia Hotel while other passengers boarded. Just a block away on Mound Street, where legend says Indians were buried, Peter noted the imposing white three-story Victorian house with a sign in the front yard that read: 'Jack L. Anubis Funeral Home. Your sorrow is our joy'.

The bus lurched southward towards Lufkin.

On the drive down Highway 59, Peter, peering out the window, mulled over his life. With his parents dead and no siblings and no friends, with his dream of becoming a minister deferred, if not defeated, the boy felt adrift. And with less than a hundred dollars in his pocket, he feared he might soon be sleeping with other deadbeats under bridges.

The bus traveled slowly through the sleepy little town of Nazareth where Peter had been born and raised. It passed the school where children strove at recess in a ring. He glimpsed his childhood home sitting vacant at El Paradiso Trailer Park. The site of the run-down trailer rekindled agonizing memories of being mocked all through school because of his goofy appearance. In elementary school, Peter's classmates dubbed him 'Bonehead,' a nick-name that stuck until he graduated from high school at the bottom of his class.

He eyed the little roadside church where he had been baptized. Other than his mother's arms, the only place Peter had ever felt welcomed was in the Little Hope Church of Nazareth where every Sunday morning he had lit the altar candles and rang the steeple bell. He had no other aspiration than to preach one day in this tiny sanctuary disappearing behind him in the bus window.

Within an hour, the bus paused before a large billboard proclaiming: Live it up in Lufkin! On one side of the road, Peter viewed a scrapyard; on the other, a cemetery.

The bus had no sooner stopped at the Lufkin station when a flame-red Ford Pinto with a door reading 'Cerebus Taxi Company' careened around a corner and screeched to a halt. The driver, a pointy-eared troll grinning with sharp teeth, approached Peter. "Where you headin', young feller?"

"Goin' t' Deadpecker. Know where that's at?"

"Well, if I didn't, I could follow my nose t' Loco Pollo. You can smell that stinkin' hell hole from miles away. Hop on in. My name's Charley Sticks. Here's my card. You'll prob'bly be callin'."

Since the stench of ammonia from the poultry barns had run off most residents long ago, only a foul-smelling ghost town awaited its newest citizen. Other than Loco Pollo, Deadpecker offered little more than a run-down nursing home called Nugget's Lazy Acres; Nugget's Last Stop Gas n' Grocery; and an abandoned gothic-style red brick church with boarded windows, a tall steeple, and a sign out front reading: 'Space for Rent. Dirt Cheep. Contact Colonel Nugget.'

Peter noted the words on the office door of the processing plant: 'Loco Polo! You just can't get enough'.

"Pardon my protrusion, but is this where I apply fer a job?"

The stocky man with pouty lips under a beaked nose swung around in his office chair, cocked his head from side to side, and scrutinized Peter as if the boy were a sack of poultry feed. "You got the right place, alright. My name's Colonel Nugget. Take a seat. Let's talk some turkey."

Peter was surprised the job interview had lasted only two minutes. Colonel Nugget's single question had been "Whut's yer 'pinion 'bout chickens?"

Before answering, Peter pondered his response; he wanted to make a good impression. "Dumbest bird in the barnyard."

Colonel Nugget cocked his head and smiled. "Young feller, you got the job. You're workin' the night shift in the packagin' department Monday through Friday, ten in the evenin' t' six in the mornin'. You git a five-minute break each hour an' all the leftover chicken patties you can gobble up. Git payed ev'ry Friday. Any questions?"

"Ugh, can you tell me 'bout that church fer rent?"

"It belongs t' me an' my wife Ima. She manages our nursin' home. I gutted that ol' church fer storin' chicken feed, an' I'm rentin' the steeple. There's a little bathroom downstairs. No hot water, an' it ain't got no shower. How 'bout twenty-five bucks a month, bills paid."

As Peter climbed the rickety wooden ladder to the steeple loft, he wafted away cobwebs and flying insects. Once he reached the top, he pushed open the wooden trap door. A sudden rush of flapping wings greeted him as dozens of crows fled madly through the open arches. In the center of the belfry floor sat a large, rusty cracked iron bell inscribed with gothic lettering: 'I give you the keys to the kingdom of heaven'.

❖

Peter had no idea how chickens were processed; he was used to seeing them neatly wrapped, labeled, and displayed in grocery stores.

"Now, listen up," crowed Colonel Nugget as he walked Peter through the processing plant. "Once we crate them chickens in the poultry barns next door, we cart 'em on in here fer slaughter an' packagin'. First, we shackle 'em by the feet an' hang 'em upside down on this here rack."

Even hanging upside down, the chickens kept clucking for their lives.

"Next, we slit their throats, cut off their heads, an' send 'em down t' soak in that tank of scaldin' water so's t' loosen their feathers. After we yank their feathers, we chop off their feet, gut, clean, an' disinfect 'em. Then they're sent on that conveyer belt t' this here whole-bird station fer stuffin' an' packagin'."

The packaging station was little more than a raised platform surrounded by plastic bins filled with chicken guts. Peter ran a hand across the oblong metal work table; it felt cold and bumpy.

"Now, you're gonna grab in these here bins an' stuff a liver, gizzard, heart, an' neck into a paper bag. Next, you yank a bird off this here belt, an' stuff the bag of guts inside the carcass. Then you squeeze the bird's legs together, tie 'em real tight, wrap the whole bird in plastic, seal it sturdy, weigh it on this here scale, an' attach a label. This job's so easy, even a stupid clown could do it. I expect you t' wrap thirty birds an hour. If you can't wrap thirty—you're fired. Any questions?"

Observing a dead-tired worker standing on a ladder and stirring the steaming, stinking contents of a large vat with a canoe paddle, Peter queried, "Whut's that tub over there?"

"That's Horace Ragsdale."

"Not him. Whut's in that vat?"

"He's boilin' leftover chicken guts into sludge t' make our Loco Pollo chicken patties."

After that first week of grueling work, Peter's back, shoulders, and neck ached from bending over; his arms hurt from reaching for chickens; and his feet throbbed from standing eight hours each night. Even his wrists and fingers pained him from bagging and stuffing guts into carcasses. The poor lighting, revolting odor of chicken sludge, and constant chorus of clucking chickens made Loco Pollo a dismal underworld of suffering and torment.

Making matters worse, Colonel Nugget routinely observed Peter work. The boy, packaging as fast as he could, noted the disgruntled man's surveillance. The Colonel would point a sharp-nailed finger and admonish, "You're gonna have t' work harder, boy. You're baggin' an' taggin' only 'bout twenty birds an hour."

By the time Saturday arrived, Peter wanted to treat himself to a movie. From the gas station, he called Mr. Sticks, and soon the flame-red Pinto sped to the church door where Peter stood waiting.

"Hey there, feller," greeted the troll. "Hop on in. So, you like workin' at Loco Pollo?"

"It's hell. I gotta be 'round people instead of all them dead chickens. I wanna live it up in Lufkin!"

"Lufkin's deader than a doornail. The only movie theater we got is the Pines, an' it's showin' *Killer Klowns from Outer Space*."

"Ferget it."

"The next closest theater is the Red Bluff Drive-In. An' that won't work 'cause you ain't got no car t' drive in. An' even if you did, I doubt you'd want t' see this week's feature: *The Ghost and Mr. Chicken*."

"Gotta be some place I can go fer fun."

"I bet you'd enjoy happy hour at Grumpy's Roadside Tavern."

"A tavern? My Mummy done warned me t' stay outa places like that."

"Yer Mummy! Feller, you're a big boy now. Besides, a lotta funny lookin' folk hang out at Grumpy's. You know...birds of a feather. You'll fit right in."

Halfway between Lufkin and Nacogdoches, in early evening, against a backdrop of tall pines, the lights for the large letters G, Y, and S in the sign over Grumpy's, a dingy sawdust-floored roadside tavern, had burned out long ago so that only the remaining letters R U M P flashed in pink neon.

Inside this East Texas barroom flocked a forlorn congregation of oddballs, losers, drunks, potheads, hustlers, lonely men in shirt sleeves, and a haggard drag queen or two. On the old jukebox, Debby Boone warbled "You Light Up My Life."

Grumpy, a burly and tattooed motorcycle man under a black leather cap, observed Peter enter, wiped the counter, and placed a bowl of pork rinds before his new customer. "Welcome t' Grumpy's. Whut can I git fer you, bub?"

Peter climbed on a barstool, looked around in wonder, and announced, "I'd like me a root beer float, please."

Grumpy shook his head. "Sorry, ain't got no root beer, no ice cream, an' no floats. I got beer, though. How 'bout an ice-cold bottle of Jax?"

"Ugh, I ain't never drunk no alcohol before."

"Hmmmm. You strike me as a rum an' Coke kinda guy. This first one's on me." As Grumpy mixed the cocktail, he inspected the newcomer. "I ain't never seen you here before. Whut brings you t' these parts?"

"I jus' got me a job at the chicken processin' plant near Lufkin."

Grumpy set the drink in front of the boy who, after taking a sip, wrinkled his face and uttered, "Tastes like strong cough syrup."

The bartender grinned at the novice. "It's an acquired taste. Now tell me, you happy workin' at Loco Pollo?"

"I ain't never known such mis'ry. But I'll work in that dungeon 'til I figer out whut t' do with my life."

"Well, whutever you do, keep away from troublemakers. The world's a frightnin' place. Demons an' dogs are prowlin' everywhere. They'll use you, rob you, an' gobble you up."

Wide-eyed, Peter listened to the prophetic bartender.

"My name's Grumpy. Whut's yers?"

"My Mummy done named me Peter—after St. Peter, keeper of the keys t' the kingdom of heaven. Call me Pete fer short."

"Tell me, Pete, whut would you really like t' be doin'?"

Peter swallowed a gulp that shot right through him. "Whew! Makes my head spin. I wanna be a min'ster in a little church. But I done flunked outa Bible college in Jacksonville."

"A lotta drop-outs from that college pass through here on their way t' Houston."

Peter took another swig. "Mmmmm. Hey, this rum an' Coke ain't half bad."

"I thought you'd like it."

"Yep, I wanna' spread the word. I know I'd be good if I could jus' git me a start."

Grumpy thought a moment. "Say, I had a preacher from Houston in here last week who done started up a new business." He walked to the bulletin board next to the jukebox and pulled down a thumb-tacked business card. "Here, take this. Jus' might int'rest you."

Peter read the card: 'Clowns for Christ Ministry Correspondence Course'. Underneath the words were an address and slogan: 'We're all fools for Christ's sake'. The word 'clowns' unnerved him. He guzzled the remainder of his cocktail. "Grumpy, I'll have me another rum an' Coke."

❖

Peter returned to Grumpy's every Saturday evening. There had to be some happiness after each week of grueling work, wretched conditions, and Colonel Nugget's menacing scrutiny.

Not yet relinquishing his dream of becoming a preacher, Peter sat one Sunday afternoon in his steeple and examined the card Grumpy had given him over a month ago. The boy's logic was that if he could simply disguise his goofy appearance, no one would notice he looked funny. After careful thought, he wrote a letter requesting to be enrolled in the Clowns for Christ Ministry Correspondence Course.

Two weeks later, a large package arrived at the church door. Inside were an instruction booklet titled *Clownin' 'Round*, a red and white striped baggy costume, big floppy shoes, make-up kit, red rubber nose, curly red wig, some basic magic tricks, and juggling balls.

According to his booklet, Peter needed to select a clown persona and name. He pondered the matter long and deeply. He wanted to be a good clown, a gay clown, a clown for Christ. He decided on Rainbo de Clown.

After six weeks of practicing magic tricks, juggling balls, and experimenting with clown make-up, Peter received a certificate of completion in the mail. With its gold seal and red ribbon, the diploma framed in black plastic looked official. On it he read the words in gothic lettering: 'Reverend Rainbo de Clown'. He had never felt so proud. And his first flock congregated a short walk away.

❖

Late Monday morning, Peter walked to the dingy liver-colored cinder block building and noted the sign on the withered front lawn: 'Welcome to Nugget's Lazy Achers. We're at the end of the road'.

Mrs. Ima Nugget looked up from her desk. The matron pushed aside the bright red flap of hair down one side of her face, greeted him, and clucked with delight over his offer to preach the word. "Currently, we ain't got no religious services. I've tried t' recruit preachers from Lufkin an' Nac'doches, but once they git a whiff of Deadpecker, they don't never return."

When Peter informed Mrs. Nugget that he would preach dressed as Reverend Rainbo de Clown, she was particularly thrilled, for she was also always looking for some cheap, if not free, entertainment for the residents. "A min'ster dressed as a clown? Perfect! I'll be killin' two birds with one stone."

"Well, sorta," remarked Peter.

"Rev'rend Rainbo, I want you t' start preachin' the word this Sunday. But first you must meet our res'dents enjoyin' a happy time in the dinin' hall."

When Peter approached a decrepit woman in a wheel chair, she muttered, "You lose time 'round here. Each day's the same. You eat, you sleep, you take a dump."

"When you're old an' dyin'—you're already dead," bemoaned the aged biddy next to her.

A grizzled old man tottered over to Peter and grumbled, "They should hang a sign outside: 'Abandon hope all ye who enter.' Me, I wish I'd jus' die."

Mrs. Nugget took Peter aside. "Ignore those birdbrains! They're all sufferin' from academentia. Now then, would you like t' join us fer lunch? I'm servin' chicken patties an' creamed corn cas'role."

"Ugh, no thank you."

A scruffy gent who had overheard this brief exchange hobbled over to Peter and griped, "Creamed corn cas'role an' chicken patties! That's all we git in this godforsaken scrapyard day after day—breakfast, lunch, an' supper. Them patties ain't nuthin' but chicken shit!"

"So, Peter," said Mrs. Nugget calmly, "Now that you've met these crazy lazy achers, do you want t' deliver yer first sermon before or after Sunday mornin' med'cations?"

"Ugh, how 'bout after."

On the following crisp October Sunday morning, Halloween by coincidence, Peter woke ready to preach the word. All week he had been carefully composing the address, honing each sentence, laboring over each word, memorizing his grand oration.

Before the bathroom mirror, he applied his pancake make-up and painted on a big red smile. Next, he slipped into his baggy costume, adjusted his curly red wig, and positioned his red rubber nose. His red floppy shoes fit perfectly.

Colonel Nugget greeted him at the entrance. "Mornin' Rev'rend Rainbo. Lookin' mighty fine there. Let's pray you can preach the word better than you can package chickens."

In the dining hall, Mrs. Nugget rang her hand bell. "Ev'ryone— listen up! You've jus' had yer breakfast an' med'cations so let's all pay 'tention t' Rev'rend Rainbo de Clown whose gonna preach us the good word."

The words 'Rev'rend Rainbo de Clown' energized him. Peter felt lit by divine fire. His soul quivered at white heat.

Peter began a juggling routine but soon fumbled his balls and stood empty-handed.

Several residents hollered, "Boooooooo."

Peter quickly began a magic trick, passing an egg through his head. He fumbled it, too, and accidently broke the egg on the side of his face.

An irritated old man yelled, "Hey, bonehead! Can't you do nuthin' right?"

With egg yolk dripping down his ear and neck, Peter thought it best to begin his address. "T'day, my sermon is titled 'The Keys t' the Kingdom.' Now, ugh, in the beginnin'...ugh...was the word, an'...ugh, an' in the beginnin'...ugh...thine is...life is..."

"Whut kinda stupid clown are you?" interrupted a fussy old dame.

The first chicken patty that pelted Peter took him by surprise. By the third one, he was dodging not only chicken patties but also other leftover food. One angry old man catapulted a large spoonful of creamed corn casserole that splattered dead center on Peter's forehead.

"Git that funny-lookin' jackass outa here!" yelled a cantankerous crone.

A grouchy geezer shouted, "I don't want no damn fruitcake deliverin' the holy word!"

Mrs. Nugget vigorously rang her hand bell to silence the altercation. The matron approached Peter. "I'm afraid this ain't gonna work. You've done given the res'dents a bad clown experience."

Colonel Nugget cocked his head and took Peter aside. "Mr. Boggs, I ain't happy with whut I done seen here this mornin'. An' I also ain't happy that after three months, you still can't package no more than twenty birds an hour." He cocked his head again. "Somethin' jus' ain't quite right 'bout you."

"Whut d' you mean, Colonel Nugget?"

Colonel Nugget sharpened his glare. "You look funny. Now, I'm gonna cut the chit-chat an' git right t' the point. You ain't got no potential fer chicken stuffin'. Truth is, you jus' ain't cut out fer packagin' chickens or fer preachin' the word, so I'm term'natin' you. I want you packed an' outa my steeple by t'night."

The clown shuffled back to the belfry where he lapsed into a deep sleep.

❖

When Peter woke, still dressed as Rainbo de Clown, his head ached from the enormity of his termination. He smashed his diploma against the iron bell. After packing his suitcase, he thirsted for Grumpy's stiff cocktails. It was Halloween, and he was dressed for the holiday. As the evening darkened, he called Mr. Sticks. For the last time, they passed the setting sun. Or rather, it passed them.

Grumpy's was never busier or gayer than on Halloween. On this one night of the year, even outwardly respectable, civic-minded businessmen who would never be caught dead in Grumpy's during the light of day could don costumes and masks, satisfy their naughty urges and unusual preferences, and the next day return to the life of any ol' Joe next door.

"Is that you, Pete?" asked Grumpy as he stared at the clown slumped on a bar stool.

"That's me alright—I'm Rainbo de Clown. Give me a rum an' Coke. A stiff one."

"How's that cor'spondence course comin' 'long?"

"That stupid cor'spondance course is over. An' so's my career as a min'ster."

"Well, maybe you can find some other way of spreadin' the word."

"Nope. I ain't cut out fer spreadin' the word—if there's even a word t' spread. Grumpy, t'day I've done seen the light—an' there ain't no light t' see. We're all livin' in darkness. An' once we realize that, we're free t' face the truth. An' the truth is I ain't nuthin' but a down-an'-out funny-lookin' bonehead."

"This don't sound like the Pete I know! Whut the hell's wrong with you? An' whut you got yer suitcase fer?"

"I'm hitchin' t' Houston."

"Dressed as a clown?"

"That's right."

"Houston's a wicked city, Pete. I hate t' see you move there. You might git gobbled up."

"Gobbled up here or gobbled up there, in the long run, we're all gonna git gobbled up somewhere by somethin' or other."

The tavern door swung open, and all eyes focused on the newest costumed arrival.

"Well, fer Pete's sake!" exclaimed Grumpy. "He looks like some kinda Egyptian pharaoh. I seen that scary dog creep in here dressed up like that ev'ry Hal'ween fer the past four years. Can't help but wonder who he is. One thing's fer sure—that demon is a troublemaker."

The Egyptian scoped out the masquerade, fixed his eyes upon the clown, crawled through the crowd, and sat next to Peter. The reveler wore a cheap black plastic dog mask with a protruding snout and long pointy ears covering the upper part of his face. His black mane flowed down to his shoulders. He was bare-chested and wore a knee-length black fur skirt with a bushy little black tail and black leather sandals.

"Trick or treat, dog face," greeted Peter. "Whut you doin' this Hal'ween night?"

"Oh, I jus' dropped in fer a few cocktails an' some scavengin'."

"Whut's under that mask? Let me see yer true self."

"Truth is, I look like any ordin'ry dog cravin' an ol' bone t' chew on."

"Come on, take off yer mask."

"I better not show my face in here—bad fer business."

"Jus' whut kinda business we talkin' 'bout?"

"We'll talk 'bout that later. So, t'night you're a clown. I like clowns."

"Yep, I'm Rainbo de Clown. But you can call me Pete. My Mummy done named me Peter, after St. Peter, keeper of the keys t' . . . ah, fergit it."

"My name's Jack."

"Jack, can I buy you a cocktail? I feel like cel'bratin'."

"You bet. A Bloody Mary sounds good."

"Grumpy, I'll have me another rum an' Coke an' a Bloody Mary fer this here dog lookin' fer some ol' bone t' chew on."

"Comin' right up." Grumpy whispered, "Now, Pete, you remember whut I done tol' you. I'd hate t' see you end up as that ol' bone."

"Yeah, yeah, I'll remember."

"So, clown face," asked the dog, "jus' whut are you cel'bratin'?"

"My freedom."

"I wanna hear all 'bout it. But first I'm gonna play some music on the ol' jukebox."

Jack inserted a dime, selected B 13, and pressed 'play'. He grinned and muttered, "Dumb as a clod." Soon Debby Boone warbled "You Light Up My Life."

Peter sipped his cocktail. "Jack, seems like ev'rywhere I go, I hear that new song."

"I'm playin' it jus' fer us, Pete, 'cause you're startin' t' light up my life. You started the minute I done walked in here an' seen you sittin' at the bar all dressed up as a clown."

"Are you tellin' me you're attracted t' clowns?"

"I am."

"Yeah, sure. You mus' take me fer some kinda fool." Peter took another sip.

"So, Pete, whut d' you do fer a livin'?"

"Don't do nuthin'. Got no job. No place t' live. No parents. No friends. No damn nuthin'."

"Well, I'll be yer friend, Pete." He smacked his lips and placed a comforting hand on the boy's shoulder.

Peter was struck by his sincerity. "Really?"

"Yes—really. Hard t' keep good friends these days. I don't have many. Come t' think of it, I could count the number of friends I got on one hand."

"All right—friends it is." Peter held out a hand for a strong shake confirming their new-found alliance.

"An', Pete, if you need a job, I got one fer you."

"I'm afraid all I know how t' do is package chickens."

"That's valu'ble experience. I'll teach you ev'rything you need t' know. An' I got a little room fer you t' stay—rent free."

"Rent free! Jack, you're the best friend I ever done had."

"Pete, I hope I'm not too forward, but since we're best friends, may I kiss you?"

"Ugh huh."

Jack leaned forward, grabbed Peter, and kissed him long, deep, and hard. A bolt of lightning electrified the boy's skinny frame. However, the protracted kiss caused Jack's dog snout to smudge Peter's make-up so that his overdrawn clown smile morphed into a lurid horizontal red smudge.

"Jack, that's the first time I ever done been kissed by anyone 'cept my Mummy."

"Whew! I'm outa breath. So, I'm yer first. Tell me, Pete, d' you ever feel urges—sinful, naughty urges?"

"I'm startin' t' now! Hey, Grumpy, I'd like me another rum an' Coke. Make it a stiff one, too. T'night I'm cuttin' loose!"

"A stiff one—comin' up."

"An' another Bloody Mary fer my new friend—my new best friend."

"An' make it a stiff one fer me, too," added Jack.

"Two stiff ones comin' up."

"So tell me, Pete, would you like t' explore them naughty urges a bit further—with your new best friend?"

"Yes, I think I would!" Jack's exciting offer made Peter uninhibited and fearless. "I'm ready. Got ev'rything I own in my suitcase. Jus' say when."

"How 'bout now?"

"OK, but where?"

"My place in Nac'doches."

"Yer home?"

"Heavens no! I gotta wicked wife an' three horrible little monsters. Let's go t' my office."

They guzzled their cocktails.

Peter stumbled off his barstool. "Jack, I gotta ask you a question."

"Go on."

"Tell me the truth—am I funny-lookin?"

Jack got right in Peter's face. He could see the slovenly buffoon's beard stubble under the white pancake make-up. His breath smelled bad, too, like strong cough syrup, and his eyes looked red. "Pete, you're the handsomest young man I ever done met."

"Thank you, Jack," he slurred.

"Besides, Pete, I have a partic'lar fondness fer clowns. Years ago when I was a poor college student, I used t' make money as an amateur clown performin' tricks at birthday parties."

Jack slowly drove; he knew no haste. The long black station wagon braked before a three-story white Victorian house on Mound Street. Jack steered around back to where a wooden ramp led from the pavement to the door of what had once been the kitchen.

Peter looked wide-eyed. "Are you 'Jack' as in 'Jack L…'"

"Anubis. That's right."

"An' you got a job fer me here in yer fun'ral parlour?"

"Yes, I do. You start t'morrow."

"Am I gonna help you 'balm dead people?"

"That's right. Unless, of course, you want t' help me 'balm livin' people."

Peter smiled uneasily.

"'Balmin' a body ain't that much dif'rent from makin' a fruitcake—or fer that matter packagin' a chicken. Come on in an' make yerself at home."

Peter gazed at the starkly lit room. Still resembling a kitchen, it was clammy and had a vinegary odor. In the center stood the embalming table. From the ceiling hung a metal shower head that pointed to a drain on the white tiled floor. Near a chrome gurney, he eyed the countertop of stainless steel tools and jars of make-up. Somber pipe organ music played on a recording system.

"Can I mix you a drink? You're a rum an' Coke man. Right?"

"That's me alright."

Jack opened a cabinet labeled 'Embalming Fluid' and reached for a bottle of rum and a bottle of vodka. He mixed a rum and Coke and handed the cocktail to Peter. "I'm havin' me a Bloody Mary."

"Whew!" exclaimed Peter. "This here is strong stuff. Jus' buzzes right through me."

"I like 'em stiff. Almost strong enough t' 'balm a body. Only the best for Pete, my new boyfriend."

"Boyfriend!" Peter looked wide eyed and apprehensive. "Did I hear you right—boyfriend?"

"You heard me right. Here's t' us."

"T' us."

The Egyptian dog and the carnival clown clinked their glasses.

"Pete, you look nervous. Chill out. You'd think I was gonna gobble you up. Maybe we should play a little game of spin the gurney."

Peter chuckled.

"Let's put on some cheerful music." Jack removed the cassette of dirge-like organ music, inserted the Chad Mitchell Trio singing "It's a Dying Business," and pressed 'play'. As the trio sang, Jack lip-synced the words 'It was a hell of a funeral' and danced comically around the embalming table. He had to stop, though, after growing short of breath.

"Ha-ha! Oh, Jack, I'm gonna die laughin! I ain't never had so much fun."

"You gotta admit—ol' Jacko sure knows how t' put the 'fun' in 'fun'ral.' Say, I'd like t' show you somethin' special. Only my closest friends know 'bout it." The demonic undertaker got right into Peter's face, smacked his lips, and slurred, "Would you like t' see whut's in my secret room?"

Peter nodded.

"Mum's the word. Okay, Chicken Little?"

"Mum's the word."

Jack pried loose a wall panel exposing a rickety wooden stairway leading down to a basement. "Ain't a whole lotta ol' houses in East Texas got somethin' like this here. I discovered it by accident one day right after I bought the ol' place. It was like unearthin' King Tut's tomb." He pulled a chain that turned on a pale, dim light. "Let me show you the fruit cellar."

❖

Peter peered down into the little box of a dark, dank, dusty room and could barely discern the oblong metal table on the dirt floor.

"This here room is jus' fer me an' my closest friends."

"Looks kinda spooky."

"Climb on down. While I light some incense, you hop on the table an' lie back. I'm gonna give you a massage."

Peter reclined on the table; it felt cold and bumpy.

"Ummmmm. That incense smells good—kinda like Pine-Sol."

"That's right. Jack's gonna take good care of you."

"Hey, whut you doin?"

"I'm removin' yer silly clown costume."

"With scissors?"

"You don't need this outfit no longer. Yer days of clownin' 'round are over."

"Jack, ain't that the truth. I ain't never again gonna dress up like a clown. In fact, I hope I don't never see another clown long as I live."

"Trust me—you won't."

Jack removed Peter's floppy shoes and cut loose the legs and sides of the baggy costume.

Still in his clown make-up, nose, and wig, Peter lay naked except for his flimsy underwear, which Jack next snipped off. "There now, how d' you feel all stretched out an' butt neked?"

"I feel like a plucked bird."

"Would you like another rum an' Coke?"

"No thanks, I still got a damn good buzz from the first one you give me. You make 'em even stiffer than Grumpy. I jus' wanna cut loose an' enjoy this happy time with you, Jack. T'night I'm givin' in t' all my naughty new urges. An' if I'm a sinner—then so be it."

"Then so be it. Here, let me rub yer feet. How does that feel?"

Peter giggled. "You're ticklin' me t' death! Don't stop. Ha-ha-ha!"

"That's right—ha-ha-ha! Laugh, clown, laugh. Now I'm gonna do somethin' you'll really enjoy." Jack opened a box of cellophane and pulled out and cut off an arm-length sheet. "I'm gonna treat you t' a soothin' Egyptian foot wrap."

Jack worked quickly. Within minutes he had wrapped not only Peter's feet, but also his bird-like legs.

"This is fun!" exclaimed Peter. "At last I'm livin' it up."

"You lucky stiff. I knew you'd like it. Let me wrap yer arms next. It's ther'peutic."

"Ummmmm. Feels good."

Like an old pro, Jack methodically wrapped the boy's arms, except for the elbows. "Pete, you're gonna have t' sit up now."

The mortician unrolled large sheets of plastic wrap and swathed Peter's upper torso first under the armpits and then around his chest and down around his stomach. Next, Jack bent and crisscrossed Peter's arms. Using more cellophane, he packaged the boy's arms against his chest.

"You can lie back down now."

Next, Jack carefully enveloped Peter's loins, occasionally turning him on his sides.

"Lookin' mighty fine there! I'm gonna work on that handsome face of yers a while." Jack removed Peter's red rubber nose and curly red wig. "We'll start with this here blindfold, an' then I'll wrap yer head. A blindfold guarantees complete darkness. I don't like no gaps."

"I like darkness."

"Me too. I'll leave yer nose open fer breathin'. I ain't gonna wrap yer ears either. They say hearin's the last t' go."

He then wrapped Peter's crown and forehead and quickly wound the Saran Wrap around the rest of the boy's face, mouth, and neck. When he pulled the plastic tight, it pressed against Peter's lips, flattening them, exposing his teeth and gums in a macabre grin.

"One last thing. I'm gonna squeeze yer legs t'gether an' tie 'em real tight. Gotta be sturdy t' hold the weight."

Peter mumbled, "Mmmmmmmmmmm."

"That's right, Pete, mum's the word."

"Mmmmmmmmm."

Jack smacked his lips. "Pete, you funny-lookin' monkey, I jus' can't git enough of you."

"Mmmmm."

"Well hell, high water, an' damnation! I'm outa Saran Wrap. This ain't never done happened t' me before. I'd finish wrappin' you with duct tape, but it jus' ain't the same. Gotta run t' the grocery store. I won't be gone long, so don't go nowheres."

While climbing the rickety wooden stairs, Jack paused to catch his breath, turn around, and look down into the dim box of a room. Flipping on a bright overhead bulb, he smiled as he inspected the far back wall of the fruit cellar. He took not only pride in his work, but also joy. There—side by side—hanging upside down from a rack attached to the ceiling, dangled four perfectly mummified human forms, each cocooned in cling wrap, each with a grotesque and toothy grimace.

In the bathroom directly above the fruit cellar, Jack removed his dog mask and costume. When he donned a pair of jeans and a cheerful T-shirt reading 'Cadaver de Clown. I'll die laughing', he looked like any ol' Joe next door.

At the late-night Food-Fest on North Street, Jack gathered about twenty rolls of Saran Wrap and headed to the checkout. "You jus' can't git enough," he joked with a stock boy placing wrapped Loco Pollo chickens in the refrigerated meat compartment.

They both laughed heartily.

Then suddenly Jack felt the sharp pain—the tight clamping in his arm, chest, and heart—the shortness of breath. "Help me! Somebody help me!" As he blacked out, he heard boxes of Saran Wrap fall to the floor.

The night manager called an ambulance.

The medic who took Jack's pulse shook his head. "Looks like a bag an' tag t' me."

By the time the ambulance arrived at the hospital, Jack was wearing a label: 'Dead on Arrival'. The night doctor, following routine protocol, ordered him stripped, weighed, tagged, zipped into a plastic body bag, and sent to the basement morgue.

Earlier, after Jack had sealed the entrance to the fruit cellar, Peter at first felt calm. He liked the stillness in the room and enjoyed the pine scent. Anything was better than the stench of ammonia permeating Deadpecker.

He thought of Jack. *Oh, the joy!* He entered into a mysterious realm of sensual delight.

But in the eerie silence, as the effects of rum began to wane, he sensed a growing discomfort. The plastic wrapping began to feel tight—too tight.

He felt short of breath.

He tried to scream.

"Mmmmmmmmm!"

Surely I shall not die, he thought.

Peter lost track of time. *How long had Jack been gone? Thirty minutes? An hour? Two hours? All night? A century or more?*

"Mmmmmm."

His breathing diminished.

His blood, he thought, ceased to flow.

His muscles felt formal, stiff, clod-like.

"Mmmm."

Jack! Oh, Jack . . . Jacko?

"Mmm."

Gobbled up.

He vaguely remembers Jack's words: "Hearin' is the last t' go."

All his being is an ear.

A steeple bell tolls.

In a minor key, Debby Boone warbles "You Light Up My Life." Her voice dampens, deepens, winds down, and dirge-like, melds into the mournful bass pipes of somber organ music until they, too, diminish. Softer—softer—softer.

And then, upon his earlobe, there interposed a large fly with blue uncertain stumbling buzz.

And then the boy—wrecked and solitary—could not hear to hear the keys to the kingdom fall to the floor.

ELEUSIS
ROBERT HYERS

Standing in the baby aisle at Wal-Mart, Adam tried to ignore the fact that he had spotted his nemesis, Thomas, and Thomas' new boyfriend, Vinnie, roaming the store. If they spotted Adam and Adam's boyfriend Justin, Adam would have to talk to them. Adam occupied his mind with deciding which pacifier he wanted, the one with the little gray elephant logo that matched his gray running shoes and thin, polyester raver pants that hugged his tiny waist and widened as they moved down his legs, or the pacifier with a powder blue star that matched the tight powder blue shirt clinging to his naturally flat chest and stomach. Perhaps he should try matching a pacifier to the candy bracelets he was wearing. The bracelets contained a rainbow of different shapes and colors and stretched from his wrists to his elbows. The outfit was more colorful than he was used to, but he wanted to fit in at his first rave. He'd been living with Justin for the past year and had made excuses for not being able to attend any of the raves Justin was spinning at because Adam thought he'd feel uncomfortable. But with each day together Justin meant more to Adam, and he wanted to attend at least one for Justin. Adam held a pacifier in each of his delicate hands and moved the pacifiers up and down, his face hard with intent.

"Just pick one," Justin said, annoyed.

"Give me a minute," Adam replied. He never had to buy a pacifier before and was hesitant, but Justin said it was necessary so that Adam wouldn't grind his teeth or rip open the inside of his mouth after the ecstasy kicked in. Since one's handbag should match one's shoes, Adam concluded the same must be true for a pacifier.

"I'll take this one," Adam finally declared, holding up the elephant logo and sliding the star back onto the display.

Adam scanned the aisle. Even at this late hour the store bustled with white trash taking advantage of everyday low prices, dressed in jeans with expandable waists and faded corporate giveaway T-shirts. Before Adam knew it, Thomas and Vinnie had turned the corner. Adam and Thomas' eyes locked. The target had been found; the two were now fast approaching.

Thomas was a queen Adam knew casually from the clubs. Thomas had always rubbed Adam the wrong way because Thomas never had to work for anything. He floated through life, using his good looks and charm to get whatever he needed from his current boyfriend, which now happened to be Vinnie. Adam vaguely remembered Vinnie from early adolescence; both of their families had lived in the same government-subsidized apartment complex for a few years. Adam had avoided Vinnie whenever possible. On the few instances fate had them cross paths inside the complex; Vinnie would interrupt his football game with the other tenants' children to call Adam a faggot. Now gossip whispered that Vinnie was a bisexual mess who shot steroids in the gym during the day and snorted cocaine in the clubs at night.

"So, Adam dear," Thomas said after an insincere hello and peck on Adam's cheek, "that's a...colorful outfit you have on there."

"Yes, Thomas. Well when in Rome...you know the rest." Adam inspected Thomas, making sure that Thomas could follow Adam's eyes as they moved up and down Thomas' profile. Thomas wore black slacks and a tight button down shirt. "I see you've pulled one of your gay classics off the rack."

Thomas ignored the remark. "So, Adam, my love, did you remember to put us on the comp list like you promised?"

"Of course I did. Just tell them to look on Justin's list."

"Is this Justin?" Thomas' big blue eyes, which must've been contacts since Thomas had brown eyes, inspected Justin.

Adam smiled as he watched Thomas look Justin over because Adam knew Thomas was jealous. Justin was hot, but a different kind of hot than Adam or Thomas—a natural, rugged kind of hot. Justin never had to keep exercise regimens to remove those persistent ten pounds or stand naked over a mirror to apply baby powder and Vaseline for razor burn or rub in dabs of cover-up over pimples pushing through his skin like Adam and Thomas had to. Now Justin was sporting a three day old untrimmed beard. Justin's dark brown hair was always messed up. His eyebrows always needed a trim. His cuticles were picked at and traces of dirt clung to his pale fingertips. Sometimes Adam thought Justin's kind of hot was better than Adam's or Thomas' because Justin never had to work at it.

"Yes," Adam replied.

"Were you going to introduce us?" Thomas said though the half-smile he only used for flirting.

"Justin, this is Thomas," Adam said half-heartedly, waving a hand in Thomas' general direction.

A shopping cart turned the corner, preceded by the sound of its squeaking wheel, filled with canned vegetables and powdered fruit juice and tacky knickknacks like a green sign with lavender writing that read something about home and the heart. An obese woman pushed the cart; her labored breaths accompanied each slow step. Her eyebrows raised slightly when she noticed the group standing there. Her beady eyes widened, lifting some excess cheek skin.

"I know the four of you can't be up to no good," she announced.

"Excuse me?" Adam said.

"Have you all accepted Jesus Christ as your personal Savior?"

"Lady, don't waste your time with that Jesus shit on us. Don't you have a cousin you should be fucking?"

"Don't get smart with me, boy. The end times are near. The rapture will be upon us. I'm just tryin' to help you all out." The woman passed them and turned into the next aisle, her labored breaths and squeaking cart wheels moving with her.

"That was strange," Thomas commented.

"She reminds me of your mom, Adam," Vinnie said.

"No, she doesn't," Adam replied.

"Yeah she does. Remember when we were kids? She used to stop me and my mom all the time and talk about that rapture thing."

His mother's obsession with religion was brief but intense. Adam remembered how his mother would drag him out with her to their complex's curb when she was just drunk enough to function. She'd make Adam hold the stack of flyers containing images of rising suns and gleaming crucifixes while she gripped his hand like she was afraid he might flee. If he closed his eyes he swore he was clasping hands with a skeleton, her hands an emaciated and cracked copy of the soft and full-figured hands in her high school yearbook. She'd wave one flyer with her free hand and proclaim her knowledge of the coming rapture—when God would scoop up his chosen few and leave the rest to suffer unimaginable torture—to cracking stone stoops seating uninterested audiences of men drinking from brown paper bags and pregnant women watching strollers.

"Oh yeah, that," Adam said, shrugging it off. "She was a little crazy with that stuff. But it didn't last long."

"She must've given the crazy to you then," Thomas remarked and laughed, placing his outstretched hand at the base of his thin long neck and throwing his head back.

Anger burned in Adam's gut. He had spent years quarantining those experiences with his mother and keeping the details of his home life contained. And here, Vinnie, this little piece of white trash, was trying to undo all of Adam's hard work.

Something pulsed in Vinnie's pocket.

"We really need to get out of here," Justin said.

"All right—"

"Shh!" Thomas interrupted. Vinnie looked at Adam who now held his cell phone to his ear. Vinnie signaled Adam to keep quiet by raising his stubby index finger to his fat mouth and said hello into his cell. He hurried to the far end of the aisle.

"What's his problem?" Adam said.

"Nobody knows Vinnie's into guys too and he doesn't want his straight friends overhearing," Thomas said.

"Overhearing what?"

"Overhearing, like…our voices."

"Why? Because we sound gay?"

Thomas didn't respond.

"And you put up with that?"

Thomas pointed his long moisturized index finger at Vinnie. "But look at him. He's so hot."

The anger ignited again and Adam's muscles tightened. That mess might've been able to tell Thomas when he could and couldn't speak, but not Adam. "Hold this," Adam commanded Justin, handing him the pacifier and water bottle. Adam picked up a telephone attached to a pole nearby and hit the intercom.

"Ladies and gentlemen," Adam said, making sure to annunciate his "s" sounds; he wanted the fag to come through in his voice. "The short guy built like a truck and on his cell in…" Adam looked up at the aisle sign, "…in Aisle 17…sucks cock." Justin tried to pull Adam from the phone but Adam pushed Justin away. Adam watched with elation as Vinnie's eyes widened with panic. "Yes, his name is Vinnie and he sucks cock—the bigger the better." Vinnie abandoned his phone call and ran towards Adam. "Tell your friends and neighbors," Adam continued, "Vinnie likes nothing better than a big fat cock in his mou—"

Adam held an ice pack below his eye. The scenery along the interstate highway passed by the open car window. A hot summer day had turned into a comfortable night and the city had turned to country; where crowds of square towers had stood now stood crowds of trees behind an unfolding silver ribbon of guard rail. The pain from Vinnie's square fist and Adam's resulting anger had dulled. Although Adam knew how to fight and had the high school suspensions to prove it, he was proud he didn't punch back; he'd left that behind when he'd graduated. Violence was for trash like Vinnie who couldn't control themselves. Trash that made themselves spectacles in a routine mess of broken teeth and blood and beer. Trash who would never understand why they couldn't break free of government housing and food stamps.

Justin's mixes sounded tinny through his twenty year old car's speakers, like the mixes were coming out of an old transistor radio. It reminded Adam of the one his mother used to listen to in the kitchen on the rare occasion she was sober enough to make them both dinner. The sounds of 1970s classic rock would mix with the smells of cheap meat burning and secondhand smoke.

"You ready for some dinner, my baby?" she'd ask, unaware that the question caused the cigarette hanging from her lip to ash into the boiling potatoes.

"Sure, Mom," Adam would respond curtly. Her voice always bubbled over with pride when she asked that question, thinking that this poor excuse for a meal once every other month somehow made her a good mother.

Adam recognized the song playing, the heavy beat and soft bass line, then the synthesizers that hung in the air, waxing and waning, and the melody plucked by something resembling an archaic version of the guitar: *Eleusis*. He'd heard it countless times while Justin practiced. Adam had considered telling Justin about the ancient mystery cult surrounding Eleusis, a cult Adam had learned about in his Ancient Greece course, where followers simulated death through the ingestion of hallucinogens in the hopes of living a better life. But Justin was always focused on his records and Adam never got the chance.

"I need to tell you what to expect on these drugs," Justin said.

Later that night Adam would be candy flipping, taking acid and ecstasy. Justin had mentioned it a few weeks ago. He had told stories about his friends' life changing experiences, about mystical visions, about seeing and feeling God. Although Adam didn't care for the kind of religion his mother had exposed him to, in the year after he'd left his mother and moved in with Justin, he'd been trying hard to improve himself physically and mentally by doing things like getting up early to exercise and enrolling in community college. And now he wanted to improve himself spiritually.

"Okay," Adam said. He sat at attention.

"The ecstasy's gonna make you think you love everybody. Everybody's gonna be cool."

"And the acid?"

"Because you're feeling so good on the ecstasy, you should have a good trip."

"Should?"

"There're no guarantees with acid."

"That doesn't sound good."

"Don't worry. No matter what this will be a life-changing experience. And just remember, whatever's happening, it isn't real. It's like a dream. If you like what's happening, enjoy it. And if you don't, just wait it out. Sooner or later you'll wake up."

The dream talk brought him back to his mother. Her relationship with postmillennial Christianity had introduced her to a short-lived fascination with dreams. She had believed that when man closed his eyes to the world, he opened them to God. She had preached the importance of dreams to Adam; how according to some Biblical passages, God prophesied pivotal, life-changing events in our dreams, and that he should imitate her in keeping a spiral notebook and pen at his bedside. He never took her advice.

❖

By the time they reached the campground, the ice pack had warmed and Adam abandoned it. Justin pulled into the last empty parking space. Adam used the rearview mirror to apply cover-up gingerly to the portion of his face now turning purple. Justin pulled out his record bag and the two got out of the car. The admission line stretched in curves for what seemed like eternity, and Justin motioned Adam with a raised index finger to follow him to the front of the line. Justin flashed his laminated pass and they were admitted. Looking back at the poor souls still waiting in line, Adam had to admit he loved being the DJ's boyfriend.

The first time they had met, Adam assumed he'd hit the queer jackpot after spotting Justin in the local gay club Adam frequented and learning Justin was a DJ. Dating the DJ brought one a certain amount of status in Adam's circles. The DJ was a god perched atop his booth, the place that allowed him to survey the dance floor, to use his innate sense of others to select the music that would manufacture the necessary escape from the crowd's daytime stresses, transforming the dancers into something larger than themselves. When drugs and drink were thrown in, the DJ was kind of like a modern day psychopompos—the guide during the Eleusinian mysteries. This divinity automatically transferred to the DJ's boyfriend.

But on that first night Justin explained that he spun a genre called uplifting trance at raves, and he was only at Adam's favorite club for a friend's birthday. Adam was disappointed; none of his friends liked raves since these events weren't focused on fashion and featured instrumental music that couldn't be lip-synched to. This meant Justin's occupation wouldn't improve Adam's status after all. But then the two found a dim, neon-lit alcove away from the invasive mixture of heavy house beats and confusion of queens' chatter, and started talking. Justin had a benevolent nature which attracted Adam. Justin lived in the present, but was unlike the queens who did it in the name of hedonism. Justin felt having goals meant stepping on people, what you obtain someone else has lost, and he wanted to limit his negative impact.

The campground, illuminated with large overhead lights, was large and flat and green and stretched out to the shadow of a skyline of evergreens. Beyond the overhead lights hung blackness, interrupted by a full moon and clusters of stars. Small tents of various sizes and colors dotted the grounds and crowds of ravers walked around in flowing pants that resembled Adam's. Most carried water bottles. The tips of their cigarettes glowed red as the ravers inhaled. Some wore different combinations of piercings: noses, lips, ears, eyebrows. Others had dyed their greasy and matted hair unnatural colors bright purple and neon green.

Justin took Adam off to one side behind a group of tents and ripped open a bottle of water. "Swallow the pill first. Then put the blotter on your tongue," he said, handing everything to Adam. Adam followed instructions. The acid blotter felt like construction paper as it disintegrated on his tongue.

Adam felt anxious in this foreign world as he followed Justin towards the outline of the main stage. Adam was used to being surrounded by crowds of gay men dressed in European cut slacks and holding cocktail glasses of glowing pink cosmopolitans.

But now he moved through crowds of straight ravers with a completely different sense of fashion. Some wore dark earth tones and black leather bracelets with metal studs; others wore neon necklaces made from the same beads as their bracelets. A few more practically minded ravers had attached their pacifiers to their necklaces. The sweet smell of pot smoke passed through the fabric of crowded tents and settled on Adam's clothing. At last Adam and Justin stood at the foot of the stage. To soothe his anxiety, Adam scanned the crowd and quickly picked out the handful of queens. They were easy to spot in tight brightly colored shirts, their heads held high and chests stretched out, forever assuming the queen's natural stance that resembled the star being aware of her spotlight.

Out of the crowd Thomas appeared, pulling Vinnie behind him. There were no disingenuous pecks on the cheek this time. Thomas' hand rested on his bony hip. Adam knew what Thomas was about to say. With one eyebrow raised, Thomas announced, "So Adam, they couldn't find us on Justin's list."

"That's funny," Adam responded, letting his lips form just the suggestion of a smile.

"It's very funny. Did you really put us on Justin's list?"

"No, I did not."

"Why not?"

"Because your bitch ass gets comped everywhere you go."

The lids around his eyes scrunched inward.

"You know you shouldn't do that when you're angry," Adam said. "You'll end up with crow's feet."

Thomas's long fingers curled up into two pathetic fists that hung at his waist.

"What are you gonna do now? Sick Vinnie on me?"

"What was that?" Thomas asked. "You stuttered."

Adam didn't realize it but he had stuttered. His tongue and lips felt numb.

"You look like you have cat eyes," Thomas continued. "What are you, fucking tripping right now?"

Adam didn't answer.

Thomas moved in closer, his eyelids still squeezed with anger. He lifted his head slightly in what Adam assumed was a bid for superiority. "Vinnie told me stories. About your mother. You know, you're just like her. A fucking crazy-ass addict fuckup."

The anger glowed again in Adam's gut. He wanted to knock Thomas to the ground, to put aside all the hard work he'd been doing to improve himself and show Thomas why Adam had all those high school suspensions. But his body felt too weak. Adam felt the faint echo of a calloused hand from behind squeezing his shoulder. It was Justin.

"Come on," Justin said. "I have to get ready to spin."

"Yes," Adam said, feeling a smile appear on his face and a weak sense of superiority. "I have to go with my boyfriend, the DJ, because he needs to spin."

Thomas' face stiffened. He grabbed Vinnie's hand and pulled him back into the crowd.

"You better dance," Justin said playfully, "I'll be watching." He gave Adam a small kiss. Adam didn't respond. His toes and fingertips had lost feeling. He felt like he was fading away. What if he disappeared?

"Are you okay?" Justin asked.

Adam nodded slowly. His head felt light on his neck.

"Just wait it out," Justin instructed.

The crowd had grown thicker. Massive speakers towered either side of a DJ spinning breakbeat while a row of hanging spotlights burned above; his bandana darkened with sweat. Adam looked down. The grass had turned translucent. It resembled that green glass they use to make those tacky glass sculptures of flying fish that always end up at white-trash yard sales. On stage, Justin searched his bag for just the right record. Adam noticed a kid with the faux-hawk staring at Justin. This kid's skin was still tight with innocence; he couldn't have been older than sixteen. He was definitely gay and just as attractive, if not more, than Adam. This transformed the kid from a harmless distraction to competition. Normally Adam would be jealous, the instinct to protect his boyfriend leaping out like a predator to protect his fresh kill. But this instinct never materialized. It must have been the drugs.

The DJ signaled the end of his set by hitting the turntable's power button, which slowed the record to a stop, causing the beat to slow until it sounded demonic and finally ceased to exist. Justin called out the DJ's name and the audience responded with shouts and applause. Justin put on a record and soft synthesizers filled the cool night air. Adam felt lighter, like his body was dissipating, like he was becoming translucent.

A bass line rose up from the synthesizers. Adam moved his head back and forth. Soon he found that the bass was all he could concentrate on. He found himself sitting on the ground; the moist earth seeped through his pants and made his boxers damp, cooling his bony ass. The synthesizers lay on top of the beat. Adam's body felt weightless and expansive, like he could reach into the blackness above and collect the stars and moon and focus their light and heat inside himself. Now he understood where uplifting trance got its name. He felt teeth grind against each other. He hardly felt the pacifier as he pulled it from his pocket and popped it in his mouth.

Adam looked up and watched Justin. As the first record spun, Justin searched his bag and pulled out a new record. He placed it on the turntable, spun it back, and let it go. The first record's bass line repeated itself for a few measures, matched perfectly to the beat of the new record. Adam recognized the new bass line as *Eleusis*. After a few more measures the beat and bass line stopped with an echoing cymbal crash. The stage lights and the moon turned black, leaving the turntables' green glow as the only light. The new synthesizer waxed and waned in the darkness. The archaic guitar notes plucked again, dancing through the black spaces once occupied by the stars. Images of people faded in and out of the darkness: Thomas and Vinnie, the kid with the faux-hawk, the Wal-Mart woman. There was no difference between them and Adam. Justin was right; the drugs were changing Adam. The moon returned. Another cymbal crashed and the moon exploded, blanching the blackness. Justin and the equipment became black against the white light.

Adam massaged his cheekbone. It no longer hurt. *Eleusis* didn't stop playing but the ravers had stopped dancing. They lined up single file, the neon colored ones and the dark earth toned ones, all different heights and weights and hair colors. The Wal-Mart woman waited in line somewhere towards the middle. Thomas and

Vinnie stood last in line. The anger in Adam's gut the two had created had been extinguished. His insides felt empty, a vacuum, void of oxygen.

Slowly the line moved up the few steps of one of the stage's side entrances and onto the stage floor. Adam looked up at the stage, his body so light he could hardly feel the movement. The music still played but Justin wasn't behind the mixer. Justin stood at the entrance to the white void, holding a clipboard and a pen. The first raver in line, with bright purple hair and a barbell through his nose, told Justin his name. Justin flipped through a few pages on the clipboard and crossed something off. He looked up and nodded quickly. The barbell raver walked towards the rear of the stage, passed through the whiteness, and disappeared. One by one, Justin repeated this exchange with the next few waiting in line.

Adam ran towards the stage. Somewhere below, he felt his foot turn the wrong way. His ankle twisted and he dropped to the ground. He felt a dull smack as his face made contact with the wet grass. He picked himself up and brushed the dirt from his face; both his face and fingertips felt numb. Cover-up had bled onto his hands. He feared everyone could see the bruise now. He feared they would point out the imperfection, and conclude that there must be more profound imperfections below Adam's surface, push their dirty, raver fingers against his face and puncture his skin, then feel blindly inside him for his mother's God pamphlets and dream journals. He continued to the stage. He pushed himself through the line and up the stage's stairs.

"What's going on here?" Adam demanded.

"I'm doing my job," Justin replied, keeping his eyes on the clipboard.

"Your job?" Adam said, frustrated.

"Psychopompos," he said, his eyes still fixed on the clipboard.

"Will you look at me! What do you mean psychopompos?"

Justin lifted his eyes from the clipboard. "You know what a psychopompos is. You learned about it in college."

"I know what it is. How do you know?"

Adam could sense the contours of his body again, his physical limits.

"Let me get back to my job please."

"But—"

"Please!" Justin exclaimed. He returned to the clipboard.

Why was Justin so angry? Adam hadn't done anything wrong. Adam wasn't the one keeping secrets. Adam felt the anger again, reigniting the piles of dry kindling and tinder with the help of a few smoldering embers.

A few more ravers passed through. Then the Wal-Mart woman entered the light, weighed down with her heavy breaths. Now the kid with the faux-hawk was up.

The kid slid his gaze up and down Justin's rugged profile while Justin inspected the clipboard papers. Watching this awakened Adam's familiar jealousy, now crouched and ready to pounce on its target. Who the hell did this kid think he was? Adam wanted to reach out and strangle this horny teenage faggot's skinny neck. Finally Justin looked up and nodded. The kid with the faux hawk entered the light.

Thomas and Vinnie stood next.

"I wouldn't bother looking," Adam said in Justin's direction while keeping his eyes pinned on Thomas. "Their names aren't there."

Justin flipped through all of the pages then started double-checking the names last through first.

"I told you they're not on it, Justin," Adam said, both hands secured on his hips.

Justin nodded quickly. "You're both in."

Thomas smiled, pulled his bony shoulders back, and tilted his triangular head. "I guess we are on the list after all," he said, still staring at Adam. He turned to Justin. "Thank you, gorgeous," Thomas said though that flirtatious half-smile. Angry flames rose up from inside Adam's stomach; they licked the bottoms of his lungs and restricted his breathing. Thomas pulled Vinnie along and the two passed into the whiteness.

"Now it's my turn, right?" Adam said.

Justin started inspecting the pages again.

"No need to check. I know I'm in. If that trash got in, I have to be on that list."

"What about me?" someone said.

Adam recognized the slight whistle that sometimes accompanied the voice's vowels, produced by years of heavy smoking. Like an insect, embarrassment crawled back inside Adam, its antennae and shell wings brushing Adam's insides, its strong mandible helping it to burrow deep into Adam's gut. Adam had never wanted Justin to meet her, to meet the alcoholic mother who only loved her son in the moments she was so drunk she forgot how much she loved her booze, a woman who chose to stay drunk and float through life using government housing and food stamps rather than doing the hard work necessary to sober up and improve her and her son's lives.

He turned and faced her. The years of hard liquor had eroded deep lines into her skin; her lips, smeared with her favorite red lipstick, looked like crumpled gift-wrap from decades of pulling on filters. Her yellow hair, which always reminded Adam of straw, fell wildly around her face. He hadn't seen her anywhere in the line.

"Adam, my baby." she said.

"What are you doing here?" Adam said.

She pointed to the white light beyond Justin.

Justin looked up from his clipboard. "So you're Adam's mother?"

"Yes."

"It's very nice to finally meet you, ma'am." Justin smiled.

Adam's mother smiled back; the crumpled gift-wrap stretched to reveal her yellowed teeth. She turned to Adam. "I wish I could turn back the clock, my baby. I wish I could go back and make things different, make them better for you. I love you, Adam. I hope you know that."

"Wishing is cheap." Adam left it that. He didn't want to argue this again; she'd been wishing his whole lifetime.

Justin looked down at the list, then up again, and addressed Adam's mother. "You're good to go."

"I hope I see you on the other side," she said to Adam. She kissed him on the cheek. He recoiled. With her face drawn in disappointment, she disappeared into the whiteness.

"Why are you so mean to your mother?" Justin asked.

"It's a long story," he said quickly. "Now am I on the list?"

Justin checked again. "I'm sorry."

"What? That's impossible!" Adam felt every part of his body again. He felt his fists tighten. He felt his arm swing at Justin's chin. He watched Justin pull back. He felt the air between them brush against his knuckles. What had Adam just tried to do? In the past year had he really evolved? After all this had work, was he still just a beast like Vinnie?

"Are you going too?" Adam asked.

"Yes."

"What am I supposed to do here by myself?"

"Remember what I told you?"

"Wait it out," Adam said calmly, as if saying it calmly would help him accept his new reality.

Justin's rough lips kissed Adam's. Justin moved into the whiteness and disappeared. The whiteness closed behind him.

Adam turned around onstage and looked out at the empty field. The moonlight returned and illuminated the trash: empty water bottles and miniature sandwich bags used to hold pills. These ravers are pigs, Adam thought. *Eleusis* had stopped; Adam didn't know when. He felt a breeze sweep past him. It animated flaps of fabric attached to the abandoned tents. He wondered how long the acid would last; Justin had never told him. Or maybe this was a dream. If so, he wondered how long it would be before he would wake. For now he had to get out of here.

The streets were empty as Adam drove Justin's car. He needed to be someplace safe, someplace familiar, where he could make sense of the night. He returned to the place he'd been running from for the past year.

He screeched into an open spot at the curb of the complex. The apartment buildings looked the same as when he had left, armed with metal bars across the first floor windows and lined with trim the color of shit. He searched through a few bags in the backseat and found his old key.

Doug, a drunk who'd lived in this complex as long as Adam could remember, sat on the stoop. Doug was the one who had gotten Adam's mother involved with that church.

Adam remembered the first time his mother had taken him to that church. Even at his young age he was leery of any referral from Doug, but of course Adam's mother was always too drunk to notice how drunk Doug always was. Adam remembered the echoes of a pipe organ playing and people shouting as he and his mother searched the parking lot for an empty space. The church contained a theater to host its annual passion plays, a Christian retail store, and a sanctuary larger than the first floor of Adam and his mothers' entire apartment building. Once inside, Adam witnessed a fiery sermon which spiritually armed the congregation for the coming apocalypse, accompanied by screams and jumps to cymbal crashes. Finally, the pastor asked if there were any new members. Adam's mother stood like a shot and yanked Adam up along with her. The pastor asked her if she had given herself over to Jesus. "Yes!" she proclaimed before the pastor had finished the question. "Hallelujah!"

"Adam?" Doug's face was weathered from the years of cheap booze and the construction jobs he had held down periodically when he could still stay sober for a few months at a time.

"Hey, Doug."

"What are you doin' here now?"

"Visiting Mom."

"She ain't here."

"Where is she?"

"I dunno. She hasn't been around for a while. Nobody has."

Adam considered telling Doug about the rave; nobody would believe drunk Doug anyway if he tried to retell the story. But Adam decided against it. Either it had actually happened or he had inherited his mother's mental imbalance; both options were unattractive and voicing the events would only make them feel concrete in a way he didn't want to deal with right now.

"Maybe she got caught up in the rapture," Doug suggested.

"That religion shit's ridiculous."

"How dare you say that. Just because you don't believe somethin' doesn't mean it don't exist."

"But you're a God-fearing man, right, Doug? You've accepted Jesus Christ into your life. If it was the rapture, why were you left here with me?"

"Anybody who believes they deserve the rapture, don't." He came in close; the liquor's medicine odor sat between the two. "God works in mysterious ways."

"Where did you learn that? Your last court ordered AA meeting?"

Adam moved past Doug, listening to the brown paper bag crinkle as Doug took another swig, and entered the apartment. Everything looked the same as when Adam had left. The tiny metal box of a sink in the galley kitchen was still cluttered with dirty pots. The transistor radio sat on the small window above. The coffeepot, stained black from the inside, occupied the counter corner and the green linoleum floor still curled at one end.

The memory of their last clash assaulted him—the screaming, the deep gulping sounds of amber and clear liquids as Adam fed them down the sink drain, the crash of black and brown bottles onto the floor as Adam struggled with his mother's skeleton hands at the sink.

"Why are you doing this to me?" his mother had screeched. She grabbed her coffee cup and dropped to the kitchen floor. She tried to scoop up the black puddles of alcohol that had pooled into the warped linoleum. She screamed as the glass shards drove into her knees. Finally the pain was too much and she had to stand again.

Adam stood motionless at the sink.

Supporting herself with one hand gripping the sink, Adam's mother whimpered as she pulled out each shard with her other hand. "Don't just stand there," she yelled. "Help me!"

They had no first aid supplies so he pulled a few kitchen rags from the counter, soaked them in the puddles of alcohol, and used them to clean the wounds.

"Why did you do that to me, Adam?" his mother asked between dramatic winces as the application of alcohol burned her wounds. "You know this isn't my fault. You know I have a disease."

Later that night, after he knew his mother's wounds weren't serious enough for an emergency room visit, he shoved as many clothes as he could into his messenger bag. He waited for her to finish a pocket bottle of vodka and fall asleep in front of the flicker of the living room television. He considered giving her a light kiss on the cheek, or at least covering her with the ragged afghan from her bedroom. But he didn't want to risk waking her. And besides, she didn't deserve that kind of care. So Adam tiptoed through the kitchen. He slowly closed the front door. He inserted the key and gently turned the padlock until he felt the soft click and knew she was locked safely inside.

Now with his mother missing, Adam regrets not kissing her goodbye. What if she never returned? What if Doug was right and this was the rapture? Adam reprimanded himself. There was no such thing as the rapture; this was an effect of the acid and ecstasy. Period. His mother would return.

He moved from the broken linoleum of the kitchen to the discolored and uneven shag carpeting of the living room. He sat on the beat-up couch he'd helped his mother pick up off a curb years ago, the one she'd been sleeping on when he had abandoned her. He absorbed the faint and familiar smell of mold. Next to the couch stood the scratched and nicked end table holding a half-drunken bottle of vodka and a spiral notebook with a pen shoved into the spine's thin metal rings. Adam was reminded of his mother's dream journal and hoped she hadn't returned to Doug's church. Adam opened the notebook to what looked like the rough draft of a note addressed to him:

I understand why you felt you had to leave. Being your mother. Being a mother isn't easy. I know I wasn't the best mother but I really tried. This disease. This problem of mine—

Adam jerked away in frustration. He'd heard similar words a thousand times. He listened to the buzz of the refrigerator. He wished she was here. He wanted to hear those words again; maybe they wouldn't turn into arguments now.

He entered his bedroom. Everything here was the same as well. Pictures he'd ripped from various fashion magazines were still taped at odd angles to his walls; his faded sheets and worn blanket still sat tangled on top of his bare mattress. He wondered if his mom hadn't touched his room because she hoped he would return or because she'd rather spend her free time drinking than turning his room into something usable like a guest room or storage. He pulled apart the blanket and sheets, made the bed, and slipped in. He derived a new comfort from the persistent hint of cigarette smoke in his blanket and sheets. Adam wanted this dream to end; he had waited it out long enough. He closed his eyes. He prayed that when he woke he would hear the groan of the living room couch as his mother sat up, stretched her neck like a hungry nestling, and drank from a new pocket bottle of vodka.

SAMPLE DAY
JERRY RABUSHKA

Hank looked at himself in the mirror. "What tie should I wear, Keith?"

Keith didn't answer.

"This one today, then." He pulled his knot tight. "Still love ya, Keith," he said. "I wonder what you would look like now. All blown up and nowhere to go."

People were used to Hank at Sample Day. He'd smile. He'd eat. He'd thank people for the smallest portion like someone had cooked all day just to feed him from a petri dish. He took another look in the mirror. The good thing about his problem was that sometimes he could see Keith in the flesh. Not today, though. Keith was sulking. Post-Traumatic Stress Disorder had its drawbacks.

There was a ghost behind Hank's good looks that kept them faded. It made head-turners wish they'd known him before whatever happened to him happened. They looked into his face and longed to experience what it had been before. He looked good at first glance, then take another look and there was a whole new plane of handsome after you rode out the first one.

Mostly gone now.

❖

Lila was on her way to pick Hank up. She'd never been to Sample Day. Hank met her on Thanksgiving. He was poor—so many vets were poor—and he limped into a nearby church kitchen to have some dinner. His left leg still worked, but not so well. He dragged it behind him, along with Keith and the grenade.

Lila was putting mashed potatoes onto his plate and ladling on some gravy that was probably from a mix. Someone had opened pack after pack of brown gravy to give the homeless and helpless a homemade meal. Hank smiled innocently and gratefully when people gave him food. And he had on Keith's favorite tie—no one knew that Keith had never seen it.

Lila smiled at him. "Happy Thanksgiving, soldier."

"How did you know?"

"I just know," she said.

Everyone knew. The limp was most likely from either a car or a grenade. After the grenade, Hank didn't drive.

Lila was older than Hank, probably fifty-five. She wore comfy clothes—feeding the poor didn't call for glamor. Twenty years into her loving relationship her partner announced that she was straight. Grizz left Lila for a man. Left her floundering alone with three cats that all died that same year. Abandoned by all her companions, she was forced into making choices she didn't want to make and decided that the best idea was to start life over again—to get back the innocence she thought she'd never need.

In volunteering, she was appreciated where in love she was not.

She saw Hank often. She returned his smiles and played along with his childlike happiness about a plate of green beans and mashed pot. He liked the glow that shone around her when she filled his plate—just like the ladies at Sample Day.

Not all that much to look at, many considered her "dumpy" and she did indeed fill out her clothing unflatteringly. Hank saw past the hanging triceps and out of date outfits with a dog's innate sense of judgment. *This is a really good person.*

Keith would have been thirty-three, but twenty-three was all God had given him. Just a short time with Hank, a short wonderful secret love that only revealed itself in Keith's dying moment. As Keith lost blood, the color drained from Hank's face, as if Hank had tried to die along with him, but failed.

Keith liked Hank's hair, his eyes, his top lip, his mustache— Hank kept it especially for Keith. "It's bigger now that I'm not in the army," he explained to Keith. He tugged some hair on his chin.

"It droops now like you wanted it. I'll keep it so you'll recognize me. I'll be so much older than you."

Hank didn't go to church, but he got religious. God having a plan was the only thing that explained anything to him. He even had sex when God told him to. When God said, "Hank, you're a man and you deserve this." Then he would do it. Since Keith, he hadn't been with anyone more than once.

Lila was the same. She had been living a perfect life, but it was based on someone else's goodwill. Someone with the power to take perfect, put it in the garbage disposal, turn it on and watch her scream. Now Hank and Lila moved through life like shades in Hades, paying the penalty one does when love matters too much.

It wasn't love that ruined Hank. It was the grenade, then the betrayal that was the USA.

"Have you ever been to Sample Day?" Hank's face lit up with the words. A big innocent smile, a little less ghost.

"What's that?" Lila asked.

"Oh, wow, you should go! It's where they have all the samples out at Whole Foods in these little cups. It's free! It's really tasty."

It was about the only time he ate more than a sandwich with mashed potatoes and a veggie of the day.

"They mix stuff all together!" he said.

"Really? That's exciting!" She played along as if she'd never seen a plate with more than two ingredients at the same time.

Keith loved Army-grade mashed potatoes. He called it mashed pot from the ubiquitous abbreviation. It was fun. Mashed pot and grrrr beans. He had black hair over a light complexion and as much mustache as the army would allow. Deep eyes with long dark lashes and a protruding rounded nose gave him a unique and jaw-dropping appearance. Even the straight-straight, oh-so-straight guys in the army unit used their nimbler hand while wondering what it would be like to make out and stretch out with Keith. There weren't so many girls around, and Keith was awesome enough that they could tell him to his face that he was so beautiful and no one thought anything of it. No one knew about him and Hank until the grenade.

❖

Everyone knew about Lila and Grizz. Everyone. When it ends, who knows what's worse—when everyone knows or no one knows. She felt the grenade and it had never been thrown.

"I wish I could be more like you," she said to Hank. "You appreciate the smallest thing."

"It's all I have."

Hank didn't know she was a lesbian at first. There wasn't much she liked to say about Grizz waking up one day announcing that she liked men and always had. Lila lying wounded like she'd been stabbed forty times during a home invasion.

"It's what God wants," said Grizz. "He wants men and women to be together. Oh, and you've really let yourself go."

God wants me to help vets, Lila figured out. *Homeless. People who can't help themselves and who everyone else gave up on. God brought me this far to show me that. I can do this,* she thought. *People say I can't be a lesbian and love God, but now I realize that God put me in this position so I can give love to more than just Grizz. I can give love to people that need it and deserve it.*

Innocence. Turkey. Mashed potatoes. Green beans.

Happy Thanksgiving.

Merry Christmas.

The most important days were spent with strangers. No more lesbian issues, lesbian cliques, lesbian politics, lesbian bars, lesbian catfights. *Just live a life where preference doesn't matter; just sometimes to remind yourself you are human, you succumb to it.* Just sometimes. Hank's ghost walked around, Lila locked hers away.

❖

Hank liked the feel of the car versus the bus. It was smoother, more comfortable. "I haven't ridden in a car for a long time. It's such a privilege." He looked out the window with his head bouncing off the glass; people would pull up close at stoplights to get a better gawk at his lost brand of handsome. "Do you like my tie? It's getting old, but I don't want new clothes. Keith might not recognize me."

"You look handsome," she said.

"I dress up for Sample Day."

Same old thrift-store clothes, but everyone acted otherwise. Everyone was in on the game that Hank had some great threads.

Whole Foods bustled on a Saturday afternoon. Hank usually took a bus from Jefferson Avenue to Brentwood Square—from the city into the county. So many people spending so much money on so much stuff. He'd forgotten what it was like to spend money just because you could.

He stood back and watched a Taliban extremist blow up the entirety of Whole Foods and most of Brentwood Square. Bodies went flying, people went screaming, metal and concrete rose into in the air and crashed down, almost silently. Bones, blood, heads, arms, general craziness. He'd seen this countless times so it didn't affect him much. Keith would come recognize him in the chaos and pull him away to safety. He could see Keith in the flesh. Feel his touch. Talk to him. Keith would save him, and sometimes he could almost feel Keith's lips touch his. *Your face is so unique*—he would say it even then. *Where are your eyes? So deep, so deep, but once I find them they will lead me to safety.*

PTSD, they said. It is my only refuge.

Most anywhere Hank went got blown up before he went into it. But it was always alright, because he could see Keith.

Brentwood Square had changed over the years; its down-home marquee harkened back to a time the square itself forgot. Over the last half-century or more it had turned from a sleepy and affordable shopping strip to an upscale adjunct of some larger malls nearby.

People buying stuff. Buy before you die.

"It's safe to go in now," he said to Lila.

"What happened?" She'd never gone anywhere with Hank.

"I have to blow it up first. After the worst happens, then it's safe to go in. I see him. Like he is still alive and he can still know it's me."

"He always will."

"I'm afraid if I like someone he'll get sad. So I never let myself."

"Maybe he'd want that," she said. "For you to be happy."

"I am happy," said Hank. "It's Sample Day! I just saw Keith. And I dream sometimes. What about you?" he said. "Who remembers you?"

"No one anymore," she said. "Please don't make me go there."

"*We* all do," Hank assured her. "We all recognize you. All of us vets know who you are. We know that you're there for us, and not just so you can tell everyone else you did it."

Bag after bag of merchandise left the stores with their momentarily happy purchasers. Buy before you die.

❖

"Tell me about Keith," she asked on the way over.

Color came back to his face. Only then. Hank was twenty-five, Keith was twenty-three.

Hank talked out the window. "We were in the worst place on earth, far from everyone and everything. Far from home. We would smile at each other and no one would know why. He could make a bowl of mashed pot so much fun. You had to keep your love a secret there, and every look, every smile, every time I would say 'can you pass me that' our hands would touch just a little longer. I never took any of him for granted. I remember all of that. And he was so stunningly beautiful. Even when he was broken and dying. He was so beautiful. There was nothing I could have done."

He didn't tell her everything. How they made out so fiercely when they were alone, how they had to bite, chew and spit each other's lips because who knew when another chance would come. How it was different from the others, who had wives far away at home. They were right there, together, and on occasion could actually have sex. "I knew it was real love, because it was all in the heart," he continued still out the window. "And now people say it's been too long, they say I should move on, but I am poor and I can't afford to move. Afghanistan was not a good place to us. But God brought us there to meet. I met him and he just smiled and smiled at me, and I smiled back, and we knew…this is where my heart will rest."

He got out his wallet. "Oh, here," Hank said. He took out his favorite keepsake. Someone took a picture of them and for a while they were poster boys in the states.

Send Christmas cards to the troops. Keith and Hank waving.
Write to the troops.
Make out with the troops.
Love you, Ma!

❖

Whole Foods was a culinary playground of the rich. Organics, naturals, health trends, make-your-own almond butter. As a master of display, this store could make red leaf lettuce look unbeatable. Lila could afford it on occasion; Grizz had money and it trickled down.

They all knew Hank. "I'll treat you to something," Lila offered.

Wow, to actually buy something! "Just a bag of pot and some gr beans and I'm happy," he told her. "Thank you!"

"We'll get some before we go."

She got a small double-decker cart and watched Hank pick the potatoes. He looked at bag after bag of organic potatoes. "They're so good! Eyes like Keith. So deep."

"I wish I could love like you do," Lila said. "She's gone too, but still here."

"You will find someone," said Hank, confidently, still ogling his potato eyes.

"Don't want to," Lila heard herself say.

All kinda stuff in small cups. Hank always wore a tie for this. It was 'going out'. His upper lip protruded just a bit; it added to his past sexiness—what that lip could do, who knew? Get up under it and lick. Not these days. He was self-conscious about it. It set him off, it drew looks and he didn't remember why. Couldn't remember if he was born that way or it came after the grenade.

Lila looked ahead, noticed some bright eyes flashing their way. "The deli guy likes you."

Hank got scared. "I know. I like him too," he said quietly.

"Ever thought of…"

"Yeah, I have." His breath got heavier. "This place gets blown up every time I come and he gets torn apart and his head lands at my feet. Then Keith comes and takes me away. He dies every time I come to Sample Day."

"Do you think there's a message?" Lila asked him.

"Keith is afraid." Hank approached the deli area slowly, his heart beating with love, fear, anticipation. He hated feeling like that—adrift in a blizzard of emotions. Wanting someone who wasn't Keith. Wanting someone who was still alive. What a crime that had become. "It's all innocent. No, it's not," he corrected himself. Hank took a sample sandwich bite from a nice lady. He gave her a big smile. "Thanks! This is really good!"

"You're welcome, soldier," she said. Everyone knew. He was a little off, but they treated him like he wasn't. They wished they could experience his utter joy at getting a free sample.

Then Hank got scared again. He'd never talked to anyone about the deli guy. Never. Sometimes though at night under the ministrations of his own right hand Keith would disappear and Deesh would take his place. He'd pretend Deesh was lying on top of him. His sweat, drool and cum would water him and bring him back alive like a parched desert blooming after a spring rain.

"I'll buy you some turkey if you ask him out," Lila encouraged. "Keith will understand, won't he? I'm sure he wants you to be happy."

"I know he does," Hank said. "But I will have to betray him. Either way it hurts."

Another lady had some kind of 27-ingredient salad-with-mayo right in front of the deli counter. Hank was beaming. He'd never mixed so many things together like that.

"This looks great. Thank you so much!"

"You're welcome, soldier."

The limp and the lick.

"Get two," Lila encouraged. "You should eat good food."

"Nope. You only get one, or you're being greedy. It's just a sample."

Deesh, short for DeShawn. A black guy with a broad face and a broad smile. A smile that never ended, that you could look into and see clear skies and everlasting sun. Close cropped hair. He was smaller than he looked, his uniform and his job on a raised platform made him look more imposing than he actually was. He loved Hank so much. He hadn't missed a Saturday in a year, making sure he was there in case Hank came in for Sample Day. His heart would race as he scouted over Hank's form, the light gray eyes, straight nose, drooping 'stache, even how he walked and how his hand picked up a sandwich sample and put it to his mouth. He even liked that ghost of the past that looked so much more like the ghost of the future.

"It's just a date," says Lila.

"Not really," Hank stuttered with repressed love. "It's been going on for a year. I come in, and we look at each other. And he gives me a free piece of turkey. And I see in his eyes. I see it. He's the one. And I can't. I feel so guilty. I can't let myself feel what I feel."

"Maybe it's God saying you've mourned enough. After ten years."

"I don't mourn," Hank replied. "I live with what I'm given. If it's a memory, so be it. What if Keith sees me with him? Then what? I don't know what to do."

Lila wasn't sure she should keep invoking God, but it seemed to explain things. "I think God will sort it out." It wasn't religion that was the problem after all; it was the religious that had cast them out.

Hank approached Deesh, who was smiling, who had seen through Hank to his heart, his soul, who had already imagined the many ways he could make Hank feel bright skies and sunshine. They'd hardly ever talked. The Saturday afternoon line was impatient. People had more stuff to buy and more lives to lead. Hank got a special dispensation because he was so strange—people were drawn to him or repulsed. Or they wished whatever happened to him hadn't happened.

"Have a sample." Deesh passed Hank a small slice of turkey on a tissue. Their hands touched, slid over each other like oiled gears. Electricity strong enough to power all of Whole Foods jolted those two men.

Hank exercised his jaw like he needed to remember how it worked. Finally he spoke. "I live in an efficiency on Jefferson," he stammered. "Every night I have a sandwich and mashed pot. And a veggie of the day."

"Mashed pot," said Deesh.

"Lila got me a bag of new pot," he said. "If you come over I'll make you some." Then very quietly, "I love how you smile, Deesh. I think about it a lot."

Deesh was smilin' bigger than ever. "It's all for you, army boy."

"I am very poor and have nothing to offer but a broken heart. But if God wants this to happen, we should do His will."

"Gotta trust the man upstairs!" Deesh agreed.

Hank took a card and scribbled down his address and home phone.

"Six o'clock?"

Keith was standing behind Deesh. Hank couldn't tell if he was crying or encouraging him.

"Sorry," Hank said.

"What for?"

"Oh, nothing. I'm really looking forward to seeing you."

"You have no idea, army boy. No idea." His heart was pounding, he'd have jumped to the ceiling but it was probably against company policy. "Patience pays big," he said to Lila. He went to slice Hank's turkey, again their hands brushed together as he handed it over, this time with the confidence of fulfillment. Hank was used to it; so many touches with Keith were, to untrained eyes, unintentional.

Another sample, another smile. It was like the church kitchen line, but for delicacies. People grabbed, kids were shoving smaller hands underneath. Moms were scolding. They come here to buy stuff and that's the difference. What a grenade would do to this place. Hopefully DeShawn would survive the next three hours.

Pot. and beans and turkey in the basket.

"I haven't cooked for someone in so long," Hank said. "I hope he likes it."

"I'm sure he will. And Keith will be so proud of you."

"Keith is crying at the deli counter," he observed. "I pledged my heart to him forever."

"His forever is over."

"But it shouldn't have been!" Hank was a little too loud for the moms and their ubiquitous Kaylas, Kalyees, and Kaycees. "I am so lonely! It shouldn't have been! Let's get another sample. These are good days. And maybe we won't be lonely anymore." He had to calm down. Breathe. Cry. Survive. Why? Maybe it wasn't sinful to love Deesh. He'd built his whole life as a memorial. It was so hard to let go, and so wrong. After a year of longing, denying and fighting his own truth, he found himself still desperately wanting this man. He already knew how it would go: Deesh would come in the door and they would hug each other brutally tight. Try to compress a year into a minute. Love would express itself through tears, *oh God, Keith, I am so sorry.*

Lila looked around at the happiness that was Whole Foods. "These are good days," she agreed.

"You aren't having any samples," he noticed.

"No thanks. This is your day." If you are busy giving, you don't have to worry about taking.

❖

He dragged his bad leg to the apple pie with cinnamon and vanilla. Nothing drives a man crazier than apple pie with cinnamon and vanilla. It's a man trap. Deesh was watching, his eyes strong from all the way across the store. He was still smiling. He was a happy guy but so lonely for so long. He had the same fantasy: come to the door, grab his man and hold on for dear life.

Hank knew the pie lady too. She was like a mom to him, a nice lady with food. "Hi Hank," she said. "Here's the best piece just for you."

They gave him a bigger sample because they all knew. He was poor, and he appreciated it so much. He acted like they gave him his entire order free.

A very young girl, maybe four, maybe six, no one knew for sure, one of the Kaylas, Kaylees or Kaycees that wandered the store under occasional parental supervision, had never seen anyone like him before. She looked at his leg swinging a few steps behind rest of his body. Something in his face scared her and fascinated her. Such an odd color for a white guy.

"Did you get in a accident?" she asked. Everyone was so nice to him, so she thought he was important. She should know what happened.

"Shhh!" said her Mom. "I'm sorry," she whispered to Hank.

"It's Okay," he said. "It's totally innocent. I like that."

He knelt down to the little girl. "My name's Hank. I was in the army."

Her Mom relented. "Tell him your name, sweetie."

"I'm Kaylee. So was my dad."

Lila was apprehensive. What if Hank would break down or shoot everyone? Deesh strained to hear, to find out more. He knew so little about the one he was destined to be with forever. He just knew that much was true.

Hank could feel Deesh's heartbeat from across the store, like a drummer beating the back of his head. It was time that everybody knew. Everyone always wondered anyway, and they all talked about it after Hank went home. For now, it was as if the store management allowed things to come to a halt so he could tell a story. The Sample Day people were the most special people in his life. So they had a right to know.

"It's a short story, really," he said. "I was in Afghanistan. We were resting. We'd had a hard day and it was hot. We were playing cards, a few of us, just having a good time after a dangerous day. I remember laying down a heart." He looked up to a growing circle of people watching him tell a story to a little girl on the floor. "No one saw it coming. We were looking around, keeping watch. No one saw." He was losing track of the fact that Kaylee was so young. "A grenade. Mayhem. Blood. Fear. You train for this and train for this and when it happens you don't know what to do. See?" said Hank, tapping his skull. "I am okay. I didn't lose much, but my brain."

"Mommy says daddy doesn't use his sometimes."

"Mommy loves your daddy, I'm sure."

"What happened to you? Did you get blown up?" Kaylee asked.

"I was injured. My leg got messed up. But Keith, my friend, he was blown up. There were parts of him that were blown away. They weren't on him anymore. There was blood over his eyes. He had these beautiful deep eyes." He took out the picture. "See?"

"He's pretty," said Kaylee.

"He couldn't move. Of everyone there, he got it worst, and we all knew he was gonna die. And I loved him so much. I couldn't just let him go without telling him. I kissed him on the lips. I said 'I love you Keith, and I'll never forget you.' He said 'Hank I love you too. I will always be with you.' These were the last words he heard: 'I love you.' I held him and I cried and he died in my arms. Just like he said he wanted to, only so many years later after we had lived our lives. Back in the day there was no tolerance in the army for people like me," he said without much emotion.

"What's a people like you?" Kaylee asked.

"Because I loved a man. And that was considered wrong. He was sent home in a bag, and I was discharged. I was sent home because I loved Keith. That's what my country did to me, but I still love my country and I still love God. Now I am disabled in a small apartment and the army doesn't remember or recognize me." Hank sat on the floor. "And I still love Keith."

Lila was shocked. In her insular world, most moms wouldn't let their daughter hear a gay love story full of blood and guts and tears. Maybe things were changing.

"You did the right thing," said Kaylee. "If you love someone, you have to say so. That's what Mom says."

Her Mom added quietly, "You're the only one who did the right thing."

Hank looked around, scared, people watching him sitting on the floor, tears falling in Whole Foods, the one place he felt human. He saw Deesh, who had escaped from behind the deli and offered a hand to help him up.

Hank had another piece of pie. He'd forgotten he had the first one, and no one wanted to remind him.

"Time to go," he said. "Whole Foods needs to make a living. You still wanna come over?" he asked Deesh. Wasn't sure what answer he wanted to hear most.

"More than ever," he said. "You wait till I get there, and I'll cook them potatoes with you."

They're not potatoes! he wanted to scream. *You never say the whole word.* Things were different now.

Lila rang up the turkey and green beans and fresh potatoes. Hank had never bought anything from Whole Foods. It was such a treat!

"I will think of you," he told her. "When we make this, I will think of you."

"You are a good man" said Lila. "Deesh is very lucky."

"You are a good woman," he said. "We are both still here because we still need to be, so we need to figure out why. Maybe you will have a special friend one day."

She paused and thought it over. "You are my special friend," she said.

"I haven't been anybody's friend in so long."

They drove in silence for a while, back to the city on Highway 64. He could explode any building at will, until the entire city was in rubble, a bleeding mess of concrete, vehicles and humanity. Lila thought things over. Grizz had influenced her life far too long; she had chosen seclusion because of someone that didn't even care about her. But she was happy, living quietly and giving of herself. And mostly, making her own choices. Maybe it'd be nice to have someone to come home to again. Whole Foods wasn't quite her style. Maybe she'd try Sample Day at Sam's Club.

"We need to go to the thrift store." Hank said in a panic. "If that's okay," he calmed down. "I need some new clothes. I've betrayed Keith, and I don't want him to recognize me tonight. Just a new shirt and a new tie."

"I think Keith will see you either way. I think," said Lila, "that Keith made this part of his plan. It just took you a year to figure it out."

"Once someone said it was wrong for me to love another man, and that's why God blew him up. So I didn't tell the story after that." Lila was shocked into silence. "I just want these feelings to be okay," Hank thought out loud. "I have to break a heart to save one. I have to break my own heart to save it. After the grenade, after Keith, after seeing his eyes dripping with blood, I just wanted to be innocent again. I wanted the chance to love him like we had planned to after we got home. So these ten years, that's what I did. What Deesh makes me feel, it's love, too. And it's innocent. I never thought I'd have to forgive myself for it."

Back at home, Hank took off his shirt—Keith's shirt—and put on one for Deesh. Looked at himself in the mirror. *Someone still wants this?* He hadn't worked out in a long time, but he looked okay; ten years of simple food kept his weight the same. He buttoned up his new used light blue dress shirt. He had bought a thin tie because it was more informal than a normal sized one. It was an old purple tie someone first took home in about 1982. *Wow, almost as old as me.* He tentatively got dressed, then took a few of the best-looking potatoes out of the bag and put them on the kitchen counter. Looked around his small place. White walls decorated with his own hand-drawn pictures of flowers and happy bears to calm him down. Furniture from the Goodwill. *Would it be enough?*

A knock at the door at exactly the appointed time. Hank's heart jumped. *Keep it quiet! Nobody can know.* Deesh looked different out of his uniform—t-shirt, jeans, ball cap. *Was it the same person?* He looked lithe and limber. And shorter because he wasn't on an elevated platform. A lot more approachable, actually. He had three red roses in a vase. Wow he looked so happy! A half-smiled cocked his face up sexy. "Heeeyyy…"

Hank had so many conflicting feelings: relief, fear, betrayal, love, lust, need, all flashing from one to the other and beating him up like a fistfight. "Thank you," he said. He took the flowers and put them on a small table and closed the door.

Four arms wrapped tightly around two bodies. They had been denied this for so long. Their little exchanges over the deli counter finally relieved themselves into a huge deep hug that wouldn't quit. "Man, I have wanted this for so long," Deesh exhaled. "So long."

"Me too," Hank allowed himself to admit. He let himself feel someone he cared for all up and down his body, guilty guilty guilty. He broke the hug and ran his hand slowly down Deesh's face. Held Deesh's hand in his own. Looked it over. Kissed it. Took Deesh's hand and put it up to his own face. In every instance asking Keith's permission and forgiveness for breaking a ten year drought on having feelings for another living being.

"You can do this," he said. More to himself, but Deesh took it as permission. It wasn't as if they didn't know each other. Eyes, glances, and small touches told stories. Howled long wolf-cries of *you belong in my soul and I don't know how to get you there*. Now Deesh knew too, he was in competition with a dead man, with a past, with an explosion. He let Hank take the lead. Hank hadn't kissed anyone since that fateful day in Afghanistan. It felt like he was putting a knife to Keith's heart. But part of him knew he either had to do this or jump out a window.

But he mattered to DeShawn. He made the difference. Lila often told him she felt her place on earth was to make a difference in people's lives. If you have nothing left for your own, you can still live to matter to someone else. She was happy with Grizz, but had lived selfishly and conspicuously and paid the price.

"I really have loved you all this time," Deesh said. "This feels more right than anything else. I know we've never actually been together, but I think about you every day. I gotta turn it into reality." He picked up the vase. "I will always keep flowers here for you."

"I'm crazy," Hank said. "I live in two places at one time. I can't look at anything without seeing it explode. I've seen you explode too. I've seen your head bounce at my feet in a bloody mess. Are you hungry? I have some pot and grrr-beans. Well you saw, Lila bought it all for me. Well, for us. She said she would get the turkey if I would share it with you. I can't afford it."

Kiss. Hank plowed ahead, his lips pushing and plowing into Deesh's face, heart and soul. His voice moaning into the other man's throat. Once started there was no turning back. *Keith is screaming, Keith is crying, Keith is bombing a five block radius of Jefferson Avenue.* Hank always knew this would happen, but he kept at it, like running a tank over impossible enemy terrain. He gripped Deesh by the back of the head and held on for dear life, his tongue anchoring itself inside Deesh's mouth. Deesh in the triple-ecstasy of being overpowered by hands and lips, unaware of the carnage this brutal kiss was creating.

Deesh caught his breath and put his jaw back into place. "Whoa, soldier!" was all he could say.

Hank went to the window and gazed out on a war-torn and battered St. Louis as smoldering, burning, innocent victims pieced their loved ones back together. Keith walked slowly away carrying a backpack and a rifle, turned around one last time with a dirt-smudged tear-stained face, his tears washing away the dirt in streaks. "Don't leave me!" his mouth shaped. "Please don't leave me!"

"Why are you doing this to me?" Hank shouted at the ravaged city. DeShawn came up slowly and hugged him tentatively from behind. He knew he'd have to be patient. He could wait another year for a kiss like that, if need be.

Miraculously the metro track survived. Hank watched as Keith quietly waved good bye. He meticulously put down his backpack, then he laid down on the tracks so an oncoming train could slice him in two. Hank's brain spared him nothing of the gore. Then, like a video game on reset, the city put itself back together. *This is not the innocence I wanted,* Hank thought. He got angry, he grabbed his head and ran his hands tightly over his hair and face and shouted out the window.

"You've been trying to kill Deesh so I can't be with him!" He ran his purple tie through his fingers. "You still knew it was me," he said sadly. "I got these clothes so you couldn't see me and it didn't work!" He turned around, calming himself, letting his flowers and happy bears coax him back to real life. He talked to Deesh, who was trying to look as nonplussed as possible. "He tried to kill you but he won't anymore." Hank sat on the window pane, drained, tired and dejected. "Sorry. Not so good for a first date," he said.

"We're well beyond that," Deesh assured him with a small kiss that quickly turned into a big one.

"I got some fresh potatoes," Hank offered. "Usually I use instant. But for you, we'll use the real thing."

In this small efficiency, the kitchen was an enclave behind a bank of cabinets. Deesh took Hank's hand gently and led him those few steps. He picked up the potatoes and juggled them a few times. "You got some butter?"

"Yep! And parsley…"

"We'll make these the best ever," Deesh promised.

Time to try something new. It was Sample Day.

Stinkbug
Rich Barnett

Sitting naked in front of the computer doesn't feel as odd as Francis had expected. It's actually quite pleasant, he thinks, looking around the writer's study he's created from the small bedroom on the first floor of his cottage. It is furnished simply but smartly with his grandfather's bookcases, a large pine writing desk, a retrofitted glass oil lamp, a decanter of bourbon whiskey, and a computer, of course. The only tchotchkes Francis permits are a silver cup filled with pencils and a large crystal paperweight he'd picked up on a trip to Ireland a few year ago. The man who sold it to him said it had once belonged to Oscar Wilde.

Through the open window of the study, he can hear blue jays frolicking loudly in the carved stone birdbath in the boxwood garden. While not exactly on the beach, the cottage is close enough for him to taste the sea when the wind blows from the east.

He had created the perfect place to write, yet the words didn't come.

This is not the outcome Francis expected when he left his long-time job with Delaware's senior senator to fulfill his dream of becoming a writer in Rehoboth Beach, the quaint little beach town originally founded as a Methodist retreat but now attracting an increasing number of gay men and lesbians from throughout the Mid-Atlantic region. In Washington, the inspiration and ideas had flowed like Republican filibusters. He'd filled notebook after notebook with plots and characters, even skipping the occasional hearing, so engrossed was he in a plot point that he just had to jot it down on paper. Now he had plenty of time to write, but found himself stonewalled.

For nine months he had waited for his muse. Desperate for inspiration, he had turned lately to a book on the writing habits of well-known authors because it included stories about how they dealt with writer's block. Francis dutifully followed John Steinbeck's advice and pretended to write to a friend. He forced himself to write two thousand words a day like the prolific Nicholas Sparks. And he wrote nonsense, like Maya Angelou sometimes did to show the muse she was ready and waiting. None of it helped.

Money, thank goodness, wasn't an issue. He and his husband Luke had banked plenty during their successful careers in the nation's Capital and Francis had a sizable trust fund from his grandfather.

After umpteen shots of whiskey and a couple of hours perusing literary magazines on the Internet, Francis is about to give up the possibility of writing for the day and just play a game of 'five against one' when he hears a familiar buzzing sound. The stinkbug!

Unlike most people, Francis doesn't abhor the insect. He finds it quite amusing the way it minces across his desk and turns somersaults when he shooed it away. Three days in a row he had tossed the bug out the window and into the garden. It always returned. Francis was beginning to enjoy its company.

The insect careens across the room and landed awkwardly right in the middle of his computer screen. The bug's bumbling arrival reminds him of the Aunt Clara character on the TV show Bewitched.

"Welcome back, little stinkbug. I hope you're not here to watch me write," he says as he begins peeling an orange, "because that's not gonna happen today." Francis read once that stinkbugs were attracted to citrus fruit. He puts a few mandarin slices on a little plate for his visitor. "I bet they remind you of your native home. Perhaps that's how your family got here, stowaways in a crate of mandarins on a slow boat from China," he says out loud.

"I beg your pardon; my people are from Alabama." The voice is tinny with a slight southern accent. "But, I do love the song *Slow Boat from China*, especially Rosemary Clooney's rendition. Liza Minnelli sang it well too…oh the times we had at Studio 54."

What the hell? His computer screen is dark and he can see Luke outside in the garden. Strangely, it sounded as if the words had been spoken by the stinkbug. Impossible!

With his finger, Francis flicks the bug off the computer screen and watches as it buzzes about like an angry little helicopter before landing upon the plate of orange slices.

"Just because you do not appreciate the talents of Liza Minnelli is no reason to be rude." By God, it was definitely coming from the stinkbug. And with a slight lisp!

"I despise Liza Minnelli and I didn't know stinkbugs could talk," Francis replies, eyeing the insect warily.

"Please refrain from using that word. It is so undignified."

Francis gasps and leans down to take a closer look at the insect. "What should I call you?"

"My full Christian name is Truman Streckfus Capote, but you may call me Tru."

This was getting more bizarre by the minute, Francis thinks. He rubs his eyes and downs another shot of whiskey. "Is this a joke?"

"Sadly not," the insect replies. "My current existence, though, feels rather burlesque: brilliant raconteur reincarnated as lowly insect sucking on fruit slices and dodging Hoover vacuums."

Francis gently extends out his index finger and the stinkbug hops on, much like a trained parrot might. He brings the finger closer to his face, looking for some explanation.

"Are you a figment of my drunken imagination?"

"I assure you, I am real."

"Prove it."

"If I must. These past few days, I've watched you waste time sharpening at least two dozen pencils and reading back issues of the Oxford American."

Francis nods. "Go on."

"I am also very aware that you are struggling to put words on a blank page."

Francis raises an eyebrow. If Virginia Woolf heard voices and Charles Dickens claimed his characters spoke to him, sometimes telling him dirty stories in church during Sunday service, what's so crazy about Truman Capote reincarnated as a stinkbug?

He decides to play along. "If you've been stalking me, why didn't you reveal yourself earlier?"

"Reconnaissance. I needed to be sure before the big reveal. When I spied you sitting naked at your desk today, I knew it was time."

Francis's cheeks grow warm when it dawns on him that he's buck naked in front of Truman Capote. He feels the blood rush up his neck and throughout his face as he reaches for the red plaid lap blanket.

"There's no need for modesty now," says Tru. "I've seen everything. You're in good shape for a man on the downside of fifty."

Compelled to explain his nudity, Francis babbles on about how the renowned French novelist Victor Hugo used to write in the buff when he was feeling blocked and that Hugo would instruct his valet to remove all clothing from his study until he had written for at least one hour.

"Yes," replies Tru, "we all have our methods to draw forth the creative juices. I could only think while lounging on a sofa or in a bed, preferably puffing a cigarette or sipping a cocktail."

"They called you a horizontal writer," Francis nods incredulously.

"They did, didn't they? Now listen up, Francis." The insect's tone of voice changes, suddenly becoming more serious. "I've been searching for someone like you, a kindred soul, and a fellow writer who might empathize with my plight and who might be motivated to help.

"How can I help you?"

"Take me to Paris."

Francis's eyes widen. "France?"

"It's where Princess Lee Radziwell resides. You know, Jackie O's sister."

"I'm aware of who she is."

"Princess Lee was one of my favorite swans. A woman of legendary beauty and style like Babe Paley, C.Z Guest, Gloria Guinness, and Slim Keith, the ladies who ran New York high society during my heyday. Alas, most of my swans have passed away. But, if I can convince Lee to forgive me, my prayers will be answered and I shall finally ascend up and out of the insect class and into my next reincarnation."

"I don't understand," says Francis.

"It's Karma, my dear. Souls who have sinned and have not properly repented while alive are forced to undergo a second round of life in this world as rehabilitation for their past sins. Or so the Hindus and Buddhists believe. Oh, don't look so surprised. At one time I was very keen on the Oriental religions. I'm being punished for my wicked behavior."

The crazy explanation makes sense to Francis. Truman Capote had turned on Lee Radziwell and all his wealthy benefactors, skewering them and revealing their most intimate secrets in a series of short stories published in Esquire. He bit the proverbial hand that fed him and now he was paying the price.

"What makes you think she will forgive you?"

"Lee and I had a special connection. She was so jealous of Jackie. I'm the one who persuaded producer David Susskind to cast her in *Laura*. I even wrote the script especially for her. Of course she was terrible and in the end I convinced the poor dear to give up the movies and focus instead on being a socialite. But, I digress. Once I explain to Lee how it all got to be too much—the movie, the parties, the pressure…"

"The booze," Francis chimes in.

"Look who's talking! In any case, I shall beg her forgiveness. I never expected everything to fall apart after the Esquire stories. I didn't mean to bust up all the furniture in her guesthouse during my last stay. Things just got out of hand. To think, I even lost control of the prized lunchtime banquette at La Côte Basque."

At the sound of Luke clomping down the hallway outside the study, their conversation died.

"Hey," Luke yells, "What are you doing in there?"

"Playing with a stinkbug," Francis replies, not yet ready to reveal Tru. He knows Luke will be a tough one to convince. Luke is a man of logic, not dreams.

Luke enters the study. He is shirtless, having just come in from working in the garden. Whoever said men in cargo shorts were passé hadn't seen his younger husband. Luke stood a bit less than six feet with close clipped blonde hair and an easy almost shy smile. A former lawyer, he was now employed at a local nursery and enjoying going to work in shorts and sporting a heavy scruff rather than a suit and tie. Life at the beach agreed with Luke—the physical labor these past few months had toughened his physique.

He squats down to take a look at the insect sitting on the plate. "Mon grand, are you certain it's not a box elder bug?"

"I'm positive. Note the distinctive shield shape. The coloring—brown shell with white and black marking on its legs and antennae—definitely identify it as a brown marmorated stinkbug. A box elder would be oblong and black with red stripes."

"Hmm, well, please get rid of the damn thing. Wallace and Arthur have a full-blown infestation in their home. They found dozens of them clinging to the lining of the chintz drapes in their living room and Arthur even found some hiding behind his paintings. I just couldn't bear something like that happening here."

"Worry not, Mon petit, we do not have bugs. We have an insect, a very unique insect."

Luke picks up the plate of mandarins and stares closely at the stinkbug.

"It looks like a Zantac pill to me. I see nothing fabulous about it." He swiftly tosses the fruit and the bug out the open window and returns the plate to the desk.

"Haven't you seen the TV reports, Francis? These invasive Chinese bugs are destroying fruit crops. They also feed on ornamental plants. Once they get inside a home, it's virtually impossible to get rid of them."

"Since when did a little bug bother the big master gardener?"

Luke shrugs. "Most bugs don't. These bugs do. Box elders I could tolerate. They sound sort of aristocratic and British countryside-ish. But stinkbugs? Awful! Now, thanks to you, I've got to check behind all the drapes and paintings in the cottage. These pests are sneaky."

Luke playfully grabs Francis' cock. "You need to get back to work. How about you write for an hour and then I'll come back and give you a blowjob."

Francis usually likes it when Luke initiates their sex play, but he's not into it at this moment. When his husband exits the study, Francis bounds over to the open window and leans out, looking for the insect. "Tru? Are you there? The coast is clear if you want to come back."

After a few minutes, Francis hears the buzzing sound and the stinkbug zips in through the window, crash lands again on the computer screen.

"Your partner…"

"My husband," Francis interrupts.

"Oh yes. I still can't believe all that is legal now. What's the fun of being homosexual anymore? Never mind. Your husband is very handsome, but quite the killjoy. I'm certain he will not approve of our trip to Paris."

"Who says I'm going on this crazy expedition of yours? The French customs and security inspectors won't like it either if I bring an invasive stinkbug into their country."

"That word again…."

"Sorry, but you know what I mean."

"Rest assured I have no intention of running amok and breeding. I do extremely well in captivity. Just pack me up in a pill bottle or a cigarette case and slip me in your shaving kit. If you check your bag for the flight, I'll be fine and the authorities will be none the wiser." Tru continues, now in a singsong manner, "I'll make it worth your while…."

"How so?" Francis is intrigued.

"I'll help you write the novel you so desire, a stunning masterpiece that will explode onto the New York literary scene like nothing since, well, since me. I'll make you a star."

"Can you really? The critics said your best work was behind you."

"Preposterous! Tru is clearly offended. "Failure, my friend, is merely the condiment that gives success its flavor. And besides, what do you have to lose? The piece you are writing about the conservative politician and the prostitute is dreadful."

"It's a true story."

"It's trite."

"Have you read it?"

"Just hearing you talk to yourself about it tells me all I need to know," Tru said.

"What would you suggest we write about?" In a moment of self-awareness Francis knows his only true passions are politics and drinking. "How about a drinking and driving story from back in the days when it was a sport and not a crime? My dear mother used to hand me a beer whenever I drove back to university, to take the edge off that long drive up the Shenandoah Valley."

"Talk about a mad mother. I'm afraid that is just too immature," critiques Tru.

"Sophomoric sells. Look at the success of Tucker Max."

"He's misogynistic and a one trick pony. Boredom, not hilarity has ensued."

"He achieved some fame," Francis counters.

"He achieved notoriety, and he was never published in *The New Yorker*."

"How do you even know about Tucker Max?" asks an exasperated Francis.

"I might be an insect but I still keep up with literary trends."

"What if we change the gender of the prostitute character in my novel into a man?"

"Yesterday's news. Francis, please stop worrying about all that right now. The idea will come. And like a wave, it will sweep you—us—safely to shore."

Francis pours himself a glass of bourbon whiskey and gulps it down. He still can't fully fathom that this is happening. But at the same time, he knows he very much needs the help to jumpstart his writing.

"What the hell," he tells Tru. "It's a deal!"

"Bravo!" Truman takes a celebratory flight around the study, buzzing loudly and lighting upon the Oscar Wilde paperweight. "When shall we depart for Paris?"

"Can we wait for at least two weeks, so I can get a good price on a flight?"

"Absolutely not. Too much could happen between now and then. You might change your mind. You might overcome your writer's block."

"Oh, I doubt that. But tell me, truthfully, do you think Lee Radziwell will believe you are Truman Capote?"

"Not at first. No one ever does."

"How many people have you approached?"

"Alas, I've lost count. Initially, I searched for assistance in Paris, which seemed logical because the French are so romantic and Princess Lee, after all, is a Parisian expatriate. I'm certain my inability to speak the language hindered my efforts. And while I will never admit it to her, the fact of the matter is that most people today don't even know or care who Lee Radziwell is or was. The Parisians were not empathetic to my cause."

Tru pauses a moment, then continues. "I next traveled to Washington, catching a ride in the sleeve of a fabulous mink coat right after Barack Obama was elected president. With the comparisons to the Kennedys and to Camelot, I felt certain I'd find a sympathetic ear in the politically attuned city. You might not remember, but we met there about a year ago."

"We did?"

"I flew into your Washington apartment one evening. I was looking for prospects in Georgetown, because I knew the neighborhood was full of self-important wannabes and has-beens. The silver cup of Ticonderoga pencils on your desk caught my eye."

"I remember that. You walked all over my pencils."

"And you tossed me out the window several times before finally closing it and shutting me out."

"So you followed me here to Rehoboth Beach?"

"No, I unsuccessfully approached a few other prospects in Washington, but the image of the attractive writer with the silver cup of pencils stayed in my mind. I always wrote with Ticonderogas too. I overheard someone say you had moved to Rehoboth. One day I threw caution to the wind and caught a ride to the Delaware shore in the beach bag of an aging homosexual. And here we are!"

"How did you know I'd be receptive to your offer?"

"Darling, I can smell your desperation."

"That's not very flattering," Francis says with a slight smirk.

"Yes, well, sometimes you've got to be cruel to be kind."

"How do you know Lee Radziwell won't be cruel and try to kill you when you confront her? Not everyone looks kindly upon, well, your kind."

"I assure you, Princess Lee does not kill insects. She would summon someone to do that for her and I'd have plenty of time to hide. I'm wily. Eventually though I'd wear her down with my charm and persistence. And once she says she forgives me, well, Karma will be satisfied."

❖

Later in the day, Luke re-enters the study. He is wearing just a towel, having come from a shower. He sees Francis with the stinkbug and gives a loud sigh. "Why is that bug back in the study."

"He's entertaining me."

"Bugs do not entertain, Mon Grand, they break down waste and spread disease."

"Bees make honey."

"And they sting," Luke counters.

"You say tomato and I say tomahto…"

"Francis, stop being so damn clever. You've been in here all day naked and playing with a stinkbug instead of working on your novel. What the hell is going on?" Luke glares at Francis.

Might as well spill the beans, Francis thinks. Luke isn't going to overlook this. "I, uh, didn't want to tell you, but this bug that you so despise is the reincarnation of Truman Capote."

Luke frowns. "You've got to be kidding."

"I know it sounds crazy, but if I take him to Paris so he can apologize to Lee Radziwell, he's promised to help me overcome my writer's block."

"Paris! Good lord, you should hear yourself! Reincarnation? You don't even believe in God."

"Actually, I'm feeling more agnostic than atheist these days, but that's beside the point. Lots of writers believed in reincarnation—Thoreau, Emerson, and Whitman. Certainly even you can see the black humor in Truman Capote coming back as a stinkbug?"

"What I hear are the ramblings of a drunkard." Luke looks over to the almost empty decanter of bourbon whiskey. "Wasn't that decanter full yesterday?"

"Tru has been hovering by my side the last few days. He says we're kindred spirits."

"Stop calling it he! It's an ugly little insect with neither the capacity to speak nor the ability to help you write. You're neither St. Francis of Assisi nor Doctor Doolittle."

"Well, unlike you, Tru is offering some support."

"You've got to be kidding…"

"All you do is badger me about writing."

Luke says nothing, but Francis sees he's fidgeting, sighing. He starts to say something, then stops himself. Finally, Luke speaks. "I pester you because you've started drinking so much. That wasn't part of the deal when we left Washington so you could try and become a writer."

"Look, I'm not Hillary Clinton. Publishers aren't throwing book deals at my feet. Success doesn't happen overnight."

Luke's face is turning red. His jaw clenches. "Success," Luke yells, "won't happen at all if you keep fucking around. I supported our move to Delaware because I thought it would be good for us to slow down and enjoy more out of life. But now you won't socialize with our friends. You don't go to the beach. You've given up the Sunday political talk shows. All you do is sit in your study and drink. Now you're talking to an insect! What's happened? You used to be so level headed and optimistic, a man people turned to for advice and assistance."

"Tru says…"

"Tru says 'bye-bye'."

In a flash, Luke snatches up the crystal paperweight, shakes the stinkbug off of it, and then tries to squash it. Francis grabs Luke's hand, slowing the downward force just long enough for Tru to buzz off and escape out the study window.

Francis scowls at Luke. "You've no idea what you almost did!"

"Sure I do. I tried to kill Truman Capote. *In Cold Blood*!" Luke sets down the paperweight and starts walking out of the study. Turning his head, he speaks to Francis. "Do not bring another stinkbug into this house and do not mention any of this crazy nonsense to me ever again. And you can forget about a blowjob until you pull yourself together."

❖

Francis' breathing slows down and his anxiety lessens the moment he exits Charles De Gaulle Airport. Tru is still tucked away in a pill bottle inside his leather shaving kit in the belly of the big Louis Vuitton suitcase. No one had suspected a thing.

He hails a cab to Hotel Pont Royal in the city's chic 7th Arrondissement. It has always been one of Tru's favorite places to stay because the service is impeccable and the champagne is always cooled to just the right temperature. Their room is small, but it has doors opening onto a Juliet-style balcony with a beautiful view of the Eiffel Tower. Once they are alone, Francis unpacks Tru.

The first order of business is for Francis to call and place an order for a very lavish arrangement of pink roses, Princess Lee's favorites, from Eric Chauvin of Un Jour de Fleurs. "Eric does all the flowers for Dior's fashion shows. And he is very sexy," says Tru.

With Tru sitting discretely on Francis' shoulder, under a shirt epaulet, the two conspirators next pay a visit to Tru's favorite stationery store on the Saint-Germain-des-Près to purchase a box of deluxe white note cards with yellow and orange borders. "I used the same design for the invitation to my Black and White Ball back in '66," says Tru.

After a short visit to the Rodin Museum, they return to the hotel and Tru explains the details of his master plan. Tomorrow Francis will write in black ink a very simple message on one of the cards: *Forgive me?* There would be no signature. The card itself would say it all. Francis will then go pick up the flower arrangement. A little flirting with Eric will allow Tru time to slip unnoticed into the pink roses. Francis will hand deliver the flowers and the card to the concierge at Lee Radziwell's apartment building. Once Tru and the roses physically make it inside the Princess' apartment, Tru will emerge from hiding and make his presence known.

"It's a brilliant and simple plan," Francis says to Tru, "but how will I know if you are successful in your mission?"

"You won't until I return to the hotel room."

"You will come back?"

"Don't you trust me?"

Francis hesitates. "Well, it's just that writing the novel will be a time-consuming process. You might become impatient. I know how long you've been waiting for Lee's moment of forgiveness."

"Worry not, my friend. Truman Capote is a man of his word. We'll begin working on the novel immediately upon my return. As soon as we finish the last word of it, you shall kill me."

"What?"

"Death is required if I am to evolve up."

"I don't think I could do that," Francis says.

"But you must kill me. It's an essential part of our bargain. You see, we are in the same boat. We both must trust each other in order to achieve our dreams."

Francis bites his lip. "I suppose I can kill you if I have to. But how?"

"I suggest you use a book and quickly and efficiently crush the life out of me. Anything written by Gore Vidal would suffice. His work always bored me to death. It might as well kill me. But, Francis, whatever means you choose, I implore you not to flush me down the commode. That method will not kill me and I just can't bear the thought of fighting my way out of the Paris sewers."

"If you die, how will I get the novel published?"

"I have a plan for that too. You will send the manuscript to Tina Brown, a trusted literary friend, along with one of our note cards and a message that references a white swan. We had an agreement, Tina and I, that whenever I found a rare and exquisite talent, I'd send said writer to her. When Tina sees the magic words again, she'll be stunned, but I guarantee she'll read the novel and steer it to a top-notch New York publisher. You will become an overnight sensation."

"Wouldn't it be better if you were to make the introduction to Tina Brown?"

"You seem to forget I will be dead. Now please order us some supper. I'd love to nibble on a green salad."

Francis calls down to the restaurant for some cheese, a salad, and a couple of bottles of Veuve Clicquot champagne. Tonight they will toast to dreams and success.

"How long do you anticipate it will take you to convince Princess Lee to forgive you?"

"It might take a day or two. She is very headstrong, always has been. How long do we have the hotel room?"

"Three days."

"That should suffice. I am very anxious to shed this unbecoming brown shell."

"And I'm excited to get started on the novel. How will we collaborate?"

"I don't know yet, but we will find a way that works. Francis, please quit worrying. Come watch. Dusk is upon us and I want you to witness one of the true wonders of the civilized world."

The bellhop brings in the food and champagne and begins setting the table for their supper. When the Eiffel Tower outside bursts into lights, the bellhop slams down the silver cloche and squashes the bug he sees crawling on the starched white tablecloth.

Francis screams when he hears the ringing from the impact of the cloche on the table. The bellhop tries to explain but Francis doesn't listen as he pushes the apologetic and confused young man out of the room.

Alone, Francis sinks to his knees as he absorbs the reality of what has happened. They were so close and he'd banked so much on this trip, including his marriage. Luke had threatened to leave him if he went to Paris. Now his last hope of becoming a real author lies crushed on a table.

Dizzy and needing to think, he pours himself a glass of champagne and carefully picks up the remains of Tru in a linen cocktail napkin. He walks over to the chaise by the balcony doors and reclines softly onto it, clutching both napkin and glass of champagne in his left hand. Everything is in shambles. There is no way he can go back to sitting naked in front of a computer or writing pretend letters to friends. Returning to his job with the Senator is out of the question after the fanfare he'd made about leaving Capitol Hill to follow his dream. The Washington establishment would forgive but they would not forget.

As he lies looking at the illuminated Eiffel Tower, he suddenly gets the glimmer of an idea. Or, he should say, the scent of an idea. The cilantro-like odor coming from the crushed remains of Truman Capote in the wadded up cocktail napkin is his story.

By God, it's brilliant, Francis thinks, a fresh take on the classic American buddy story, a man and a bug, with a nod to Kafka's Metamorphosis. It could even be movie worthy! Images in his head begin flashing from one scene to another and he feels like he's going to jump out of himself, his thought stream is going so fast. Leaping to his feet, he dramatically sweeps the dinner, plates, glasses, and silver cloche from the dining table onto the floor. He opens up his laptop computer and begins typing as fast as he can.

Two hours later, and two bottles of champagne consumed, he finally takes a break from his writing to contemplate things. He decides to hole up in the hotel room and continue to work for a couple more days. When he gets back to Rehoboth Beach, everything will be fine. Luke will be pleased he is writing again and most certainly will forgive him for taking off to Paris. Francis literally feels the inspiration of the tragedy swelling up behind him and guiding him forward to the safe shore, exactly like the wave Tru predicted.

IF ON A DARK NIGHT
TWO STRANGERS SHOULD COME
WILLIAM HAWKINS

When the gods were still around, they'd tell this story about Jupiter and Mercury, about this one time they hit up a couple of geezers for a goose. See, Jupiter and Mercury were wandering around, shooting the shit, dressed up like mortals and knocking on the doors of some piss-poor village, looking for a place to crash. They must've knocked on twenty, maybe a hundred doors, but no one would let a couple of shabby looking strangers inside, no matter how remotely possible it was that there might be gods beneath such filthy skin.

For a while, it looked like no one was going to let them inside, and that pissed Jupiter off, because he was a pissy kind of god. But just when he was ready to introduce the planet to the wrong end of a lightning bolt, he and Mercury came to a little hovel of a home, and at that door they were finally let inside by a kindly old couple named Baucis and Philemon.

They made the strangers feel at home; they even tried to kill their pet goose so they'd have something decent to eat. They didn't because they couldn't catch it, but Jupiter gave them an A for effort. They'd treated him, a stranger, as if he were their own son, and so he revealed himself as the god he was and made them priests of a shining temple on top of a hill. He asked them if there was anything else they wanted. They put their heads together, and when they came back up for air it was to make a single wish. They asked Jupiter that they might die together, that neither of them would be burdened with the curse of outliving the other. Jupiter was pleased and granted them their wish.

I read that story in a book I'd bought in Mickey and Lennon's store, a used copy of Ovid's *Metamorphoses*, translated by Rolfe Humphries. Its pages were yellow, dog marked, and stained in places with splatters of some dark liquid I hoped was coffee, but the book had saved its face. The cover was glossy, almost new, and I could appreciate the effort it must've taken the thing to keep it up. The cover featured a stark piece of artwork, a geometrical tree in the rough shape of a woman—boughs and limbs knotted in rough paint strokes. I saw it and had to have it. The story just came along for the ride.

Talking about Jupiter and his new priests seems as good a way to start as any. I don't even remember when I read the story, or if I liked it when I did. But stories sometimes stick themselves up somewhere you can't reach and wait for the chance to fall on top of your head. I guess this is one of those times. I just want to be clear here; I knew better. I'd read the whole sad thing before. But knowing and doing is the difference between the first and last sip of a bottle of bourbon. That's what Mickey says.

See, Brazil needed poppers. The person, not the country. I don't really know what the country needs. I'd guess more money, because everyone needs more money, even people who've got plenty. But no one would have to guess what Brazil the person needs, because Brazil the person isn't known for being subtle. Just ask her mirror. And that night she needed poppers.

We'd been at Paul Mascagni's twenty-second birthday party up on Carondelet, invited by his latest boyfriend, an LSU student on an impromptu break courtesy of Hurricane Gustave—which people in Baton Rouge couldn't quit bitching about. He planned to show up at Paul's party as a surprise and invited us all to come see. We came and saw. It was a great surprise, especially when Paul's two current boyfriends met each other for the first time.

So it was drinks and a show. We gargled jungle juice and gossiped and watched until only one boyfriend was left standing. Since it wasn't the one that invited me, I took the hint fate left and went to find new entertainment. I just didn't have enough money for the cabbie to get me there. It was a piece of luck to catch Brazil coming out of the powder room with some of it still on her nose.

She stopped short when she saw me. For a second I thought she was going to pretend I wasn't there, go right on by the boy in the hooker wig. But bitch has at least a piece of backbone in her, and, besides, she'd had a line of courage. I could tell she was in a Rawhide kind of mood, and an Uptown party just wasn't going to cut it. I suggested we share a cab and ignored the stories on shelves above my head.

We called a cab, drank some more, and stumbled outside when it arrived. But we weren't two minutes driving before she turned and screamed into my ear, "I need poppers!"

That was when the story fell on my head, hard enough to knock my senses, I guess, because I said, "We can go to Mickey's." I bet she didn't look too happy about that, but her makeup was too thick to notice.

The cab driver hadn't blinked when Brazil shouted, and when I asked him if we could stop he pulled up to the curb with a gentle twist of his wheel and let us out. I gave him a nice tip for the trouble, and he told us to have a good night with his own tip of an imaginary cap. Brazil and I giggled and kept ourselves standing by linking arms. The cabbie's taillights drenched us in electric red.

So we went down on Jefferson, two twenty-two year old boys dressed like thirty-four year old hookers, wigs and all. We got a few honks from the road, and they got a few middle fingers for their trouble. Otherwise the night was halfway to peaceful. The sky was overcast, and the city lights bounced off the clouds in a slow kind of strobe.

I could've walked us to Mickey's bungalow home with my eyes blindfolded and firecrackers stuffed up my ears. The brick walkway, the light blue paint, the white gingerbread trimming, the dead azalea bushes memorialized below the porch. I led us there and wondered how many times it took to walk up to a house before you were walking up to your home.

Mickey had lived there for the long side of twenty years. He'd bought it when the neighborhood was bad and given it a fresh coat of paint when it'd gotten better. He'd been in the city longer, making a reputation that, by the time I met him, had settled comfortably around his shoulders like a well-tailored suit.

They say Mickey broke hearts. They say he left them trampled underneath streetcars, lying in Quarter gutters, smeared on the walls of the old convent, buried in the Bywater mud. They say Mickey was something. They always use that word. Something. He was something. They use it because they can't think of anything else to call him. You think, *no shit*, but it deserves to be pointed out. But something. Something with broad shoulders and a tight chest. Something with black scruff on his chin. Something with burning between the russet specks of his iris. Something that reached out in a smoky, dark bar and slipped its hand on your thigh and the only thing more surprising than it being there was how gently the fingers creased the denim of your jeans. They say he was something. They say he broke hearts.

But when I met him, he was just Mickey.

Katrina had finished her visit less than a day before. The city was dark, and that was fine. It had been dark before. And it was wet, but it'd been wet before, too, plenty of times. It looked battered and wrecked and abused and any other word you might want to pick up and dirty it with, and it still didn't look like anything I hadn't seen the morning of Ash Wednesday.

But the bitch took something. Something small, or at least hard to notice, something from beneath us, like a threadbare rug you'd never noticed was there until your foot landed on hardwood floor instead. I was trying to figure out what to name the feeling when we met.

By that night Mickey had become an obtuse angle of a man. His belly extended itself near a foot past his waistline and suffered him to waddle instead of walk. His hair had gone gray with specks of white. He kept it cut short across his scalp, with a neat goatee of matching color hanging off his chin. At nineteen I was taller than him by a head, and I was no giant. He had a chubby, round face, but he usually split it with an earnest smile and warm eyes. He embellished his round head with gold studs in each of his earlobes and only ever wore bowling shirts that kept his stomach poorly covered. That night, he wore a navy blue one with a cobalt stripe running off-center, paired with dull brown slacks to pop out the color all the more.

He was cute in an old queer kind of way. A normal night, I would've talked to him and laughed at his jokes. Maybe, if he was lucky, I would Google the references I didn't get later that night, those allusions to divas long since dead, or worse, old.

But it wasn't a normal night. It was the night of that kleptomaniac bitch of a hurricane, and we'd come to Bobby Schaeffer's home with the loads of our refrigerators and freezers on our backs, feasting on food destined to be spoiled and transmuting our blood to forty-proof, all the better to ignore the humidity, the heat and, worse of all, the feeling something was gone. So that night when Mickey told me his jokes, I laughed, and I didn't leave.

The only thing that grew in Bobby Schaeffer's backyard was a thicket of bamboo that lined his back fence. All through the day and night guys lined up at it like a urinal trough and pissed long and hard between the bamboo shafts. Mickey and I sat in foldout chairs in the backyard and watched the brief flashes of ass when they unzipped their pants. He invited me back to his place. I accepted with a shrug.

He was a good fuck. Most old, fat men are. If you're good in your twenties there's no reason you shouldn't be in your fifties. It's just that no one wants to watch you do it anymore. It's one of the great bitches of living, I guess, right under dying.

After he was finished, and right after he finished me off, he climbed out of bed to clean himself up. I asked him for a towel. He grabbed one from a bathroom rung and ran it under the faucet before he tossed it toward me. I wiped it over my stomach and didn't flinch. Because he'd ran it under warm water, waited until it was just the right temperature. I admit, I fell for him a little then, because that's some classy shit.

Just a little. Only ever a little. And, yeah, I saw a little more of him, even after Katrina was long gone and Isaac was asking after her. But I never slipped all the way down, down to that point where you lose yourself and all you have is him. I didn't, but I was sure he did. I could see him falling for me hard, and it gave me a kind of thrill to know.

So Brazil and I walked to his house to get poppers. We walked up to that bungalow of a home, and I knocked on the door and drew up a smile fit for the space between a flint and a knife. And Lennon answered the door.

For a moment, I wasn't sure what to do with my smile. I felt it stretch out of control, corners slipping off into the hinterlands of my cheeks. I became aware of how we were dressed, the way Brazil had put her makeup on, the way my leather jacket stopped about three inches from my waist. But I persevered through his inquiring expression and opened my mouth.

"Hey, Lennon. Is Mickey in?"

Lennon looked down at me and tilted the corner of his mouth up in a half-hearted smile. His grey hair fell a little over his eyes, symptom of a head of long, tousled hair. A rather impressive moustache stood out in an otherwise small and tender face and hid the rest of his good humor. He had eyes too blue to be stuck with another shade, eyes that drew you away from the paunch of his stomach and the legs overrun with navy veins, away from the stooped shoulders and the sullen overbite.

"Let me see. You boys come on in," He hesitated only a little before 'boys', but he made up for it by opening the door wide and letting us inside. We came in; I pulled my wig off my head as I did.

"Hey! Mickey!" he called out in the direction of the stairs. "Friends of yours!"

"Thanks," I said and looked at Brazil.

"Thanks," she said. Her face didn't handle the indoor lighting well; if I have to be bitch, she looked ridiculous. I suppose she looked just as ridiculous in the dark, but at least out there it was fun. At worse, funny. Under sixty-watt light bulbs, she just looked sad.

"Ya'll come on in the living room, have a seat. He must be upstairs; I'll go get him."

I watched his back as he trudged up the stairs. Lennon had been living with Mickey as long as Mickey had the house. He probably lived with him before then. They lived together, they owned the bookstore together, did everything worth doing together, so of course most of us assumed they were a couple, two men in an open relationship or whatever kind allowed for the occasional boy Mickey managed to wrangle into bed.

Only after I'd been the one wrangled did I learn the truth, as boring as it was unbelievable. Lennon was just a friend. A straight man who became a good friend, a good friend who'd become a bookstore business partner, a business partner who'd become a brother-in-law. "Lennon is just Lennon." That's what Mickey says.

They'd met when they were both graduate students at Tulane. They had fun together. Mickey told me the stories. The time they drove the wrong way down Royal, straight though the Quarter, just on a dare. The time they snuck on a Mardi Gras float and threw beads the whole of the parade route. And the time they'd driven to the Florida Keys on a whim, just to see how the sunset looked there.

He usually told me these stories after we'd finished fucking. He wanted to keep me in the bed a little longer, give himself a little more time to rub my body and memorize its shape with his palms. Or maybe he told me the stories because I reminded him that people being young was still a thing. They say Mickey broke hearts, sure, but it's always 'broke', never 'breaks'. But when I was in his bed, he could imagine them speaking in the present tense again. He could fantasize about returning to those days, dream of bending space and time around his swollen belly while we folded ourselves into sexual positions resembling irrational geometric shapes.

So he told me stories of when he was young to keep me, and I stayed and listened. Mickey wasn't dumb. He kept the lights off so I didn't have to see him, reached out to touch me from the far side of the bed so I wouldn't have to feel the press of his fat against my lower back. He spoke in a voice lower than the Earth's crust, and the sound of him passed through me, swept up under my hearing and uprooted it with a casual indifference. No, Mickey wasn't dumb. He knew the dark made it hard to find a reason to leave.

One story, in particular, was close beside me the night Brazil and I stopped in for poppers. It took place two years after Mickey and Lennon had opened the bookstore. Time had its knife to Mickey's throat, but it wasn't pressed against the skin quite yet. He still broke a heart or two in his spare time.

It was the late eighties. AIDS was old news; they'd even knitted a quilt about it. But even if it was old news, it was still scary shit. It was a death sentence. I guess it still is. Mickey's friend, a man named John Alvin, succumbed after a decade's worth of bareback. He chose Mickey's bed to be bedridden in, and Mickey was nothing if not accommodating. No one else would take care of him, not his family, not the hospitals, not really. Mickey thought it was his duty. To the Community.

Mickey was always going on about the Community. The Community this, our Community that. He was very critical of the Community, at least he was when I met him. He found the younger queens to be shallow, overly obsessed with appearance, with fitting in. He found them terribly apolitical. Terribly. He prophesied that all the advancement in gay rights would grind to a halt when my generation came into power, because none of the gays of my generation would be in power, because we of the new fagguard couldn't be bothered to vote.

I guess Mickey had never been to Washington and, you know, walked on a sidewalk. You can't throw a pair of beads and not hit a queer in a suit. I could've said this, argued with Mickey, calmed him down, but I didn't. Whenever he started up, I just let him finish himself off. I figured he cared so much about the Community because he knew it was only thing left to take care of him. Time had long since started drawing blood from Mickey's throat by the time we were fucking. Soon, he wouldn't just be an old queer, he'd be an infirm one, and only the fabled Community would be there to ease his suffering.

Usually, talking of John Alvin served as a prelude to his rantings. But one night, when there was thunder humming through the walls and a wind stranger than us beating off the window, that night he left that particular crazy alone. That night, instead, he told me a story about when he'd come home to find Lennon and his sister waiting for him.

"Your sister?"

"They'd been dating off and on for a year or so."

"That didn't bother you?"

"At first. Then I got over it."

"Was she pregnant?"

"No. But they'd just gotten engaged."

"Wow."

"Yeah. I know.

"So that's what they wanted to talk to you about?"

"No. Well, yes. But there was more to it than that. I never got a chance to congratulate them on the engagement before they threw the rest at me. Their faces. If you could've seen their faces. They told me they were getting married, and they looked like they were telling me someone was dead."

He swallowed. Or maybe he choked a little. Whatever it was, it was a wet sound with a jagged end.

"Then they told me Bobbi was going to be moving in. And I said 'OK, sure.' Didn't even have to think about it. Sounded great. I just couldn't understand why it looked so bad. Then they let me know.

"It was John. My sister didn't want to live in the same house as him. It scared her. She thought she'd catch it. Oh, they didn't tell me like that, of course. They didn't just blurt it out. We were all too goddamn Southern for that. So instead they put enough sugar on it to make an anchovy sweet. Mickey, the house isn't that big. Mickey, doesn't he need professional care? Mickey, wouldn't it be better for him? He tried to protect her. Lennon. He told me it was his idea, his fear. Shit."

He drew the word 'shit' out like Brazil did. One long 'e' trailing into a short 't' sound somewhere down the length of the Mississippi.

"I knew," he whispered to my shoulder. "My sister was afraid. Afraid of John, who couldn't even get out of bed without me helping him. Afraid of a man who threw up water, who couldn't talk without sores busting open in his mouth. That was the John she was afraid of."

"She wasn't afraid of John," I'd said.

"What?"

I hadn't known I was going to say anything until I'd said it. I swallowed and opened my mouth curiously, just to see what else would come out.

"She wasn't afraid of John, she was afraid of the disease."

"So?"

"So? You never were? You were never just a little scared, not even a little?"

"No."

"No?"

"He deserved better."

"What he deserved has nothing to do with it. It has nothing to do with how you're feeling."

"You're wrong. You're young. You'll learn. Fear takes the backseat when there's something important, really important to do."

"But it's still in the car," I said back.

He didn't respond. He just told his story instead.

"So I told them no."

"No?"

"No. They couldn't move in with me, then. I chose John."

"Then what happened?"

"We started arguing. We ended up screaming. My sister and me. We said things, things both of us didn't mean. Or maybe. I don't know. Maybe we did mean it. Maybe they were always in there, just waiting to come out. Just waiting to slip by us. Do you know what I mean?"

I told him no. He sighed on the back of my neck.

"Lennon just sat there, watching us. He looked disgusted. I've never been so mad at him as I was when I saw that expression on his face. He looked disgusted at us. But my sister, bitch that she might have been, my sister at least would say something. My sister would look you in the eye and tell you what kind of world she saw coming in through hers. Do you know what I mean?"

Again, I told him no. But he wasn't listening to me.

"Lennon just looked like it was all so beneath him. A man's life, my sister's heart, either one you pick, there was something on the line. And he just sat there. It's the maddest I've ever been with him."

"I thought this was a story about your sister."

Mickey went quiet. I followed his lead. He'd never really mentioned his sister before. I knew she'd died of cancer, not too long back, but I heard that from one of the boys, not Mickey. I never saw a picture of her in the house, never heard him tell a story about her, even mention her. Until he talked about John Alvin. I thought it was strange, that the only time I would hear about her, I'd hear the story where she wanted to kick the man with AIDS out to the curb. The one where she screamed at her brother and called him names people liked to graffiti on walls in red spray paint.

Finally he said, "No. It's a story about Lennon, I guess. Me and Lennon. People say we're a couple, and, you know, I usually don't correct them. Isn't that funny? I just think, you know, I think a pair of friends can be a couple. The same as two lovers. Don't you think?"

"I guess."

"Don't just guess," he admonished with a meaty jab to my shoulder. "Tell me what you think."

I could tell, despite the play he affected in his voice, this was important to him. That it was probably the first time he'd ever spoke his theory aloud. I worked my tongue over my teeth and sent words out to join the fading thunder.

"I think maybe. Depends on the two friends."

"Well, there you are."

"So you and Lennon broke up. Is that what you're saying?"

"Almost," Mickey murmured. "Almost. They both left. Went to Bobbi's apartment."

"Why couldn't Lennon just move there?"

"Small apartment. Besides, he and I had been living in the house longer than she'd been living there."

"Oh."

"The next morning he showed up at the bookstore. Like nothing happened. And we did the usual. Stocking shelves, rearranged display tables, counting the register. All in absolute silence. We didn't speak until the day was over, and we were doing the same shit a second time for kicks. Then he finally said something."

"What?"

"I'm sorry. And that was it."

"You forgave him?"

"Yeah. Of course. I'd always forgive him. I hope he'd do the same for me."

"And your sister?"

"Yeah. But it took longer. She didn't make it easy."

"Then you shouldn't have tried so hard."

He laughed, low and sad. Outside, the thunder broke itself into staccato pieces.

"You forgive the ones you love."

I thought about that while Brazil and I walked into the living room. The words passed through my brain as the sound of thunder. Above us, floorboards creaked and sighed in release. Lennon had approached the bathroom door; if I strained, I could hear the low rumble of him asking Mickey a question, and under that the steady hiss of a shower on full blast. More floorboards creaked before we heard Lennon shouting from the top of the stairs:

"He just got in the shower. Give him a few minutes. Ya'll get something out of the kitchen if you're hungry. Or there's TV."

There was a pause as Lennon tried to think of something else for us to do, but failing that we heard him trudge away, followed shortly after by the creak of his bedroom door. Brazil sat on the couch. I didn't.

"I'm just going upstairs and get the poppers from his dresser. He won't mind."

"OK." She hesitated and ran her tongue over her lips. I wondered if they tasted like a Fireball candy, or if they only looked like they did with that cheap lipstick. "Do you want me to come with you?"

I shook my head. She looked relieved. I left her alone on the couch and walked upstairs, but I did so quietly enough to be silent. I knew which floorboards creaked, which ones sighed. If he was straining to listen he might have heard me. And maybe he was. Maybe he was expecting me. He certainly wasn't surprised when I reached the top of the stairs and rounded the banister to my left, the opposite direction from Mickey's bedroom. He didn't even raise an eyebrow when I filled his open doorway; he only looked up from where he was sitting at the foot of his bed with sad, understanding eyes.

"Mickey'll be right out." He hesitated. He sounded like Brazil when he did. "I told him you two were here."

"Sure." I walked in and closed the door behind me. The sad never left his eyes. Nor the understanding.

"You're drunk," he said.

"Yes," I answered. "But I know what I'm doing."

A little bit of the understanding left his eyes. It was replaced by a dim concentration.

"I'm not interested. You know I'm…I'm not."

"You've been in this house too long not to be," I said. I hadn't been planning on saying it. I had nothing planned, not even as I led Brazil up the walk to the house. But it was true. The moment it was said, we both knew it was true. I'd taken my wig off downstairs, kept it gripped in my hand, but after I said that I slipped it back on. I reached out towards his light switch. Fear, finally fear, came into his eyes, but it was too late for that.

"Pretend I'm whoever," I said as the lights went out.

I walked toward him in the dark. His room made it easy to maneuver, and so did he. He didn't stir, and I walked forward with my hands held out in the dark until they found his knees. I knelt like I was praying and reached out until I found his zipper.

I thought about the times I'd noticed him looking at me when I visited Mickey. The times I'd popped out of the room in a towel. The time we met each other in the kitchen after midnight. I thought about him saying, "You having fun?

And me saying, "Always fun with Mickey."

And him saying, "Just be careful. He's a heartbreaker."

I thought of Mickey, calling them a couple, if not of lovers then of friends. I thought about the sister that was rarely mentioned, the cancer that never was.

I pulled him out while he gripped the hair of my wig. I cradled him in the palm of my hand and wondered how lonely it must be to be in a love with a man who didn't know how to love you back. But that's a lie. I didn't have to wonder.

He was soft at first. I could hear him choking on his breath, trying to hold back tears I assume had been dammed since he'd seen that Florida Key sunset. I wetted the inside of my mouth as much as I could.

I thought of Baucis and Philemon. I thought of them on their hill, looking down at the wasteland below. For Jupiter, in his fury, had brought a great flood to the people of their village, to punish all those who hadn't let a stranger in from the cold. I wondered what Baucis and Philemon thought, if they had had friends in their village, people they shared their lives with. I thought of them looking down at a world where the roofs of houses floated on the water like inverted boats going nowhere. And I thought about what Mickey said.

"You forgive the ones you love."

He stiffened, just a little, and I doubled down the pressure of my mouth to take advantage. In seconds he filled the inside of my mouth. Somewhere far above me he groaned, and I answered in wet slurps.

We were making too much noise. I was glad. That was the whole point.

He was close to releasing himself when the door opened. Light from the hallway crashed through the dark in a long wave that fell perfectly on top of us. I flipped the hair of my wig so he could get a good look of me, of my face, and the mouth working its way down Lennon's shaft. It didn't go limp.

"Mickey," someone said. I guess him, by process of elimination.

I couldn't get a good look at the expression on his Mickey's face. He was just a fat shadow. But in seconds the shadow was on me. It pulled me off Lennon and half-dragged me out of his bedroom door. I wrenched myself free and ran downstairs. He was right behind me. For a moment I wondered if he would push me, send me tumbling down the rest of the stairs. But he didn't. He just stayed right behind me, herding me straight forward to the door. When I opened it, then he pushed me, just enough so that I would trip over myself as I stumbled out the door.

"Get the fuck out!"

I turned. His face was red; the blood vessels pressed against his skin like snakes fighting to break free and strike me. His body trembled; running after me seemed to have taxed his poor heart, and he used the door frame to hold himself up. But he straightened himself up when he saw me looking back.

"I said get the fuck out! Don't ever let me fucking see you again you little fuck!"

I didn't say anything. But I shifted my glance, just a little over his shoulder, where Brazil was walking in from the living room, her eyes wide with fear, her wig off and clasped in her hand. Mickey turned, ready to shout something else, but when he saw her a little of his anger evaporated. He looked back at me. The wheels turned in his head. I spit in his face to help lube them up. He jerked back as if I'd shot him in the forehead.

I turned and half-ran down the brick walkway, down the sidewalk, running without mind toward where I was going. I looked back to see if anyone was chasing me. No one was. Then the strength went out of my legs, and I collapsed on the sidewalk. And the only thing I could think of was the cover of my Metamorphoses. I thought about me and Brazil, Mickey and Lennon, his sister and John Alvin. I thought about our lives, twisting around one another, making tragic shapes out of nothing knots.

Then I stopped thinking. It involved standing up, straightening my wig, and walking away from that house. And later, it helped when I threw away Ovid's Metamorphoses and buried Baucis and Philemon underneath half-empty cartons of Chinese takeout.

Winner

CORSET
SALLY BELLEROSE

Hey, Mac." Jackie has called the Hawaiian guy who owns China Express Mac for as long as she's known him. It might be his name, but she doubts it. She has heard others call him Ho and Sam as well as Mac.

"Hello, Jackie," Mac says. "Where's your better half?"

"Home, waitin' on her anniversary dinner."

"Congrats." Mac scratches his chin. "How many years you been together?"

"Forty. Minus a few months in the late eighties when she threw me out for bad behavior." Jackie's not telling Mac anything he doesn't already know. She orders spring rolls and fried rice with shrimp and chicken.

While the new kid with the limp makes up the order, Jackie inquires about the poker game going on in the back room. She has forgone poker for the last few years, but always asks who's sitting at the tables.

"Only one table tonight." Mac pushes the bowl of free pork crisps toward Jackie. "Bet you can guess who's parked there."

"Henry, James Junior, Old Man Chaffee, Bad Madeline?" Jackie takes a pork crisp. Mac nods. They listen to creaking on the back stairs.

"Old Man Chaffee checking on his wife. Swollen ankles. Too much Chinese food." Mac grunts, as close to a laugh as he gets.

"Might want a fourth 'til he comes back." Jackie runs a chapped hand across the top of her buzz cut.

Mac cocks his head. "Thought you swore off?"

"Yeah." Jackie fingers the twenties in her pocket. "How much is the food?"

Mac tallies the order in his head. "Eighteen twenty-five."

Just the thought of taking a seat at the folding table makes Jackie feel more alive than she's felt in a long time. Bad Maddie will cackle like the crazy old bird she is if Jackie walks into that big back room. Jackie can already feel the edge of the table press against her belly as she pulls up a seat. She can see the shine on the cards, a new deck every time. She can feel the slide as a card slips between her fingers. She can feel the ridges on the circumference of the chips take their tiny love-bites as she rakes in her winnings. Even her ass hitting the too small seat of the metal chair would feel good.

"Eighteen twenty-five," Mac repeats.

She hands him a twenty. What's to lose? Three twenties and change from a fourth, that's all she's got. None of them will stake her, not since she lost the tax refund. None of them wants Regina in here making another scene. Sixty dollars should have been enough to get Regina the CD player at Wal-Mart. But they were sold out. The rain check in her back pocket would make a shitty anniversary gift. All she needs is to win thirty more dollars, plus tax, so maybe forty, to get the next model up, which, what a surprise, is still available. But even if she loses, since Old Man Chaffee lives twenty steps above the place, she probably won't have time to lose the whole sixty. What's ten minutes? What kind of a loser can't buy her mate of forty years an anniversary present? What the hell? Jackie's got enough will power to take a seat for ten minutes and not get pulled back in permanently. It could mean a gift that would make Regina smile. She has to wait for the food anyway. And she could win.

Mac hands her a dollar seventy-five.

"Still five bucks to get in?" Jackie holds out another twenty.

"You sure?" Mac shakes his head. "Well, none of my business." He gives her back three fives. "Bad Maddy will be happy to see you." He turns to the kid and says, "Put the order under the lights when it's ready."

The feeling she gets when she walks in the back room is as good as Jackie remembers. Madeline flings her arms around Jackie, steps back, holding Jackie at arm's length, taking the liberty of passing her red fingernails across the top of Jackie's close-cropped grey hair, pretending, as she always has, that they're both interested in more than the theatrics of the moment. Jackie wonders, for the hundredth time, whether Madeline ever did have any real attraction to her. *Unlikely. Just part of the sport.* No matter, Jackie appreciates the effort. And to make things more interesting, there are three whiskey sour glasses in front of Maddy's spot at the table. When Maddy loses, it's usually to whisky sours.

Henry and James Junior offer Jackie nods and tight-lipped smiles. She's as comforted by the familiarity of their silence as she is by Maddy's chatter. James Junior has a big pile of chips in front of him, mostly blue. Jackie counts and does the math. About $400 dollars worth. Not the most Jackie has seen on the fake leather table top, but enough to make her put on her poker face and decide not to mention that she's only got fifty-six dollars and change on her.

"I'm only in till Old Man Chaffee comes back?" she says, as if she's considering how many chips to start off with. She asks for twenty blue chips, forty dollars' worth.

"You know the rules. Chaffee comes through the door, we finish the hand and you're out," Henry says. Four at a table has always been the rule. Jackie remembers when there were five tables of four playing at the same time and people holding numbers waiting for their turn for a seat.

The shades are drawn. Tonight the only overhead light with a working bulb is above their table. The big room seems like an abandoned warehouse with just the one table set up near the back window. Until the cards are dealt. Then the room seems full of life.

Jackie notices every nuance, every shadow passing over the other players' faces—the change in James Junior's color as he labors to get a lung full of air, Bad Maddy's powdered face held a little stiffer to block an expression. The green tarnish under his wedding ring shows on Henry's finger when he spreads his hand on the table. Something skitters in the wall. The bell dings up front, sounding far off. Jackie's heart speeds up and slows down, depending on the cards.

Old Man Chaffee's wife must have needed more than ten minutes worth of help with her swollen ankles. Jackie wins fifty-five dollars, loses twenty, wins twenty-five. In between hands the players relax for a minute at a time, eat a few chips, sip a drink. Jackie drinks the warm free water. Maddy tells Jackie she looks good with a few extra pounds on her. Jackie doesn't return the compliment. After twenty minutes, Jackie's up by one hundred eighty dollars. Then the worst and best thing that could happen does. Old Man Chaffee is back and watching as she wins her biggest round yet, one hundred five dollars on her "last" hand. Two hundred eight-five bucks. Might be enough to calm Regina down about gambling. Or more likely Jackie will keep the thing to herself.

She's glad for the rules of the game. The rules will save her, get her home on time, in enough time anyway. She rises to leave. Old Man Chaffee says, "Sit your ass down. I ain't gonna steal your chance to give some of that back." Her heart flutters, steadies, and squeezes out her better judgment. She sits. She could kiss Old Man Chaffee.

She doesn't kiss Old Man Chaffee and she doesn't give a penny back. Jackie keeps winning. She wins like the heart attack that hasn't happened, knowing sooner or later this could kill her, but not right now, right now there is the pure rush of it, her arms wide, raking it in, stopping only to allow herself a half-smile at the other cardiac cases witnessing her glory. Even James Junior, who has lost most of his winnings, gives her a grudging nod.

It's Bad Maddy who finally says, "Go home, Jackie. While I still got cab money in my bra."

❖

Jackie pulls up to the curb in front of the house and takes a quick glance at her watch, 8:38 p.m. She left at 5:30. At most Regina would have expected her to be gone an hour. She might have stretched it to two hours without causing a brawl, claiming she had a hard time finding an anniversary present, which she did, but three hours on their anniversary is far beyond forgive and forget time for Regina. Jackie pats the CD player, a shiny purple thing. Maybe Jackie will hold off presenting it until she's sure it won't get smashed. Regina's a smart old girl. Even without the evidence of dried-out Chinese food, she has probably already figured out that Jackie is late because she's been gambling. Maybe she should have ordered fresh shrimp and chicken, but she didn't want to spare the extra ten minutes.

Only thing to do is walk in and tell the bald-faced truth.

Jackie tries the kitchen door, not bolted. Good. "Baby?" she says, opening the door slowly. She expects Regina to be standing there, hands on hips, fire in her eyes. If Jackie is lucky, Regina will be worried enough that a minute or two will pass while the fact that Jackie isn't dead in a ditch settles over Regina, giving Jackie time to do some fast talking. If only Jackie had remembered the damn cell phone the Senior Center gave them she could have called Regina with some bullshit about a flat.

"Baby?" she calls again, tentatively, softly, placing the grease-stained bag of food on the counter and walking into the living room, thinking maybe she can still use the flat tire excuse. No, that would never work. Regina would march out to the car and see that the tire hasn't been messed with. "Regina?" She whispers the question. Has something happened? Has that heart pill Regina takes failed her? Has she gotten a ride or taken the bus somewhere without leaving a note? Wouldn't be the first time she tried to teach Jackie a lesson by taking off and leaving no word where she went. "My own medicine," Jackie says, walking down the ten foot hall to the bedroom.

She opens the bedroom door and stops dead in her tracks. Regina is flat on her back on their bed. Jackie can't see much of Regina's face, just the bottom of her chin and nostrils, her frizzy white hair a cloud around her shoulders. She's wearing something old and impossibly tight, some kind of lingerie that makes her small breasts look larger. Jackie stares. It seems important that she retrieve the word for the garment Regina is wearing. This forgetfulness gives her the creeps, feels like something outside of herself, alive and willful that she can't control. Her mother became forgetful before she lost all memory and then all speech. Jackie holds her breath to see if she can hear Regina breathing. She cannot. Her intellect tells her that this is Regina, her partner of forty years, asleep, sprawled on the bed, wearing some old fashioned sexy undergarment. Foreboding gathers in her chest and expands to Jackie's throat. She's bewildered by the sight of her lover after all these years. She knows she's being irrational, but is afraid to take a step closer, afraid the breasts that skew her view might not have a beating heart under them.

"Some sign of life." She mouths the words inaudibly. Dead or alive, Regina does not oblige. If she is trying to give Jackie a scare, it's working. It feels like a scene in a bad movie. Whatever this is, it looks staged, which is some comfort, a staged tragedy being much more desirable than a real one. Still, the thought that it may not be Regina's face beyond those hoisted breasts runs through Jackie's mind followed immediately by the thought that her gambling may have finally killed Regina, who has always claimed it will be the death of them both. Jackie has to stop herself from running out of the room.

"Regina," she whispers, forcing herself to move to the side of the bed, where she stares directly down at what is unequivocally Regina's face. Jackie rubs her head which is staring to pound. Maybe she is losing her mind. Come home too late, gambled one time too many, and lost everything. She concentrates on Regina's swell of belly. Is it moving? Jackie is hopeful that this is the case, but is not certain. She kneels and strokes Regina's warm dry cheek with the back of her hand.

Regina's mouth is slack, until she wakes with a start and her body jerks, one quick tremor. Her eyes open for a brief second and close. Her heart pounds wildly. Her dream of Jackie coming home safely and on time merges with the reality of Jackie's hand on her cheek. Before anger comes relief as a tear settles in the corner of her eye. In the second it takes the tear to make its way down her temple, dampening her hair, Regina is furious.

"Regina." Jackie's voice is all tenderness. She sees Regina's wrinkled cheeks become pink with fury and removes her hand.

Regina sucks in a deep breath, opens her eyes and sits up. She does not look at Jackie. She looks through the open bedroom door. Jackie stands but otherwise doesn't move from the spot. "I thought you were dead," she says. Her knees hurt from kneeling.

"Because you're a fool. Alive, no thanks to you." Regina had not meant to fall asleep, had not meant to be in this get-up when Jackie finally made it home. "Stop staring." After an hour and then two went by Regina had meant to be in street clothes, sensible shoes, with her purse near in case she got a bad phone call and needed to be ready, ready to do whatever needed doing to take care of Jackie. In case some legitimate misfortune had happened. "Give me my robe," she yells. Then, with a break in her voice where the last of the relief squeaks out, she adds, "You really are a god damn fool."

Jackie is relieved, too. Relieved that her fear of death, at least for today, was unfounded, she almost smiles, almost welcomes the tongue lashing to come. She vows silently that this is the last time, the absolute last time she will gamble. The lottery is exempt. She does not vow to give up the lottery.

The robe is on a hook on the back of the door. Jackie says, "Baby, I'm so sorry," and touches the robe's hem. She doesn't look up, because right under her expression is a smile. Regina is not only alive, she's wearing a corset. And behind Jackie's shame, before and after the fact of her addiction and loss of control, Jackie won. She won big. She won going-out-to-dinner-and-a-movie-and-a drink-after-with-plenty-left-over big. "Corset," she says, handing Regina the robe. "I couldn't remember the name for it. That was your mother's. I remember now." She nods with her eyes closed. "Our little apartment, a walk-up on the fifth floor."

Regina scowls, how dare Jackie call up past sex acts, as if she had the right to mention making love at this moment? Simultaneously, Regina is thinking what Jackie is also thinking— sex on the kitchen floor, witch hazel on the scratches from the cracked linoleum on Regina's back and Jackie's knees.

Regina spits out, "Grandmother's corset," as if the mistake about which dead relative was the original owner of the corset is another transgression to be thrown in the black hole of Jackie's sins. She will not let herself be moved by the fact that Jackie, who once had an almost photographic memory, has started to forget the names for things. Regina is suddenly mortified to be wearing this ridiculous piece of clothing. She ties the robe's belt in a double knot. She stamps her foot. "How much did you lose?"

Jackie is careful not to let the pleasure she takes in seeing Regina stamp her foot, a gesture full of vigor, bleed through her expression of sincere remorse. Years ago Jackie was made to understand that you're beautiful when you're angry is a cue for Regina to pack Jackie's bags.

"Over five hundred," Jackie says. "Won," she adds quietly, because trying to speak over Regina is futile at this point. Regina needs to get it out. Jackie tries to tamp down the elation, the after-a-win mania building up in her. How quickly the world turns sometimes, despite how badly she has messed up, if Jackie plays her cards right, if she lets Regina see how sorry she is, despite every time she has ever fucked up, if she can show her honest feelings, like Regina is always trying to get her to do, because she is, Jackie is sincerely in love with Regina, after all these years, as much or more now than she has ever been, because she's genuinely sorry and ready to do better, ready to quit altogether, really, now and forever, if Jackie can hold out, hold back her increasingly good mood, let Regina have her well-deserved say, let her vent, do what she needs to do, if Jackie can hang in and not blow it by trying to make everything all right too soon, there will be a celebration, eventually they will have their own little party. It will be after, Jackie understands, Regina calms down and realizes this time it really is just a one-shot mistake that somehow turned out okay. After a while Regina will smile at Jackie again.

For the moment, Regina has murder in her eyes. "You lost $500 dollars," she really belts it out. "Five hundred dollars you piece of…"

"Won," Jackie says quickly. She's not sure if Regina hears over her yelling, but Regina stops short of calling her "shit." Jackie is pretty sure the window is open behind the drawn shade. Well, they've heard worse from the neighbor's house come in through that window.

Regina looks like she might explode, which she does, screaming, "You lost five hundred dollars on our fucking anniversary. Where did you get the money? You piece of," she throws up her arms and screeches, "shit." Her head shakes, her face contorts. She takes a deep breath. She takes several more deep breaths. Jackie takes a step toward her, but Regina's puts a hand up to stop her from getting any closer. Regina's head stops shaking and her face becomes blank. "I give up." She sits on the bed. Speaking slowly because the words hurt she says, "After all the time and money we spent on rehab, money we didn't have, time…" Her voice is barely audible. She gives Jackie a look that breaks Jackie's heart. "We're running out of time." She looks at the wall for a long moment before turning back, looking old and tired, looking directly at Jackie. "Do you get that, Jackie?"

Jackie forces herself to look Regina in the eye and nod before she sits on the bed next to her. She bends forward, head bowed, hands clasped between her knees, so she doesn't have to bear Regina's look. "Won," Jackie says softly. "Won," she repeats.

"You stayed away from this thing for three years. Why now? If you think I'm going to take on more hours so we can eat and have electricity…" In mid sentence, Regina cocks her head, and says, "Won?"

"Won." Jackie nods. "I'm so god-damned happy you're alive." She would take Regina in her arms, but knows this is not possible, knows that her own post win optimism will be short lived, knows that Regina's anger may well escalate for hours or days before it settles down, knows that experience gives Regina every right to fear that winning is no better than losing when it comes to satiating Jackie once she has felt those cards in her hand. Still, Jackie wishes she could hang on to the rush of the win for just one evening. She sits and cries, lets her tears fall on the grey, once blue carpet. It's all she's got, tears and five hundred bucks. Regina stands over her, hands on her hips. Above and below the double knot of its belt, the sides of her robe separate. She looks down at Jackie with pursed lips, eyes pinched and trained like the scope of a shotgun on Jackie's forehead.

Jackie's tears are mostly real. She hopes they work. Hopes the undignified sobbing and sighing makes Regina see how much she loves her. Hopes at some point she can tell Regina how happy she is that Regina put on that corset for their anniversary. Because Jackie is grateful that Regina has put up with her, stayed with her all these years. Also she's tired and hungry and all she can think about is how to get Regina to forgive her as quickly as possible. The smell of the German chocolate cake Regina was putting in the oven when Jackie left bolsters her resolve to get them both to the table. She reaches for her handkerchief, feels the money, and pulls the roll of bills out of the back pocket of her chinos, a big bundle, mostly fives and tens, more money than twice the combined weekly income from both their part-time jobs. She offers the wad, open-handed, to Regina. She has blown a chance to show Regina how good she looks in that corset. Blown the opportunity to feel Regina's soft flesh and listen to the pounding of their hearts. Tonight will not be a night when sated, pleased with herself and Jackie, Regina will sit up in bed and carry on about TV commercials selling youth by making old people ashamed of their skin and hair, their minds and teeth. Jackie won't get the wrinkles on her face and neck kissed tonight. Jackie shakes her head and accentuates the sorry in her expression. She places the wad of money on the mattress next to her.

Regina waits a few minutes before she snatches the money, and points a finger at Jackie's chest. "Stay seated on that bed. Do not move an inch."

Jackie listens as Regina goes from room to room, slamming doors and drawers, flushing the toilet, banging windows. She allows herself a smile, knowing Regina is hiding the money, taping it to the bottom of the silverware drawer or putting it in a plastic bag and sticking it in the urn with her mother's ashes. Regina is gone, making clattering noises, for a long time. Jackie hears snippets of a short phone call, words spoken softly that Jackie can't make out. It gets quiet. It stays quiet. Jackie would be wondering if Regina left, but Regina wouldn't leave wearing a robe and corset.

Jackie retraces the steps she took to get to the bedroom, walks down the ten foot hall, saying, "Regina?" several times, switching to "Baby?" as she rounds the hallway into the kitchen.

Regina listens to Jackie's approach. She has a plan, Gamblers Anonymous and her personal version of shock and awe, which she's already given Jackie a taste of by playing a shrew, that's Regina's plan, her only plan. She closes her eyes to conjure up the face of gambling. She has her own definition of poker face, it's not neutral or impassive, it's the smarmy smiling face of Richard Millhouse Nixon, arms and shoulders raised in his obscene split fingered victory salute as he debarked from a jet coming back from who remembers where. Regina doesn't care that this image is ridiculous, doesn't care that she has never, not even once, met a gambling buddy of Jackie's who had any resemblance whatsoever to this picture. Not a disgraced, smug-faced politician among them. She can't even pin this image on the people who make money off gambling. As far as Regina knows, Jackie has never been to a casino or horse race owned by some greedy millionaire leeching money from lower class losers. No, her Jackie has always been lured into over-heated back rooms of local restaurants or cheap hotels. Her consorts have always been the poor dealing to the poor, seated at a folding table. No matter, the image of Nixon doesn't have to make sense as long it fuels Regina's resolve.

Jackie finds Regina sitting at the kitchen table, her robe wrapped tightly around her, eyes closed, sitting up straight, but relaxed in her chair. She looks serene, more like a Zen Master than an aging lesbian meditating on her beloved's bad habit.

Jackie sits opposite her without speaking.

"Here's what's going to happen." Regina opens her eyes, slowly deliberately crossing her arms over her chest. "That money is dead to you. We will not go out to eat, go to the movies, buy me a new dress, order cable. You will not get one iota of pleasure connected to that money." She holds up the sales slip she has removed from the Wal-Mart bag. "Nor will you ever see me get one iota of pleasure from that money. The CD player is going back."

Jackie nods, feeling any chance that she can salvage part of this evening to savor the win slip away. "Smart of you," she says. "To kill the buzz." She reaches across the table and Regina let's her take her hand. She wonders how many gallons of bad

Gamblers Anonymous coffee she will have to drink before this is over. "Have I worn you out?" She means will you throw me out? She looks at their entwined hands, knowing that this could be Regina's last gift for a long time.

"We've been wrestling with this miserable addiction our whole lives." Regina wonders if she is completely worn out. Or does she have one more round of tough love in her. "We've lived through rehab too many times, scrounging from friends and relatives to pay for it. They're used up, some are dead, My Love," she says wistfully. "The days of tapping our friends are gone."

"My Love," Jackie repeats like a prayer. "We can beat this thing without rehab."

"We? No." Regina shakes her head. "Maybe I could do it one more time, beg or borrow the money, get you into rehab, go to Gamblers Anonymous with you, listen to endless hours of sobriety talk, but I'll be damned if I'm going to. You can do it without me or you live without me." Regina pulls her hand away.

It's only after they eat the cold Chinese food, Regina puts the uneaten German chocolate cake in the refrigerator and says, "Let's go to bed," that Jackie realizes for sure that she is not getting thrown out of the house. Not tonight.

They lie back to back and fall asleep hoping the same thing—that Jackie's need to sleep with her body curled around Regina's and her desire to see Regina in that corset again win.

THE DARK SYMPHONY
ERIC ANDREWS-KATZ

He lurked in the darkened doorway remaining perfectly still. His excitement grew the longer he watched, raising his naturally high body temperature. The cold brought some relief to his burning palms and his cheek pressing against the brick wall. His skin absorbed the chill like a porous sponge. When the couple had passed the doorway, he glided into it finding the perfect spot to unobtrusively observe them. The factory smoke mixed with the fog, but the buildings lining the alley provided a boundary filtering out most of the misty covering.

The woman moved down the alley's muddy path while keeping one eye on her prey. Taking the man's hand she lured him further along, seeking out an undisturbed place to conduct her business. Having used the spot before, she knew where to go and had no problems finding it.

The moon was a sliver in the clear sky, hanging low and casting limited light. It was enough for him to make out her dirty round face with hag-like features, heavy eye bags, and a gap-toothed mouth trying to stretch into something resembling a smile. She might have once known the bounteous duties of being called pretty, but those days were past. Liquor and bad nutrition had taken their toll aging her rapidly.

When the couple had gone a quarter of the way down the alley she stopped, leaning back against a slated wooden fence. Reaching down, her gnarled hands fumbled with the cloth layers and lifted the skirts of her dress above her knees. Pushing her hips forward she waited for him. The man had shrugged off his coat and thrown it over one of the wooden boards of the fence. He stepped in front of her temporarily blocking the view with his back. The man reached down and fumbled with his clothing until his pants lowered, revealing shirttails and pasty white flesh. Bracing himself with his palms he entered her with a quick thrust, pushing her against the fence. Once he found his rhythm, she reached around clasping onto his back with one hand, while holding her skirts up with the other. He buried his face in the crevice between her neck and shoulder fondling and pushing inside her.

From the shadowed location he watched them go through their ritual. There was no voyeuristic charge or lusting envy as he peered at their rutting. Only a feeling of disgust, sharp and deep within his bowels. The bile churned in his stomach clawing its way back up into his throat. He swallowed hard, trying his best to keep it down. This was not the first time he followed the doctor, secretly observing the temporary courtship a few coins could buy. It sickened him to watch what he couldn't have, but he never looked away.

The doctor pulled up his trousers making a show of dropping several coins into the woman's hand. Her dark moon eyes grew wider as one coin followed another, and her ragged grin spread when the last one fell with a final 'clink'. The doctor tipped his hat as if he were bidding good night to a companion instead of a common tramp. Putting his hands leisurely in his pockets the doctor strolled back up the alley alone to enjoy the remainder of the night.

He dissolved into the archway's darkness waiting until the doctor meandered passed. His dark hair added to the camouflage as he pressed himself against the brick, holding his breath with the momentary fear of discovery. It was for naught, as the doctor's familiar form strolled by the doorway never having cause to search the path's shoulders. He watched the doctor walk gracefully with ease and a confident stride until he turned at the corner and was lost to sight.

The woman was getting closer. She moved slow keeping her eyes focused on the coins in her hand, delighted with their total. As she approached he could see her more clearly. Her hair was brittle brown, strewn liberally with grey strands and pinned behind her head in a stringy ball. Her skin was pale with badly painted makeup sparsely placed, covering a complexion of dirty mop water. Flowers twisted from a dull cloth were clipped to either side of her head holding back her hair. Her dress was a nondescript brown tenting her body, compromising flattery for easy accessibility. She looked up startled when he suddenly appeared in front of her.

"Pardon me, love," she said with a guttural accent. She snorted an awkward laugh, gazing up at his six-foot frame. The top of her head hovered below his chin's level. "You gave me a fright, you did."

She shuffled aside to get around him. He moved in front of her.

"Somethin' I can helps you with?" The fine hairs on her upper lip bristled.

He held up his right fist with a shilling grasped tightly between his thumb and forefinger, his dark brown eyes sparkling with anticipation.

"You're just a boy," she said. She quickly scanned over his squared head, squat nose, and cleanly shaved appearance. "Can't be more than sixteen, I'd say. A poppet lookin' for his first time, eh?" She laughed with the stench of tooth rot and liquor.

He said nothing while waiting until her cackle slowed. His fingers formed a quick fist before resuming with a second coin. He rubbed them together to make sure she saw them both. Her saucer eyes grew beady with greed. They focused on him with capital interest.

"Well then," she whispered. Her gaze shifted from his dark eyes and locked on the coins between his fingers. "A boy's a man when he gots money to spend."

She moved for the coins and he pulled them back just out of her reach. He jutted his chin pointing down the alley. She glanced behind and returned with a broken grin. With a nod of her head she spun around leading him back to her previous spot. She resumed her position, shoulders braced against the fence and her hands busily hiking up the layers of her dress.

"No," he said in a commanding whisper. He reached up and ran the edges of the coins around the bottom of his lip, tapping the metal against his flesh. His free hand went to her shoulder giving it a brief push downward to emphasize his point.

"Oh! He knows what he wants, does he?" she said, regaining her balance from the strong grasp. "That's ok. I can give the Bishop a li'l kiss if you like."

She moved to her knees as he took off his long pea coat. Folding it in his arms, he gently tossed it over the fence's frame behind them. He stood in front of her, thick legs firmly planted and strong arms clasped loosely behind his back.

"A big boy like you...let's see now." Her hands fumbled with the buttons of his pants. She slowly slid into his undergarment like a worm wriggling through dirt. When her hand touched his flesh, she hesitated and muttered with unexpected curiosity, "Here t'is."

"And here's Jack." He whispered back in cold monotone.

His left hand reached down taking firm hold of the back of her hair, and yanked it with one forceful pull. The surprise allowed only the release of a stinted screech. His free hand plunged a razor's pointed edge into the back of her skull just above her spinal cord.

Her large eyes stared outward seeing nothing. Her lips moved in the soliloquy of a prayer's silent words said far too late. He let go of her head and one of the cloth flowers came off in his hand, as he watched the body tumble over like a ragdoll. It twitched on the ground for a moment. Then it remained still. Blood pooled down the back of her neck. He redressed the buttons on his pants. Stepping over the body he carefully squatted down avoiding the pooling blood and took hold of the dead woman's hair.

"You did this to me," Jack said sanctimoniously. He stared into the shocked and glazed-over, clouding eyes. The razor slid out and the cheek was sliced open from eye socket to the jaw. "You filthy whore." He slashed again. "You did this to me!" Each allegation accompanied another razor's cut, precise and penetrating. His hand flew as if waving a baton to a symphony only he heard. The dark music played as the razor slashed until both flesh and song were well exhausted.

With a serpent's grace he stood in a single movement and looked down at his handiwork. A tight, satisfied grin took control of his lips. His hands were still warm with her blood and he shook them off before retrieving his overcoat from the picket fence. He fixed the coat's belt around him; covering what few stains appeared on the front of his pants. He picked up the faux flower from her hair, studying it closely before putting it away into the pocket of his coat. Closing the razor he let it fall into the bottom-lining of his pocket, his hand following, fondling both of the sacred objects.

"You brought that on yourself," he muttered stepping over the mutilated corpse, never once looking down.

Jack stopped at the alley's edge letting a portly rat scamper past. Ignoring the familiar stench that lingered in Whitechapel, he filled his lungs with the crisp night air. The sounds of the tavern were less as the hour grew later, but activity still prevailed a short distance behind him. Having spent many years of his childhood here, he was quite familiar with the alleyways. For a brief moment he toyed with the idea of returning to the seedy hall, of maybe strolling the well-known streets and dispatching another. Common sense argued against it, and listening to his intuition he turned away from the lower-class taverns and slum tenements and started for home. The index finger on his left hand stroked the flower's twisted cloth stem in his pocket.

His feet automatically guided him as his mind wandered. He thought of the doctor, the briefest glimpse of the pale flesh, and wondered what it would be like to touch it. To feel the curves of his buttocks and let his fingers explore. Jack's mind teased him with replaying the scene except the doctor wasn't with that filthy creature; the doctor was with him. His heart pumped faster at the thought of touching those lips, and his blood raced throughout his body raising the temperature. This fantasy always followed the dark symphony, and he became just as lost within it.

Jack stopped walking. Enjoying the pulsing in his body, he thought about turning around and revisiting the tavern with his revived inspiration. When he realized what street he stumbled onto the feeling quickly faded. In his subconscious revelry he wasn't aware his feet led him here. Cold bitter reality washed over him, and he felt an angry shiver run through his veins.

He was too close to that house. That dilapidated hellhole his mother raised him in. Long after she fell into a stupor he could still smell the sickeningly sweet and lingering scent of opium smoke, detesting it to this day. He remembered searching the dirty floors for anything to eat and finding nothing. He could still hear the screaming when she woke and the way she struck at him while lost in hallucinating delusions.

"I'll cut it off!" Yelling. Screaming. His. Hers. His mother's high-pitched voice rang out violently, shrill and frightening to a child of five. Her breath stank of smoke and liquor. "You want to cry like a girl! I'll make you a girl!" Her face twisted in rage. One eye freshly blackened from a client that refused to pay and both eyes burning with animated madness. She grabbed him hard, throwing him to the floor. He tried to scream, but her hand held his throat tightly. He was choking, pinned to the dirt floor. She grabbed a knife and slashed. Screams filled the air. Pain ravaged through him, stealing his breath until he blacked out.

He woke only for a few moments at hospital. His terrified screams filled the room until a doctor placed a small cloth of ether over his mouth, allowing a dark and dreamless sleep. Helping him. Saving him. Much later—days later—from deep in a fog he could hear them talking, congratulating one another. "He's still a man. It won't ever get much bigger and he won't have children, but he's still a man!"

It continued at the orphanage. The endless teasing when he had to sit to urinate. "He's a girly boy!"

They were wrong. Half a man was what he'd become. The other half changed to some other thing. Something different. A desire awakened within him that he couldn't understand. Women failed to create lust. Instead they bred a rage, boiling deep within and burning until a void formed where his conscious ought to have been. It was the male form that enticed him, seduced him, and brought him desire. But something else was begotten there, deep inside. And that something developed a taste for more than just men—something far beyond—something darker.

Jack dismissed the memories and corrected his way home. He kept his head lowered. He was angry that such thoughts had resurfaced, and that he was too weak to keep them from his mind.

"This is the last," his mind told him. "This is the last time."

"The others were to be the last," he whispered back.

"This is the last time," his mind repeated like a lullaby. "The last."

His shoulders slowly crept toward his ears and he held his arms tightly to his sides. The index finger on his left hand stroked the flower's stem inside his pocket. It gave him comfort to feel it, that and the cold metal and weight of the closed razor in his pocket.

Making his way through the tree-lined streets of Hyde Park, Jack strolled easily passed the well-manicured buildings on either side of the clean road. Stopping in front of the brick office building and residence of Dr. Edward Toddington, he tried the knob before reaching for his keys. He was pleased to find the lock had not been set. He slipped his shoes off and crept in on padded feet trying to be as unobtrusive as possible, hoping to get upstairs, get washed and into bed without being noticed.

Pausing on the second step he looked past the empty chair in the hall and noticed the door to the back office was slightly ajar. Dim light and soft conversation filtered out of the room. A woman's low and frenzied voice followed by the doctor's reassuring, recognizable tone. Jack strained his ears and held his breath trying to make out any of the hushed words. Unexpectedly, the door was pulled open flooding the hallway with light.

"Jack, my boy," the doctor said. "I didn't hear you come in."

A woman led the way toddling as she went with the doctor close behind. She was dressed in an evening cloak that was many years older than she appeared to be. Her face was long and plain with a natural grace and a light coating of freckles across her clear complexion. Drying tears streaked her cheeks. Her light brown hair was parted in the center and pulled back by a dark green ribbon. Her hands were covered in threadbare gloves, leaving her fingers exposed. She held her fists laced together, tightly clasped below her bosom.

"Jack, this is Miss Mary Kelly," the doctor said. He was still dressed in the same clothes from earlier that evening minus his coat. "Miss Kelly, this is my ward Jack."

"Please to meet you, sir," she said with quick politeness, barely taking notice of him. Immediately dismissing him she turned back to the doctor. "Sir," she responded with quiet desperation. "I can't thank you enough. You don't know what this means to me."

"Don't worry, my dear," the doctor said compassionately. "I'll look after you." He reached into his pocket and took out a few coins. "Here's something for you in the meantime. Get a few good meals. Make your arrangements, and I will see you in a week."

"God bless you, sir!" She said latching onto his hand and pressing it against her dusty cheek.

The doctor allowed her a moment before retrieving his hand. Taking her by the elbow he led her to the front door.

Jack heard the door open and close from behind him without further conversation. A moment later the doctor shuffled past staring at the floorboards, his hands clasped behind his back.

"Jack, a word please?" He said before disappearing into the office.

Jack hesitantly retraced the few steps down. He entered the doctor's office to find him sitting on the edge of his desk. His arms hung loosely between his legs, but his hands were clasped tight. Jack slipped in and sat in the patient's chair opposite the desk and waited.

"Enjoy yourself at the Music Hall?" the doctor stabbed at small talk. He accepted the nod as an answer. "Jack, I've decided that it's time you take more responsibility with helping me in my medical procedures."

"Sir," Jack said with surprise. "I don't know what to say."

"Say nothing, my boy. You've earned it." The doctor stood up and meandered about the office. "I took you in when you were ten, and you've proven to be an apt pupil. Your mind is quick and sharp, and you have a great sense for keenly observing everything. Especially my work. You've become quite skilled for a boy of sixteen years." He paused to face Jack directly.

The doctor's silver hair was kept short and away from his face. His brow and moustache still held some of their original darker color, but in his beard and sideburns it appeared more random. Bushy eyebrows showed above dark rimmed glasses, framing his sharp blue eyes. He was a handsome man with an easy smile showing full rows of strong teeth.

Jack became lost in the compassionate eyes as the doctor spoke. He studied every hair of the well-groomed moustache and goatee that hovered around the soft full lips, as if becoming hypnotized by their subtle masculine movements. His mind resumed with the thoughts of what it would be like to touch those lips, to feel them on his own. He imagined whispering the doctor's name, soft and passionate.

"I've decided to hire Miss Kelly as our housekeeper." The doctor finished speaking and was waiting for him to say something.

Jack blinked away from his fantasy and quickly replayed the last sentence. "Sir," he said as irritation ignited within him. "You don't mean Miss Kelly that just left, do you?"

"Yes," the doctor stoically replied. The blue eyes turned hawkish. "I do."

"But, sir," Jack answered quickly. "Is she the kind of woman you want keeping your house?"

"And what kind is that?" The doctor fired back. He crossed his arms tightly across his chest. "Miss Kelly is a polite, kind woman and a quick study. Any matters of class or station she will pick up in time."

"She's a harlot." The words fell heavy, silencing all else.

"She is that," the doctor said unapologetically. "But she won't be if I hire her to keep my house."

"She's a common whore," Jack announced, trying to keep his repulsion from rising and coming out.

"I know what she is. I have known her for some time." He calmed himself with a deep breath and began again. "She is a woman trapped by what life has given her, and ever so eager to learn how to improve herself."

"Why bring such filth into this house?" Jack stood up thrusting his hands into his pockets. His fingers clutched tightly around the closed razor.

Something shifted in the doctor's face. The stern eyes softened and his features relaxed as if melting. His tongue wet his lips and he swallowed before softly speaking.

"Miss Kelly is afraid." The doctor spoke quietly. "And we are in a position to help."

"She is filth."

"She's a person."

"She's a whore!"

The words thundered in the room. The older man closed his eyes taking a deep breath and slowly exhaling.

"I'm sorry," the doctor said.

"Why?" The one word rejected the apology and demanded an explanation.

"Jack," the doctor stared at him incredulously. "You must know what is going on in Whitechapel. There are horrible things happening to women there. Women like her."

The boy's stoic expression revealed nothing. "Horrible things happen everywhere. That is a matter for the police to deal with, not you."

"She is with child." The doctor blurted out. He took in a sharp breath and pushed on. "I'd feel responsible if anything happened to her."

Jack opened his mouth to say something when comprehension hit. He closed his mouth with a deep breath letting the harsh understanding coldly wash over him. The motors of his mind churned, and for a brief moment he wondered if the doctor knew he had been followed all along. The idea was banished, and Jack sank back into the patient's chair, settling down before speaking.

"And that is more important to you than I am?" Jack responded. "You would bring this filth into your house? Trust her with a child?"

"She is not your mother, Jack!" The doctor pleaded. "Your mother was a sick woman, an addict with many other problems. What happened to you does not happen to most. Miss Kelly needs our help. She needs my help. And I am going to do my best to give it to her." He let out a heavy sigh signaling the finality of his decision. "Please, Jack, try to let go of your past and give Miss Kelly a fair turn."

Dr. Edward Toddington stood directly in front of his ward. He placed his fatherly hands on the boy's shoulders looking down, trying to find a way to share his compassion.

"Please, son," he said using the rare sentimental title. "Give her a chance." He offered his best attempt at a reassuring smile, stopping when he saw the stare of the cold brown eyes in return. Resigning, he patted the boy's shoulders and left the room. "We'll discuss this further in the morning. And, Jack," he paused on the other side of the doorframe. "Close out the light when you go to bed."

Jack sat in the chair as immobile as a statue. The moment the doctor's hands touched his shoulders the electrical charge set his pulse to race. For a moment he was afraid the doctor would see his heart pounding within his chest. The last few spoken sentences blurred and softened until Jack only heard the dark melody in his mind.

Inside his jacket pocket his hand shifted. Holding the closed razor in his palm, his fingers gently wrapping around it as if touching a religious icon. His thumb tracing the edge, running over the metal lip as if it were a delicate string instrument. The song called to him and he quickly became lost, only barely aware the doctor was leaving the room.

Jack stood while the music continued playing. As if in a trance, he moved about the office collecting specific items as he went. He glided back to the front door and replaced his shoes on his feet. Turning the cold handle in his warm palm without a sound, he opened the door and stepped out into the night.

The air was still, stirring only as he briskly cut through the rolling fog. The night was dark but dawn was slowly approaching. The song sang loudly to him, and he needed to answer it before morning light revealed his intentions. He wasn't exactly sure of his destination; instinct directed his movements. Jack slowed his careful pace when the familiarity of Whitechapel returned. He prowled the less traveled streets searching for prey. The moon was getting lower and a discolored skyline whispered that time was running out when he saw a figure ahead of him.

As he grew closer he knew it was a woman. Quickening his pace he was delighted to see it was Mary Kelly. She paused at the end of the street turning left down the familiar alleyway. Jack trotted slowly to catch up and, turning the corner, saw what drew her in that direction. A crowd of people, drunkards and whores with their clientele, along with two police constables had gathered in the alley since he had left. The shrill whistle called out, signaling the location to all others in the area of the newly discovered murder scene. People began running in all directions, either drawn by morbid curiosity or repulsed by the details revealed.

Mary Kelly stopped at the alley's entranceway, hesitant to enter. Jack slowly approached stopping a few paces behind. A woman rushed toward them reaching out and taking Mary by the shoulders.

"It's Martha," the woman stuttered. "Someone's done killed Martha."

"The Ripper from the looks of it," said a gentleman stopping alongside her. "Sliced her bloody face apart. Cut 'er open from belly to chin, he did."

"How do they know 'tis Martha?" Mary asked in a voice croaking with fear.

"One of her flowers," the other woman answered. "She always wore them twisted flowers in her hair."

"Poor sod," said the man. Two constables ran passed them. The crowd behind was growing thicker. "We needs to get outta here."

Jack stepped back and turned away from the group. More police and more people were heading toward them. He slid over to the side of the alley's mouth and waited. The woman and man bustled by him first. He let them disappear without moving. His pulse raced with excitement, but his patience won out and he remained still until he saw Mary moving quickly away from the crowd without looking around her. She crossed the street and continued away from the bloody scene. Keeping pace behind her, he stealthily followed. When he was sure no one else was around, he quickened his step to catch up to her.

"Mary Kelly," Jack called out. He was careful to direct his voice at her and not let it echo down the street.

The woman paused upon hearing her name but quickly increased her step without looking around. He called out again. She looked over her shoulder ready to bolt away and paused as her mind searched for recognition.

"I know you," she began hesitantly slowing her pace. "Don't I?"

"Yes," Jack said. Purposely, he slowed his walking to show he wasn't a threat and put his hands up. "I'm sorry if I startled you. We met earlier tonight. My name is Jack, I'm Dr. Toddington's ward."

A smile crossed Mary's lips and her shoulders lowered with relief.

"Oh yes, sir." She said with a nervous laugh. "I'm sorry, sir, but a girl can't be too careful. Not with what's going on back there, she can't."

"That is precisely why I am here," Jack said as he closed the distance between them. "Dr. Toddington asked me to make sure you arrived home safely, but I'm afraid I've gotten myself a little lost in catching up to you."

"Sir," she said. "Thank you, sir, but I'm just about home now."

"Let me at least get you the rest of the way," Jack stopped when he stood next to her and extended his arm. "I'd be a fiend if I let anything happen to you."

Mary looked at his offering and a flattered girlish smile flashed across her lips. She threaded her arm through his and continued walking to her home, feeling safe that such a strong, tall, and imposing young man was escorting her.

Within a few moments they were climbing a set of broken stairs to the second level of a dirty building. Watchful of the stars fading in the sky, Jack smiled as he brought her to the very lip of her apartment door. The building seemed deserted; its tenants either passed out or too inebriated to notice anything outside their own hovel.

"Thank you, sir," Mary said. She stood outside her door facing the boy. He towered above her, a clear head in height over hers. "You're very kind to do this."

"No," Jack said through a clenched smile. "I'm not."

Jack clasped his hand over her face, enclosing her nose and mouth in his palm. His free hand flew behind her head, grabbing hold and keeping it still. Her struggle was limited and he used their combined weight to force the door open. He half pushed and half carried her into the room as the fight slowly left her. Kicking the door closed behind them, and letting her limp body slide unconscious to the floor.

Jack remained still, listening to the world outside. Nothing stirred, and no one made a sound. He turned his attention to the apartment. It was small with a bed in the corner. Several crates imposing as chairs surrounded a few more serving as a table. An empty bottle of wine was turned over on the trunk next to a chipped saucer overflowing with ashes and stubbed out cigarettes.

Jack picked up Mary Kelly and moved her to the bed. He removed her clothes until she was lying naked, then gently sat next to her. Cradling her head in his large hands he gave a quick twist, snapping her neck.

He studied his pretty corpse allowing a smile to emerge. Standing up he reached into his jacket pocket and withdrew several scalpels and a surgical knife.

"We have a situation to correct," he said with quiet contentment. The instruments began the tuning-up process inside his mind. A shrill cello chord screamed, and the dark orchestra began its concerto.

"This is the last time," his mind whispered. "This is your symphony."

❖

Jack crept into the Hyde Park residence as the retreating night surrendered to a red morning. A lamp dimly lit the hallway, and as he put his shoes down, he noticed his suitcase, stuffed and packed by the front door. The doctor, sitting in the hall's chair as stiff and erect as a statue, greeted him while staring straight ahead at the wall.

"You forgot to turn the light out in the office," the doctor said. His voice was low, controlled and monotonous. "When I came down I found my tools missing. I went to your room to ask why, and you weren't there. I found these."

The doctor turned at the neck to look at Jack. He held out his hands. Overflowing like a child's treasure was a broken cameo, two severed fingers, and a scrap of a blood-crusted scarf cradling a severed ear.

"I suspected when the killings started," the doctor continued calmly. "I didn't want to think about it, but I knew. I overlooked blood spots on your shoe or an unknown stain on your pant leg because I didn't want to know. How can I turn a blind eye to this? Why? Why would you do this?"

"You left me no choice," Jack said, not moving from the doorway.

"What choice!" The doctor's voice broke and he cried openly.

"You chose them." Jack replied without remorse. "You always put them first. I was here for you, and you chose them."

"You didn't have to kill them. To destroy them!" The doctor's voice filled the hallway as he leapt out of the chair. His hands flexed at his side and he took an audible breath trying to calm down. Gaining back control, he lowered his voice. "You're better than that."

"Better than what?" Jack said with cold monotony. "Better than the whore that mutilated me? Or better than the one you wanted to bring into this house? You already love her more than you can ever love me! You want me to just stand here watching it unfold before my eyes and do nothing?"

"Jack," the doctor walked over and put his hands on the boy's shoulders. "I love you like you are my own son."

"That's not enough!" He threw off the man's arms, pushing the doctor backwards. "You will never look at me like you look at that woman." He snarled through a tightly clenched jaw. "No child deserves a creature like that for a mother. Now that's not an issue."

"Oh Jack," the doctor stammered, his eyes widening in horror. "What have you done? Tell me you didn't." He covered his mouth with the back of his hand.

Jack said nothing, remaining rigid and motionless in the doorway.

"Poor Mary," he whispered. The doctor's eyes filled, his face twisting with pain and struggle. He wiped at his eyes, sniffled and caught his breath. "You can't stay here. You have to go."

Jack felt his chest tightening; the air was pushed from his lungs. For the first time since childhood he recognized his own fear.

"Go?" He said with the tiny voice of a child. "Go where?"

"There is money in your bag," the doctor said pointing to the suitcase. His words were sharp and clear. "Enough to get you anywhere you want, but you can't stay here. I won't have it. I can't live with you under this roof knowing what you've done. I won't turn you in but you can't stay here."

"And what am I to do without you?" Jack pleaded.

"Go." The doctor repeated as if not hearing Jack's question. He grabbed the little bag shoving it into Jack's chest. "Go to France or Italy, or take a boat to America. Go far away and never come back. The sight of you sickens me."

"Don't do this," Jack beseeched, his voice creeping up an octave. "I did what I did for you. So we could be together."

The words thundered and fell hard between them. The doctor stared into the cold brown eyes trying to find something of the boy he once knew. Only a vacuous non-entity looked back.

"You're a monster," the doctor hissed. His eyes burning angry blue flames. "Get out."

"I beg you," Jack pleaded. Desperation entered his voice.

The doctor pinned Jack's biceps against the door with a strength that surprised both of them. The suitcase fell from Jack's grasp to the floor. Their noses barely touched as the doctor seethed with loathing.

"You are never to return, do you hear me?" He searched the cold brown eyes for comprehension. "If I ever see you, or hear another woman is murdered, I will turn you over to Scotland Yard and gladly watch you hang."

Jack deeply wounded stared at the doctor. The words cut hard, and he felt each slash of rejection. He could feel the bile burning in his stomach. In his mind, the instruments tuned up for the dark symphony and began to play. He couldn't let that happen. Not here. Not now. Not with him.

Jack pulled himself free of the doctor's grip, but did nothing else. The blue eyes he had found comfort in were cold. He knew there was no returning. Reaching out, grabbing hold of the doctor's head, he pulled him close until their lips touched. His mouth forced the doctor's open; his tongue furiously searched and kissed him deeply. The doctor struggled in the tight grasp, then lessoned and slowly succumbed.

Jack pushed hard and the doctor sprawled backwards.

"I loved you, and you are no better than any of them!" He picked up his suitcase, spat on the floor, and left without another word.

The morning was on the verge of lighting up the sky as Jack wandered the streets of London. In the suitcase he found an envelope with £80. That could open many doors. His rage fueled him until he realized he was exhausted and hungry and in an unfamiliar part of London.

A factory whistle pierced the air in the distance as he looked around at the shops as they began to open. He noticed a dingy eatery and started in that direction. A rounded woman with tight, dirty-gold ringlets of hair emerged from the doorway with a broom in hand. She swept the garbage from the storefront, her ample breasts sweeping along with her. The gingham dress clung awkwardly to the zaftig figure revealing glimpses of black boots on her feet. She disappeared into the shop to exchange the worn broom for a wooden chair. Sitting down she reached into the pocket of her dirty apron and pulled out a tobacco pipe. Planting the edge in her mouth, she struck a match and lit the pipe.

"Good day, madam," Jack said approaching the woman. He set the suitcase down and offered a polite nod.

"Coo," she snorted smoke like a dragon. Eyeing him carefully from toe to crown. "You must be lost if you callin' me madam. Can I helps you find your way, deary?"

The bold wantonness of her appearance and the crass dialect in which she spoke immediately brought a smile to Jack's face.

"I'm new to this area," he said. "And I'm trying to get a business set up."

The woman let a healthy cone of smoke exit her lips. "Times is hard, but I gots a room to rent. Not much, but enough for a bed, a washing area, and a space for business depending on what you doin'."

Jack studied the stoutly woman. She leaned forward resting her elbow on her knee and held the pipe to her tightly clenched mouth. Smoke smacked out of her lips, commanding attention and waiting for him to speak. "Do you mind if I…"

"I don't minds a thing t'aint my business." She replied without halting either her scrutiny of him or her smoking. "I just needs to know what exactly is your business. Make sure it ain't nothin' too out of the ordinary. That and your name."

There was something deceivingly honest about her. The smoke from the pipe rose slowly hiding her briefly behind a translucent veil. She exhaled from the corner of her mouth and the vapor parted. Jack smiled at the woman's blatant directness and took an immediate liking to her.

"Todd is my name," he said trying out the sound of it.

"Todd wha'?" She asked quickly.

"I'm sorry, it's Mr. Todd," he answered with chuckle. "Mr. Sweeney Todd, and I plan to open a tonsorial parlor. I have much skill with a razor and scalpel."

Runner-up

LOVE THY NEIGHBOR
N.S. BERANEK

O ooh! Daddy! Can I have a orange one? Pleeeease?"
Ivy pointed to the bright, photo-realistic graphic on the cooler stationed at the mouth of the checkout line, where polar blue letters festooned with icicles announced: *Freezies—50 cents!*

Fifty cents was highway robbery, considering they were nothing but frozen colored sugar water in plastic tubes, twenty cents apiece if you bought them by the gross at the Family Dollar. But the greedy bastards who owned the hardware store had Tommy over a barrel. It was a sweltering day. What father was going to tell his kid she couldn't have a cool treat when it cost half a buck?

"Sure thing," he said. "But let's get it when we go. You don't want it to melt while you're carrying it around the store, do you?"

"No, Daddy," Ivy replied solemnly. For a moment he thought she was going to start pouting but she surprised him and grinned instead, revealing big gaps where several of her baby teeth used to be. The sight made Tommy even angrier at the store's owners. More sugar was bound to mean more cavities, and her baby teeth had been riddled with them. He didn't want the permanent ones to suffer the same fate. On top of that, several of her teeth leaned or overlapped or had too much space between them. The flaw was one she'd inherited from her mother, a fact Tommy never would have believed had he not seen pictures of Amanda as a pre-teen, already gorgeous except for a mouth like a decrepit picket fence.

It was too early to worry seriously about paying for braces, so Tommy pushed those thoughts away and returned to his quest for a much simpler thing, a replacement washer for the faucet of Ben's kitchen sink, which had gone from a drip to a dribble to the sudden need to pull out everything stored beneath the sink in order to shut off the water supply.

Rounding the corner into the plumbing aisle, Tommy caught sight of two other residents of their neighborhood milling about its far end. He'd seen the pair mowing lawns in the area, the job he'd once held. He felt sure they were brothers. They looked like brothers, though one was broad and bulky and the other long and lean. They also looked like boxers, and since he didn't know their names he'd nicknamed them using boxing terms. The older one became Brawler, the younger Bantam.

Ivy chose that moment to skip away from him, moving toward something that had caught her eye. Brawler shifted his gaze. Bantam turned. Tommy's reaction was visceral; he didn't want her anywhere near the two. "Ivy!" he called, employing his sternest-sounding Dad voice. "Come back here. Now."

He'd once heard a man on the television talking about coming to the realization that the kind of father he'd always thought he would be was actually a really cool uncle. Tommy hadn't been able to relate. He'd never had any expectations of fatherhood, so he sure as hell had never imagined being a divorced dad. Growing up he'd hardly envisioned his future at all, though he'd assumed he'd get married or be in some kind of a relationship with a woman. The Brawlers and the Bantams of the world made that necessary.

Ivy stomped back over and stood at his side. Now she was pouting. Tommy was about to make some excuse to whisk her out of the aisle when the brothers started in their direction.

Brawler kept his gaze locked on Tommy's. He nodded as he passed them, a gesture which seemed friendly, only his eyes were cold. Bantam's focus was on Ivy. He held up a paper bag so small it would have been perfect for one of the baby dolls she'd outgrown before she even got to school. Though he had maybe twenty years on her eight, the smile he flashed was even more gap-toothed than hers. "We thone gosss whasss we come for, how 'bout you?" he asked, air whistling through the open spaces. He shook the bag and its contents jangled. Then he laughed and hurried after his brother.

After they were gone, Tommy pretended to search the clear boxes hung from pegs for the specific washer he needed but actually kept an eye on the brothers, watching as they moved through the checkout area. Only when they were safely out the door did he grab the correct package and steer Ivy toward the front of the store.

❖

Several Sundays later, preoccupied with thoughts of a failed trip to the grocery store, Tommy was inadvertently taking his aggressions out on Ben's lawn. After each pass he spun the mower around wildly, rocking it onto two wheels and sending bits of grass flying into the air. He failed to notice his carelessness even when he ran the blade housing right up against the field stones encircling the rosebushes and the old oak—an action which scored its bright red paint. He was so lost in thought that he almost didn't hear a voice call out behind him.

"Mornin', Thomas."

Not even his mother called him Thomas. As he knew he would, when Tommy turned he found Estill Johnson's hunter green pickup rolled to a stop in front of the house. Freshly waxed, the truck sparkled in the sun. Curling ribbons of pale blue paint trailed horizontally across the door, bearing a message in blocky white letters. Though Estill's deeply tanned, hairy arm hung out of the driver's window and obscured a section of the message, Tommy knew what it said: *Read the Word! Jesus is Lord!*

The interior of the cab was too dark to see his face clearly, but Tommy pictured the man's deep frown lines and scraggly salt and pepper beard. "Morning, Estill," he called back, following it with the down-and-only-halfway-back-up type of nod he figured the Marlboro Man would use, were he not a fictional character created by the advertising world.

Like many of the neighborhood's (and the city's, and the nation's) residents Estill was on his way home from church. It was the reason why Tommy and Ben's grocery store run half an

hour earlier had been a bust—beer sales weren't allowed until
1:00 p.m. on Sundays. The theory went that restricting access
to alcohol would force people to sober up, at which point they
would see the light and go seeking the Word of God. No matter
how sober they were Tommy and Ben didn't attend services. They
were heathens, an atheist and a secular Jew, respectively. Estill,
by contrast, fancied himself a latter-day preacher and fisher of lost
men. After Amanda had thrown Tommy out and then dragged him
into court for child support and alimony, requiring him to miss so
much work that he lost the best job of his life (which halted his
support payments, a turn of events he liked to think of as instant
karma, in spite of his disbelief in the divine), Estill had kept him
from starvation by hiring him at his roofing business. It was under-
the-table, cash only work. He was fairly sure most of the other
workers were undocumented aliens, a fact that had surprised him
until the day Estill broke into a rant about the inferiority of man's
laws to God's.

Estill always came up on the roof with them, but never to
work. Instead, he preached at them all day long against the
background track of hammering nails. The other workers rolled
their eyes when his back was turned, and Tommy frequently heard
them mutter pendejo and snicker. He envied their ability to quit
Estill's sphere at the end of the day. He'd gathered that they all had
wives and some also children waiting at home. He'd also figured
out that on most days they re-convened at a nearby bar to throw
back a few pints before heading off to their families, something
Estill would no doubt frown on, but at quitting time his focus was
always on Tommy. Estill paid him last and kept him long after
the others were gone, bending his ear with customized sermons
about a godly wife's need to submit to the will of her husband,
a righteous husband's place as the master of his household, and
loads of other Dark Ages trash. Tommy never had worked out
whether the man truly meant for him to march back into the house
he'd once rented with Amanda, toss out the would-be guitarist
with the unlikely name of Walter who was currently sharing her
bed, and declare her to be his property in the eyes of God, or if he
just wanted to make him feel so worthless that he'd go running to

Jesus seeking salvation. Regardless, after he stopped foaming at the mouth Estill always slipped him a few extra bills, so Tommy endured the tirades.

Estill had offered to pay him to attend church services, too, but that was where Tommy drew the line. Instead he earned additional sawbucks on Sunday mornings by mowing the zealot's lawn, trimming his bushes, and weed-whacking his fence line, work now handled by Brawler and Bantam.

Tommy was thankful for the money he'd earned working for Estill but it had hardly constituted a living, so he'd worked hard to build a real clientele for his mowing and trimming services. Before long he was responsible for caring for thirty yards in a fifteen block span, including—starting four summers ago—Ben's yard.

He was homeless by that point, a situation he thought of as a temporary setback. He'd slept on his cousin's couch until the cousin was evicted, then gone to a friend's only to find that the guy had a new girlfriend and his living room had begun doubling as a bedroom for her two daughters. Even the shittiest rooming houses, which let closet-sized spaces for seventy dollars a week, were only available with proof of a steady job, and Tommy's off-the-books yard mowing business didn't count. But even if it had, the season was winding down. As a last resort he'd even looked into the city's shelters. For able-bodied males, though, there was no room at the inn.

Ben might as well have dropped into the neighborhood from Mars, being never so much as late on a payment in his life, but he somehow seemed to get that Tommy's housing predicament was the result of his having exhausted all of his options, and when cooler weather arrived Ben declared that Tommy should move in. "Stop pretending you don't know what I'm talking about," he said when Tommy denied he'd been sleeping on a bench in the park. "I followed you last week. I saw you. It's dangerous and I'm pretty sure illegal, too. You're going to stay here."

A few weeks after winning that argument Ben had started a different one, right before producing an application for employment at the factory where he'd been the bookkeeper for a decade. "The lawn mowing and roofing season is over, and we're in desperate need of guys out on the floor," he explained. "It's pretty mindless work and not much pay, when really you should be on our maintenance staff, but you'd be doing me a huge favor. What do you say?"

The hourly rate turned out to be not nearly as low as Tommy anticipated and benefits were offered after three months. It was how he'd ended up with the new best job of his life, how he'd resumed paying alimony and child support and even begun making back payments. There wasn't much left over each week; still, he began saving up for a secondhand Moped, something to eventually trade in toward a reliable car. He viewed having a car as key because it would double as a safe place to sleep once Ben inevitably woke up from the spell he was under and told him to hit the road.

He never had bought the Moped, but he'd saved the cash. Looking at the truck idling in front of Ben's house, Tommy wondered if it might finally be time to go shopping.

Since he moved in with Ben he'd hardly crossed paths with the preacher, but those few times were too many as far as he was concerned. Each time Estill had found something about Ben to criticize or question. "I heard that pond he has back there is fulla Japanese fish," he said once, punctuating his words with a sneer. Another time it was, "Tell your friend Halloween is Satan's holiday and he oughtn'ta celebrate it."

Tommy wasn't in the mood for another of his admonishments. "There somethin' I can do for you, Estill?" he asked, letting his irritation seep into his tone.

The man lobbed nicotine-darkened spittle onto the street's asphalt surface and narrowed his eyes. "You never said the fella owns this house's a Jew."

The hair on the back of Tommy's neck stood on end but he did his best to keep his cool. "He's not religious," he said. "Like me." Immediately, he regretted his words. He had to stop himself from cringing.

"That so?" Estill asked. "'Cause I heard some other things about him, too."

Tommy's right leg began to shake. Much as he wanted to do the opposite, he moved forward, to close the gap between them. He wasn't about to stand in the street shouting back and forth about

Ben's predilections, or his own. "People need to mind their own Go—" He caught himself just in time. "Damned business."

"They say he ain't never been married."

"So? Women are hard to live with." Tommy shrugged for added effect. "That's why I'm divorced." He steeled himself and added, "Just like you."

He'd pieced together that Estill's wife had left six months into their marriage, unable to abide his homegrown, deeply religious ways. It tickled Tommy to no end that her name was Faith and Estill had lost her. The jury was still out on whether the two had ever consummated their union; if they had, the effort had not produced offspring.

If Estill was of a mind to ask if Ben had fathered children, having his own life held up for comparison put a stop to that. "Divorced's one thing," he said. He leaned sideways and let fly another gob of yellow brown phlegm. "It ain't natural for a man to never even try to find a woman."

Tommy forced a laugh, but the tips of his ears felt hot. He wondered if they were as bright red as they felt. "How do you know he's never tried?"

"I don't," Estill said. "But I reckon you do. You're the one what lives with him."

Tommy's leg shook harder. He needed to put an end to this most dangerous of witch hunts. "This isn't middle school, Estill," he shot back. "If you want to know if he's interested in you, you're just gonna have to ask him your damned self."

As he'd hoped, the other man recoiled. Estill sputtered denials, then threw his truck into gear and sped off.

Tommy was still mulling over the exchange as he finished cleaning and putting up the mower. He wiped his hands on a red cotton shop rag as he rounded the front corner of the house and reviewed his plan to hoof it to the corner store two streets away for a case of Corona, no limes. They'd bought those earlier at the regular grocery. For some reason the tiny neighborhood store didn't sell them, though they made room for cheese puffs and beef jerky, cigarettes and cherry-flavored cigarillos, money orders, lottery tickets, and a range of beers including Corona.

Tommy and Ben had already snagged several items before they approached the refrigerated case and discovered that the beer was still imprisoned behind roll-down bars. Still, when he saw the limes on the conveyor belt with the lunch meat, loaf of bread, and carton of eggs, the pimply-faced cashier shot them a look Tommy swore meant *Dudes! Epic fail.*

Ben had surprised them both by deadpanning, "We wouldn't have this problem if this were in New Orleans," before sliding his card back into its slot in his wallet.

And Tommy had surprised himself as they neared the front doors. "We could just go," he blurted.

"Where?"

"New Orleans."

Ben flashed a rueful smile. "That would be fun, but—"

"Not just to visit," Tommy explained. "We could move." He watched Ben's brow crease.

"That wouldn't be prudent."

"Fuck prudence."

A mother entering the store with two pre-teens in tow scowled at him, but Tommy didn't care. Like them, she was going to Hell for grocery shopping when she ought to have been in church. He followed Ben to his pumpkin-colored hatchback and set the grocery bags in the trunk. "I'm serious," he said. "Let's move to New Orleans. Why not?"

"Because you have Ivy and I have enough anxiety already trying to decide whether to stay in the job I'm in or take a chance with this other outfit."

The owners of a new manufacturing venture had approached Ben out of the blue and offered him a substantial pay increase to come work for them. They seemed like good guys, he said, but they were just starting out. What if, ultimately, their business tanked? Sure, the place where he and Tommy worked had its problems—outdated software and machinery, workers who didn't seem to care if they got fired and so couldn't be counted on even to perform the simplest tasks (if they showed up at all), and more and more business lost to China every day—but they'd been dealing with those issues for decades and hadn't gone under, so there was no reason to think they would fold any time soon. Ben wondered aloud how he could walk away from a sure thing.

That was a reservation Tommy didn't understand. He always found himself asking exactly the opposite question: How can I stay here, when there's a possibility that something somewhere else might be even better? The decision to take each new opportunity that arose had already resulted in a wild ride. He'd enlisted in the army right after 9/11 and done two tours in Afghanistan as a tank mechanic. Upon his discharge he'd spent a year working in his crazy Uncle Earl's body shop, during which time he'd nearly been blinded by caustic chemicals twice and had a gun pulled on him four times. Then he'd enrolled in night school and learned the bartender's trade, and his first job in that field had resulted in his meeting Amanda, which led to his becoming a husband and father. To be a better provider for his family he'd left bartending and taken a job on the line in a factory, stamping parts out of metal. They'd rented the tiny, two bedroom bungalow half a dozen streets from Ben's four bedroom yellow clapboard Cape Cod. Five months after moving into the house Amanda's manager pissed her off and she'd quit the cashier's job she'd held for three years, and then barely looked for another job, acting like they were the Cleavers or something instead of what they were: a pair of high school grads with blue collar jobs in 2009. Too late, Tommy realized she was popping pills with the couple renting the house next door. Soon after that she'd thrown him out, gotten a lawyer, and hauled him into court. By the time her antics cost him his job the economy had well and fully tanked. He might have sooner flown under his own power as landed another decent job.

"Thomas."

Tommy looked up and winced. The green pickup was stopped in the street in front of the house again. He'd had enough of Estill's crap for one day, but the thought that the nut job might've come back seeking revenge for his earlier wisecrack, that he might have a shotgun and be looking to hurt Ben gave him the motivation to walk over.

"What do you want now, Estill?"

"Lost my house keys."

In spite of everything, Tommy felt a pang of sympathy. He didn't want to go help the man, but he said, "Whad'ya need? Tools?"

"Nope. Got a second set at my sister's. Just retracin' my steps. Thought I might find 'em."

"You never got out of the vehicle here, and it's not like there are rust holes in the floorboards of that parade float you call a truck that they could've fallen through. If they turn up, I'll bring 'em by."

"'preciate it," Estill said. The truck pulled away.

Ben was sitting at the kitchen table working the crossword puzzle from the day's paper when Tommy entered with the case of Corona.

"Who was that you were you talking to a little while ago?" he asked calmly.

Tommy smiled. Ben wasn't the jealous type, so the revelation that seeing his boyfriend chatting with another man did actually get his hackles up felt good. Tommy set the beer box on the counter and ripped the top open. "That was Estill," he said.

"Estill the preacher?"

Tommy laughed. "How many Estills you think there are, even around here?"

The lemon yellow house with the rosebushes ringed with stones seemed out of place in the neighborhood, and the man who answered the door when Tommy knocked was even more so. He'd introduced himself as Ben Jacobs, and he'd been dressed in a lilac button front shirt and charcoal slacks even though it was a Saturday afternoon. Tommy had never seen the home's lawn in need of so much as a trim before, but it definitely needed to be cut that morning. Ben hadn't questioned the price Tommy quoted him. He readily forked over twenty bucks to have the property mowed and edged with a string trimmer and its hedges clipped, and when the job was done he handed over not only the cash, but a bottle of water, too. Tommy was used to getting drinks from garden hoses.

That gesture, along with the man's choice of dress, shy smile, and the glimpse Tommy got of the interior of his house—furniture that looked as if it had time-travelled from a Sears catalog circa 1940 along with funkier, modern touches, like a clock that appeared to be melting down the wall a la a painting by Salvador Dali—made a lasting impression. All of the following week Tommy found his thoughts returning to Ben.

He figured the job was a fluke, a one-time thing, that Ben had had a heavier-than-normal workload or family drama to deal with, something that had taken precedence over cutting the lawn. Still, the next Saturday he went back and knocked on the door. To his surprise Ben not only agreed to let him do the yard work again, but inquired after what other services Tommy had to offer, and they added cleaning the leaves from the gutters to the to-do list. The weekend after that he'd asked Tommy to tack wire mesh over a hole along the eaves where squirrels had started getting in, and so on and so on. Right after the weather turned and it looked like mowing season was over, Ben announced he had projects indoors that needed tending.

Though he'd been careful to confirm he was throwing the correct breaker, the entire time he was replacing the light switch over the kitchen backsplash Tommy felt as if he was about to get shocked. The air seemed to crackle and spark, especially during those times he realized Ben was behind him intently watching him work. After making an adjustment to a wonky ceiling fan, he'd climbed down from the chair he was on, turned around, and found himself face-to-face with the other man, who'd leaned forward and kissed him.

"You're either the bravest or the stupidest person I've ever met," Tommy told him hours later as they lay tangled in each other's limbs in bed. "What if I wasn't into guys? I might've killed you."

Ben hugged him tighter. "Nah. You felt it, too. I could tell," he said.

"How?"

"I don't know. I just did."

Tommy pulled two bottles from the case, grabbed the opener hanging on the side of the fridge, and popped their tops.

"The limes are in the crisper," Ben offered. He looked down at the crossword, then back up quickly. "Oh! There's been a rash of thefts around here apparently." He slid a folded section of the newspaper across the table.

"Thefts?" Tommy mimicked, smirking. He stuck a wedge of lime into the neck of a bottle, handed it to Ben, and picked up the paper. The article explained that items had mysteriously been going missing from homes, sheds, and garages in the area with no sign of forced entry. "Weird." He took a sip of beer and felt his stomach growl. "Hey, where's the authentic Mexican cantina fare I was promised? I'm starving."

Ben pushed back his chair. "Si, Senor. Coming right up."

❖

"Eleanor says you can't have a picture of Harry Styles in a princess-themed room," Ivy said as she and Tommy walked back to Amanda's. They'd spent the afternoon at the little neighborhood park beside the freeway, where they'd enjoyed complimentary carnival rides and skill games and even hot dogs and ice cream as part of the city's Neighbors United! campaign. "She says you can only have a picture of a prince, like William or Harry. But I don't like them. They're old."

"You can put up pictures of whoever you want."

"That's what Hayden says. She says I can have a picture of anyone because it's my room. Only she's a Belieber, so I don't really listen to her."

Tommy was only halfway paying attention. His thoughts were still on events at the park. There'd been a big police presence at the thing. They'd let the kids get behind the wheel of a cruiser, given them police shield temporary tattoos, and lectured on the benefits of canine units.

Unsurprisingly, Ivy had been most fascinated with the dogs. She'd refused to move on from them for so long that it became awkward. Tommy tried making small talk with the human officer, but she only narrowed her eyes at him. Tommy told himself that the cops were on edge because an event catering to kids was bound to draw out the area's baby rapists. As soon as he could, he moved his daughter along.

They were almost to Amanda's street when Ivy announced, "Walter said liking Justin Bieber is gay." Tommy's blood began to boil. He was already angry with his ex-wife for letting the guy continue to stay with them after what had happened two weekends before.

Ivy's bedroom had just gotten the princess makeover she'd been obsessively talking about for weeks. She'd proudly explained that everything in it, from the bedspread to the trash can to the draperies, now had a princess motif. Even the light switch plate was adorned with a pink glitter castle and unicorns. Naturally, she wanted her father to see it.

It was the first time in months that he'd been in the house. Right off, he noticed the acrid smell. Next, he saw that every flat surface in the living room was dotted with crude little charred tinfoil bowls. Then there were the signs of violence—a crack in the coffee table's glass top and an indentation the size of a fist in the drywall beside the television. He pictured screaming fights between the two adults, things being thrown, and his daughter terrified, cowering in her room.

All during the room reveal and Ivy's excited recounting of her big shopping trip—the fear she'd had all the way to the store that the princess-patterned sets would be sold out and she'd be forced to settle for a cupcake-theme instead—Tommy had tried to decide how to handle the Walter situation. The minute his daughter was back on the porch he closed the screen door behind her, flipped the snib, then gathered up as many of the foil pieces as he could find and stormed into the kitchen. He found his ex-wife waiting for him, leaning against the far wall with one arm folded across her chest and the other holding a cigarette to her lips.

"Jesus, Amanda," he hissed through gritted teeth, conscious that their daughter was just one room and a screen door away. "A meth head? Seriously? Get him out of the house!"

She stared back, emotionless, then shrugged and said "It's not your house anymore."

"Damn you, she's still my kid!" Tommy squeezed the foil pieces into a ball and whipped it at the floor. "I don't want him or his drugs near her! You got that?"

"You shouldn't listen to Walter," Tommy said. Up ahead, a police car turned onto the street and rolled slowly toward them. "I know he's an adult, but some adults make bad choices, and you can't listen to them."

Ivy nodded. "I know, Daddy. Mrs. McPherson said gay doesn't mean stupid and you shouldn't use it that way. She also said that the stuff that's happening in Russia happened in Germany a long, long time ago." She looked up at him. "Is that true?"

He'd seen headlines about the reports coming out of Russia. Apparently, gay people there were being brutally attacked, even killed. As for the Holocaust, he barely remembered what he'd read about it in school, only that it was horrible. He felt he didn't know enough about either subject to comment, and made a mental note to research both topics that night, if Ben wasn't using the computer.

Before he could reply the police car swung into an open space along the curb and the driver's door opened. The officer climbed from the car and strode briskly in their direction. "Sir," he called. "Do you have some I.D.?"

It seemed wrong, but Tommy figured it was for the safety of the area's kids. He pulled out his wallet and handed over his license. "She's my daughter."

"Where were you an hour ago?"

What had happened an hour ago? Had a child been abducted? Was there an Amber alert? Was Ivy in danger?

Or—he did a quick re-assessment—did this have something to do with the recent robberies in the area? Did the police think he matched a description of the person responsible? Was that why the officer in the park had acted so cold toward him?

"We were at the neighborhood thing at the park."

"I met three police dogs," Ivy volunteered. "Cagney, Atlas, and Lacey."

The officer ignored her. He looked at the license, then back up at Tommy. "Empty your pockets."

Tommy blinked. "Excuse me?"

"We can take a ride to the station and do it there, if you'd prefer."

There wasn't much to show: four singles he hadn't needed because the food and games at the park really had been free; a hot pink hair elastic Ivy asked him to hold for her because her dress didn't have pockets; his keys to Ben's house and car, on a ring with a flat plastic cowboy boot; two dimes, a nickel, four pennies, and his billfold.

The officer took the wallet and rifled through it. He pulled out old receipts and examined them. "What did you buy at the hardware store?"

The non sequitur threw him. Tommy had to reach back in his memory. The last trip he'd made to the hardware store was at least a month in the past. "I, uh, oh Jeez, I don't know."

"Washers?" The cop offered.

"Oh, right, the day the faucet decided not to turn off."

"You live right around the corner from here?"

He hadn't lived with Amanda for five years. He'd meant to change his license, of course, but at first he'd been all but homeless, living on various couches, and then actually homeless, staying in the park, and then he'd moved in with Ben, and hadn't been sure how long that would last. Hell, he still caught himself wondering if Ben was about to come to his senses and tell him to leave. Most of all, though, the reason he hadn't changed his license was that it was hard to get to the DMV when you worked factory hours.

He weighed which answer to give the cop. He didn't want to get Ben involved in anything, but if he said he still lived with Amanda, would Ivy correct him? As if on cue she tightened her grip on his left hand.

Worse than explaining it to the officer, if he lied, how would he explain it to her?

His stomach clenched. There was also the possibility that the cops weren't looking for child molesters or robbers at all, that really they were wise to Walter's little habit. He didn't want to be associated with that.

"No, not anymore. Her mother and I are divorced."

"When did that happen?"

Crap. "Uh, f-four years ago. But I moved out a while before that."

"And you still haven't changed your license?"

"I'm sorry. I can never get out there because I work."

"Where's home now?"

"I'm staying with a...friend...a few streets over."

The officer handed back the license and wallet, though Tommy's hands were still filled with odds and ends. "Get this corrected," he said. "And tell your 'friend' to keep her doors and windows locked, and her car, too. There've been several robberies in the area."

As he shoved the wallet back into his pocket a light bulb went on in Tommy's brain, the memory of Bantam holding up the tiny brown paper bag. They lift people's keys, have duplicates made, and toss the original set back where it's sure to be found. They wait long enough for the whole thing to be forgotten, then come back and rob the place. No one thinks twice when they see them outside the house because they're the regular lawn guys.

The cop's gaze flicked to Ivy and back. "We've gotten called to that house a couple of times," he said. "You oughta ask your ex-wife a few questions about what goes on there."

❖

"I can't believe this," Ben said for the hundredth time since learning about the encounter with the police.

Tommy and Ivy had made a pact not to tell him, but earlier that evening when they were all outside playing catch, a woman had happened along walking a German Shepherd. In her frenzy to tell the lady everything she'd learned about canine units at the park three weekends prior, Ivy let it slip that they'd been stopped by an officer on their way home.

"I can't believe this," Ben said again. He was more agitated than Tommy had ever seen him, pacing back and forth. "I can't believe you didn't tell me."

Tommy's stomach twisted into knots. Would this be the thing that finally soured Ben on their relationship? "They were working a case," he said. He'd called in his suspicion about the brothers to the crime stopper tip line and also warned Estill. Neither of them had seen Brawler or Bantam since; Tommy assumed they'd been arrested.

"He frisked you!"

"No, frisking is where they pat you down, looking for—"

"Drugs," Ben said along with him. "They think because Amanda and that Walter character do drugs you do, too."

"They were looking for the burglars," Tommy corrected. There was a tremble in his voice that he was powerless to stop. Ben's pacing had brought back painful memories, things he'd tried hard not to think of since he was eleven, when his mother took to pacing their darkened kitchen and chain smoking until dawn. Tommy had been called out of class one day only to find his father waiting in the school's front office. He figured he was in trouble, though he couldn't begin to guess what for, but instead of talking to the principal they'd headed home. On the way his father had explained the new reality of their lives. Like Janet Leigh in *Psycho*, Tommy's mother had stolen money from the bank where she worked as a teller and gone on the run.

Ben was going to run, too. Tommy could feel it. He'd run before, in a way, had come south for college and never moved back, taking one job after another here until he landed the one he currently held.

Tommy figured no one else saw the job for what it was—a good excuse to stay away from his family and the world he'd grown up in, in order to avoid having to tell them he was gay. He'd all but exited their lives, returning only for structured visits—holidays and funerals and the like. Tommy had suspected guys he was in the military with of having done essentially the same thing. Soldiers were allowed to have different life goals than civilians and all their actions got colored as sacrifices, which put them above reproach.

A man could use the service to fashion a life more to his liking than what was acceptable in civilian society without having to answer to anyone. In that regard it was not unlike the priesthood.

Ben had been afraid of what people would think or do if they knew the truth about him, so he'd run. He was afraid now, of what the police knew, of what they might do. Tommy didn't want to think what would happen if he found out about the many terrible things Estill had said.

Ben stopped pacing and exhaled deeply. "I think it's time I sold the house," he said. "The market's come back enough that I'll at least get back what I put in."

"Sure, makes sense," Tommy agreed. He felt sick. Though he didn't expect to be told, he asked, "Where will you go?"

Ben looked up sharply. "Me?" he asked. "What are you talking about? Us."

Tommy was so surprised, he couldn't find words.

"I'm not going anywhere without you," Ben said. He stepped directly in front of Tommy, met and held his gaze. "You're the best thing I've got."

Tommy's throat tightened, making it hard to reply. "Yeah?"

Ben grabbed him by the waist and pulled him close. "Absolutely. Full confession: I've been thinking about moving for a while. We don't really fit in here, do we? We should go downtown, maybe over by the university. There are some great Victorian fixer-uppers over there. With my equity and your carpentry skills we could make an amazing home—an amazing life—together. What do you say?"

The newscasts were ending when Ben finally slid his chair away from the computer. "The good news is it looks like we can get an even better price than the last time I checked. I'll call a realtor tomorrow," he said. He stretched, started for the stairs, turned back. "Aren't you coming?"

Tommy slipped onto the desk chair. "In a sec. I just want to look something up."

A moment later he felt Ben's arms wrap around his shoulders. "Like what?"

"What's happening in Russia. And a brush-up on the Holocaust."

"Let me guess: Ivy asked you about it?"

Tommy nodded. "A while ago. I keep forgetting to do it."

"You've had other things on your mind." Ben rested his chin on Tommy's left shoulder. "After we're settled again I think you should ask the court for full custody of her. That's not a healthy environment for a child."

"They'll say that about us."

"They don't know for sure that you and I are anything more than friends."

"They'll ask."

"And we won't tell. Not right now, anyway. Later, after it can't work against us."

Tommy typed 'Russian gays' into the search box and hit enter. The first result yielded a newspaper article with the headline "Russian President Condones Attacks on Gay Citizens" complete with a picture of macaque-faced, bare-chested Vladimir Putin riding a sable-colored stallion against a background of ashen cliffs. A foot long Bowie knife was strapped to his thigh.

Ben snorted. "They say the thing that bothers you most about other people is the thing you can't make peace with in yourself."

The article detailed the vicious beatings young gay Russians had suffered at the hands of thugs, and the fact that many of the crimes had been committed in broad daylight in public, yet no one had raised a hand to stop them. Even more sickeningly, a large percentage of the attacks had been filmed and then posted to YouTube. There were links, but Tommy didn't click on them.

Dreading what he might see on those pages as well, he typed 'Holocaust' into the search field.

Ben straightened up. "Come to bed."

"I just need a refresher. It's been a decade."

"Shut off the computer. I can tell you what you want to know."

Tommy chuffed. "It's been even longer for you."

"Yes, but for me it wasn't just another unit in History class. Members of my family were killed during it." He reached over Tommy, took control of the mouse, and shut down the system.

"The important thing to keep in mind," Ben began as they started up the stairs, "is that it began very, very slowly. Not over a matter of weeks, or months, or even years. I'm talking about centuries of institutionalized hatred directed toward an entire group of people, a powder keg of resentment and fear that was just waiting for a madman like Hitler to provide the spark to set it off…."

BEANSTALK
CLIFFORD HENDERSON

Once upon the future, in a town called Utonia, there was a strikingly handsome, but seriously unhappy, young woman named Jackie. It was unusual for Utonians to be unhappy because most of them were very happy, or, if not very happy, at least relatively content. And why wouldn't they be? Utonia was a beautiful town. It rested between two plump mountains and had soil so fertile, it was said if you weren't careful a seed in your pocket might take root. So everyone was well fed and strong and generally stayed that way until they dropped dead, at which point there was much crying and singing and gratefulness for having known the deceased. But most of the people were happy and even when they weren't they moved through their unhappiness quickly, never thinking that they should hang on to grudges or grievances.

You might wonder why Jackie was so unhappy. After all, she had a strong body and a wonderful mop of curly, bronze hair, green eyes that shown like peridot cabochons, and a mind that moved as quickly as light. What's more, she lived and worked in an elegant, arty little studio, which she paid for with the sales of her stunning 3-D landscapes—each one its own liquid crystal display that changed with the seasons. But while others thought her landscapes dazzling and extravagant, the edges of these masterpieces depressed her and made her feel hemmed in. At the start of each new landscape she would brace herself for her eventual disappointment.

The Utonians did not know what to make of her predilection for gloominess, but then Utonians, on the whole, were a little unclear about unhappiness (what caused it and such), but they were great believers in the power of love. They didn't much care who loved whom, some women loved women, some loved men; some men loved men, some women. It was all the same to them. Indeed, parents noted their children's gender preferences in the same light as they might note their eye or hair color. Love was simply love and it was good. Consequently, some speculated that Jackie's unhappiness was caused by a lack of love. Others disputed it. She'd had lovers before, after all. In fact, she'd loved some of the most beautiful women in Utonia. Shouldn't that have cured her? In the end, no one could come up with a definite cause.

No one, that is, except for the crone, Marta, who lived by herself in a hovel made of bones, clay, and hide. She was an ornery spit of a woman who, it was understood, was happiest when left alone with her garden of cabbages, beans, and carrots. She was also the only one old enough to remember how things used to be. And she understood exactly the cause of Jackie's unhappiness.

It was no surprise then that when Jackie was walking to the gallery one day, her most recent landscape tucked under her arm; she bumped right into Marta. Solutions are, after all, forever seeking out problems. Sadly, it takes a quick wit and cleverness to knit the two together, and while quite clever, Jackie was not clever enough to recognize her deliverance.

"Watch where you're going!" Marta said.

Startled, Jackie looked up from a smattering of withered bougainvillea petals on the ground. "Oh, Marta, I didn't see you."

"Of course you didn't. You were too busy staring at your feet."

"I was looking at these petals. I—"

"I know what you were doing, girl."

Jackie, like all Utonians, was slightly frightened by Marta. The stench of less-happy times hovered around her, an ominous fog of what could be if one weren't mindful.

"Poor, poor me," the crone taunted. "That's what you were thinking, wasn't it? Poor, poor me. That's what keeps you from looking where you are going."

"Well, I…" But Jackie could not find it inside herself to admit that what Marta said was true, that she was feeling particularly low. While the world she lived in did not have "edges" like her landscapes, it felt as if it did. Utonia was too small, too predictable, too conventional. Where was the challenge?

"What's that under your arm?" Marta asked, pointing to the landscape.

"One of my landscapes. I'm taking it to the gallery."

"Let me have a look at it."

Jackie held it out for Marta's inspection. The landscape was one of her Foggy Morning series, an 18 inches x 24 inches rendering of a willow tree by a stream.

Frowning, Marta turned her head from side to side as if to get a better angle, and then said, "Flip it upside down." Which Jackie did, although she felt insulted that the old woman was treating her artwork as if it were the ugliest thing she'd ever seen. After viewing it upside down and then right side up again, Marta said, "I'll take it!" and snatched it from Jackie's grasp.

Jackie did not want to sell it to the crone, believing it would be tossed and forgotten among her notorious collection of bones and skins. There was no arguing with Marta so she agreed to the sale. Before she had a chance to name her price, however, Marta handed her a large speckled bean.

"What's this?" Jackie said.

"Payment," Marta said.

"But it's a bean. What am I supposed to do with a bean?"

"If you have any sense at all, you'll plant it." With that, Marta began hobbling up to her hovel on the hill, robbing Jackie of the chance to quarrel.

Not that she would have. Quarreling with Marta simply wasn't done. The many tales of her turning people into worms and lizards made it inadvisable. Jackie didn't need the money anyway. Her landscapes made her a comfortable living. She only placed them in the gallery to keep them from collecting cobwebs. So, dispirited, but not much more than usual, Jackie slogged back to her studio. Once there, she had just enough energy to curse Marta's meager payment and toss the stupid pink and black bean between two prickly thistles in the weedy plot in front of her house. She then dragged her sorry self inside and flopped down on the daybed.

Her final thought before nodding off was that she might get lucky and actually die in her sleep from boredom.

The next morning she slept in, not realizing how late it was because her studio, oddly, was still dark. Lying on her daybed, rubbing out a crick in her neck, she heard an eerie humming coming from outside. Yawning, she stumbled over to the window and was shocked to see a huge, fibrous stalk with plate-sized, heart-shaped leaves coiling up and up, like a corkscrew, from between the two thistles in her weedy plot. As she was staring, her mouth agape, a scarlet flower bloomed from the stalk. Then another. And another. One on top of the next. *What the hell?* she thought. Then she remembered Marta's bean. Clearly, it had been no ordinary bean. It was bewitched. She should have known.

She slipped on her slacks and T-shirt, slid on a pair of sandals, and charged outside—her curiosity piqued. The beanstalk spiraled upwards past the house, past the trees, and was just breaking into the clouds—piercing the very edges of her world. Marta had made her wish come true!

Jackie grabbed hold of the beanstalk, wedged her foot into the axil where leaf met stalk, and tested to see if the stem would hold her weight. It did. She tried the next one up. This too held her weight. Impulsively, she began climbing, stopping only to catch her breath. The growing stalk aided in propelling her upward like an escalator. She couldn't wait to see what lay ahead, knew it must be wonderful. Why else would Marta have given her the bean? Happier than she'd felt in years, she began to sing a childhood ditty as she climbed, never once looking back at Utonia, now little more than a speck in the distance.

When she reached the clouds she started having reservations. It was cold for one thing, and disorienting, the puffy whiteness making her lose her equilibrium—both physically and mentally. What if Marta didn't have her best interest in mind? What if Marta was sending her to a place from which she couldn't return—to rid Utonia of her gloominess? But she couldn't stop now—not so close to learning what was beyond the edges. So, like a little goat, she continued on.

Having made it through the clouds, her effort was rewarded. The stalk curling up through a tunnel of solid earth toward a patch of blue sky. She scrabbled up through the wormy earth and hauled herself onto the land. It was a wonderfully warm, sunny day and before her was a long dirt road, which appeared to lead to some sort of distant city. She could just make out a jagged skyline of enormous, erect buildings, each one taller than the next.

Jackie did not stop to think what kind of a self-important place would encourage such ostentatious architecture. Oh no. She imagined it to be better than any she'd ever seen, the buildings filled with beings much more technically advanced than Utonians, much more complicated and interesting. What a ninny she'd been for doubting Marta. Clearly, the crone had only her best interests in mind.

She trotted toward the city, passing through grassy hills dotted with oversized cows and sheep. She passed farms and ranches, the houses and barns perpendicular and huge in strange contrast to the soft, undulating landscape. She spotted a shepherd trying to coax a wayward sheep out of a gulch. A pimply teenager, he was close to twelve feet tall.

"Hello!" Jackie yelled.

He looked up from his charge, gave Jackie the once-over, and yelled, "What's wrong with you?"

This took her aback. "Wrong?"

"You're so small."

She laughed looking down at all five feet five inches of herself. "Oh. That. Where I come from we're all this size. Or thereabout."

"Is your husband tiny too?"

"My husband?"

"Yeah. You know, the guy you're joined to."

"Actually, I don't have a husband."

"Sorry to hear that," he said, shaking his head. "At your age."

She chose to ignore his rudeness. "What's this city up ahead?"

"Pureland. Where every man is happy and every dream fulfilled."

Excited, she said, "Thanks!" and continued on her way, overlooking the bitter tone with which he'd uttered these last words.

Soon other people joined her on the road, peasants mostly, filing out of their giant farmhouses and heading toward the city, all of them dressed in what looked to be their finest clothes, all of them walking with a steadfast urgency. They were huge, some of them as tall as sixteen feet. But unlike in Utonia, where there was no dress code, where a person wore what she or he felt best reflected his or her personality, the women here all wore coarse ankle-length dresses, the men, simple slacks and tunics. Most would not look at her. Those who did, did so with pity. She spotted a boy, about her size, struggling along behind his parents on painful-looking stilts. He glanced at her briefly then looked away, clearly ashamed to be associated with someone of her diminutive stature. But she didn't give much thought to the Purelanders' obvious discomfort with her size, reasoning that if any of them set foot in Utonia, people would stare too. Besides, up ahead a phalanx of young giantesses decked out in flowers and long white dresses paraded with great importance. Clearly the crowd was heading to some kind of special event. It had now grown so large it was more-or-less pushing her along.

They arrived in what appeared to be a suburb of the gleaming city. Giant houses with giant lawns and giant birdbaths and decorative gnomes lined the road with military precision. But it was the people streaming out of these houses that fascinated Jackie. Not only were they huge like the peasants, they were also dripping wealth.

The giant women clung to their men's arms like pocketbooks, their faces masked in self-righteousness. They wore opulent, ankle-length dresses so snug the women were forced to take tiny steps, two or three high-heeled ones to every leather-booted one of the male—and they were draped in so many jewels they had trouble lifting their arms or turning quickly. As for the men, they strode down the streets in tight slacks featuring huge jeweled cups covering their genitals. Men and women alike held their chins so high and their chests so puffed out they never even saw Jackie trolling around beneath them. Or, more likely, they simply had no interest.

Then, amid the bustle and hubbub, Jackie heard someone weeping. Drawn to the sadness like moisture to the earth, she angled her way out of the crowd, waited until the street emptied of people, and made her way to the nearby house that seemed to be the source of the sadness. She had to climb a spiky shrub to see inside the first-story window. But it was worth it, for there, sobbing underneath a waterfall of silky black hair, was a young woman not much bigger than Jackie. She was slumped over on a bed much too large for her and was brimming with a sorrow so deep if flowers had been in the room they surely would have wilted in empathy. Jackie could not turn away. Even when a fat giantess burst into the room.

The giantess was squeezed into a shiny, pink dress and teetered on ridiculously high-heeled shoes. Her expression was twisted with rage. "I am so ashamed of you, Ivy! Twenty-two years old and still not married!"

A balding giant with large muscles and a huge gut was hot on her heels. "It's because she's a runt! What man would want her?"

"I had the Ragner boy all lined up!" A boil the size of a ripe plum bobbed on the giantess's upper lip as she spewed the ugly words. "He was ready to take her. But what did she go and do? She told him she didn't want to marry him. Told him she would make a terrible wife. Honestly! The girl doesn't know what's good for her."

The giant man slammed out of the room, yelling, "I'm going to the Joining Ceremony. And you'd best come with me, wife, or people will talk."

"What about her?" the wife wailed.

"Let her stew in her tears. Maybe she'll cry herself into some sense."

The giantess sighed a sigh so long and so suffering the pictures on the bedroom wall rattled. "I'll tell people you're sick. That should keep them from coming after you. But you miss too many Joining Ceremonies and they're going to wonder."

The young woman, Ivy, lifted her head, revealing a beauty not even anger or the puffy redness of crying could mask. "I hate Joining Ceremonies! Half the couples getting joined are miserable."

"Miserable beats alone!" the giantess said before storming out of the room.

Jackie longed to comfort the young woman, Ivy. Ivy. The name alone caused a curious feeling to rise up in her, a feeling of possibility, a feeling that maybe she could be happy—if only she could find a way to make contact. A gentle knock on the window? No. It would scare her; perhaps make her call out to her awful parents. Besides, there was such pleasure in simply gazing at her: her strong cheekbones, her long lashes, her lovely, full lips.

"What are you doing peering into Jorge Inger's house?" a hulking giant snarled from the street.

Terrified, Jackie leapt down from her perch and sprinted her way down the street and through the crisscrossing avenues of the suburb, never daring to look over her shoulder to see if anyone was following. She continued on through the rolling, green hills, her adrenalin pumping, heart thumping, and when she finally reached the hole in the rode, she dove into the tunnel and all but slid her way down to the weedy patch in front of her house. Only then did she let herself rest, slumped on the ground, winded and exhilarated. What an adventure she'd had. What a peek into another world.

But that night she was unable to sleep. She couldn't stop thinking about Ivy, about how sad she was. She became so obsessed with ways she, herself, might alleviate Ivy's unhappiness that she forgot all about her own discontent. She kept getting out of bed to look out the window at the beanstalk. Radiant with moonlight, the heart-shaped leaves glowed from within while the stalk lay hidden within the shadows. She cursed the lazy sun for taking its sweet time rising, cursed herself for being such a coward she'd scurried home at the first sign of trouble.

She picked up her palm communicator and messaged Marta. *What kind of bean was that?*

She was surprised when Marta messaged her right back. It was the dead of night. *You needed perspective.*

Irritated by Marta's elusiveness, Jackie messaged back a line of angry question marks.

Good luck with the bean, was all Marta replied.

Jackie tossed her communicator onto the daybed and continued her pacing and sitting and pacing and cursing until dawn finally had the decency to break. Then she strode outside to the weedy patch prepared to climb up the beanstalk, only to discover it had sprouted beans. Big beautiful green pods clung to the stalk like giant dewdrops. The beans made the stalk much easier to climb. She could use the pods to hoist herself up. When she reached the road this time, she took it at a quick clip, her mind whirring with scenarios of what she would say, or do, when she saw Ivy again.

The shepherd startled her out of her scheming. "Hey, shorty! Where are you off to in such a hurry?"

"To seek out a friend." she yelled back.

He waved a hand in the air. "Good luck."

She continued jogging through the hills until she reached the suburb of over-sized houses where she shifted to a brisk walk so as not to gain the attention of the giant passersby. When, at last, she came to that same street corner and that same shrub, she had to wait for a giantess pushing an enormous stroller with a pig-faced baby to make her way down the street before climbing up to the window.

Once there, she held her breath and peered into the room. Ivy was there, sitting on the floor drawing in what looked to be a giant note pad. She was even more beautiful than Jackie remembered with her black hair now tucked behind the cutest of ears. But once again Jackie was at a loss for how to get her attention. She'd spent the entire night coming up with plans on what she would do when she saw Ivy again and now she couldn't think of a single one. If she could just get up the nerve to knock, she could...

But again the giantess of the house waylaid her by bursting through the door. "Put down that silly book of yours, girl!" Her face was covered in some kind of goopy beauty cream. "The widower Thompson has agreed to take a look at you. He's coming by tonight. Prepare yourself."

"But he's twice my age! And was cruel to his last wife!"

"He needs a woman. His house is a shambles and he's been forced to eat nothing but tins of fish and peas."

"Would it kill him to pick up a broom? Boil an egg?"

"I don't know where you get these crazy ideas! Certainly not from me or your father. It would shame him to do such a thing. That's women's work and you know it. Just be ready." The hag gave Ivy one last menacing look then charged out of the room and slammed the door behind her.

Ivy flung her book on the floor, her eyes blazing with anger.

Jackie took a deep breath. Then another. When there was no more courage to be found, she tapped lightly on the window anyway.

Startled, Ivy whirled around, but when her eyes met Jackie's her alarm appeared to melt into curiosity. Or Jackie hoped that's what her expression meant.

She motioned for Ivy to open the window.

Ivy shot a look to the bedroom door then quietly walked over to lift the window. It was so large it took all of her body strength to accomplish. When at last she'd managed, all she said was, "This is different." But those three words wiped Jackie's mind clear of every single thing she'd planned to say; like a ray of sunshine lighting on sleeping butterflies, they all fluttered away.

"Well?" the young woman said.

To Jackie's utter astonishment, she heard herself say something she had not planned to say, "I think I love you."

To Jackie's further astonishment, Ivy smiled a puckish smile. "In that case, come in. It's not often I have a woman knock on my window professing her love." She glanced toward her bedroom door once more before adding, "But be quiet. My parents are on a rampage."

Jackie scrambled through the window and did her best to jump lightly down into the bedroom. She was completely unprepared for how insignificant the enormous furniture would make her feel. How did Ivy manage? She noticed a stepstool by the light switch. Another by the dresser. But these concerns were minor, compared to what she'd just confessed. Was she in love? Was that the fizzy feeling in her belly?

"I'm Jackie," she said, and stretched out her hand, a ridiculously formal move under the circumstances.

Ivy curtsied playfully and took her hand. "Ivy."

Then the two of them just stood there staring into one another's eyes, two ridiculous grins pasted on their faces, two hopeful hearts beating an unmistakable duet.

"Wow," Ivy said at last. "It's amazing to be able to look into someone's eyes."

Jackie thought: *Amazing to want to look into someone's eyes.*

"So what are you doing here?" Ivy went on. "And, more importantly, who are you?"

The amazing story of Marta and the bean came out in fits and starts, winding this way and that, like the beanstalk itself. Ivy appeared impressed if not entirely convinced by what she heard. "A giant beanstalk, huh? A place where everyone is my size, and a woman is not required by law to be joined to a man?"

"Women can be joined to women where I live," Jackie said, then felt herself flush.

Ivy raised an intrigued eyebrow. "Reeeeally…"

"Yup."

Unsure what to do next, Jackie picked up the sketchbook Ivy had tossed on the floor and handed it to her.

"Thanks," Ivy said. "My parents would kill me if they ever bothered to look at this. All art in Pureland must be sanctioned by the Committee for Moral Uprightness." An undercurrent of rage rumbled in her words, which Jackie found thoroughly compelling. Equally compelling was Ivy's ability to shift from the rage to the casual flipping of notebook pages for Jackie to see. She was so fluid with her emotions, flicking from one to another so effortlessly.

The notebook was filled with portraits, each one beautifully capturing a moment of private sadness.

"These are immoral?" Jackie asked.

"Unhappiness is considered immoral."

"But a person can't help if they're happy or not."

"That's debatable, but it certainly shouldn't be illegal."

"But your mom, your dad, they both seem sooo—"

"I know. It's this weird paradox…or denial…or double standard. I haven't quite figured it out. But it plagues Pureland. Everyone is unhappy, but they pretend not to be."

Jackie stared down at the yellow, ankle-high carpet pile. "I used to think I'd never be happy."

"What changed?"

Jackie almost had the courage to tell her, but returned to the portraits instead. "These are wonderful." She worried that Ivy would notice her sudden shift of focus.

Ivy just laughed. "Of course, you would say that. You came to me on a magic beanstalk professing your undying love."

"I just—" But the rest of Jackie's thought was kidnapped by a new one. She hadn't said undying had she?

Ivy placed a hand on Jackie's chest. "Please don't apologize. Don't ruin this." Her hazel eyes were flecked with gold, her skin a sumptuous olive, her nose a small nut waiting to be…. Unable to stop herself, Jackie leaned in to—

The sound of the front door crashing open thundered through the house.

Ivy stiffened. "My father. Back from his morning workout. He'll want breakfast."

"Can't he get it himself?"

"Just go."

"But…"

"Please. Go!"

"Ivy!" Her father's bellow made the house shudder. "Where's my triple latte?"

Ivy bolted for the door then spun around, took the few steps back, and cradled Jackie's face in her hands. "Thank you," she said, softly. "You've made today a much nicer day." Then she planted a whisper of a kiss on Jackie's lips. By the time Jackie regained composure, Ivy was slipping out the door, leaving Jackie to go out the way she came in.

She slunk around Ivy's neighborhood all morning, occasionally returning to the shrub outside Ivy's bedroom window, but alas, the room remained empty. She decided to do a little exploring and took one of the many moving sidewalks into the city. There she saw things that both thrilled and frightened her. Beautiful mirrored skyscrapers next to alleys of trash and impoverished people; gorgeous store windows full of lavish merchandise but featuring live models whose lips and breasts were hideously augmented. But by far, the most puzzling thing was a torture device in the city's center that secured the offender's head, hands, and feet in a thick wooden block. Apparently it was used for punishing anyone deemed unhappy. A nearby broadside defined unhappiness as everything from failing to laugh at the Mayor's jokes to sharing intimacy with one's same sex. Truly, the more Jackie saw of these giant people, the more she understood Ivy's drawings. These people were unhappy but they made great efforts to appear as if they weren't.

She returned to Ivy's suburb dispirited and just in time to witness the giant children returning home from school, giant backpacks slung over their giant shoulders, giant lollipops clutched in their giant fists. Their giant mothers herded them along like gaggles of unruly hippos, passing each other on the street gushing forced niceties, their faces contorted into painful looking smiles. The children taunted each other with cruel insults, but none of them ever dared cry.

Jackie was about to climb up the shrub when a melon-faced boy, as wide as he was tall, said, "Hey, you, I could squash you like a bug! Hey, Ronnie, Eno! Look what I found." She tried to dissuade the bullies from their plan, but then one of them called over his dog—a mean, snarling thing—and Jackie, her depression now paramount, soon found herself trudging back to her own world at the bottom of the beanstalk. Only now her melancholy had a twinge of something new: anger. Not at her world, or Pureland, which would have been her usual response, but at herself. *How could she have given up on Ivy so easily? Was she really such a coward? Too wimpy to step up for someone she...loved?*

Outside the pods were swelling with beans, some of them even burst open and dropped their precious seeds to the ground. Anyone could tell there wasn't much time before the magical plant began to die back, before she'd be cut off from Ivy forever.

She messaged the crone. *I have seen a place that lies beyond Utonia. It frightens me.*

You again? Marta messaged back.

Please tell me why you gave me that bean.

You needed perspective.

I can see that now. But I think I have also fallen in love.

Marta did not message back right away, which only added to Jackie's sense of urgency. When Marta did finally write back all she said was: *One does not "think" one has fallen in love. One either has or one hasn't.*

Jackie knew that Marta was right. She also knew, as strongly as anyone can know anything, that she had fallen in love. She messaged this to Marta adding the question: *How should I proceed?*

To which Marta messaged: *You're on your own with that one, dearie. Now, I'm going back to my nap.*

Jackie stared out her window. The late afternoon sun was turning the shadows long; the stalk showed signs of withering. It was now or never. So once again she forced her now-aching muscles up the beanstalk, which was beginning to shrivel and flake; and once again, she jogged down the road.

The shepherd shouted, "You? Again? Where are you off to now?"

"To rescue my love!" she yelled back, brazenly.

He smiled a snaggletoothed grin. "Good luck!"

"Thanks!" she yelled, and kept on running.

When she returned to Ivy's house she was out of breath and her calves were burning, but she barely took note of these things. She slipped behind a tree while a couple of giant children on giant bicycles sailed past. Then, careful to make sure no one was watching, she mounted the shrub and peeked into the window only to find Ivy's room still empty. Her heart sank. Then she noticed the window was ajar. Determined to risk whatever it took to rescue Ivy, she wedged it open further and climbed in. Voices were coming from the interior of the house, one of them was Ivy's. "I should warn you, I will make a very bad wife."

"Ivy!" her mother snapped. "Manners!"

A man, the widower, Jackie supposed, chuckled and said, "I see I will have to teach you to be a good one."

"Show him the joining gown I made you," her mother said. "And the shoes."

A strange ka-thunk ka-thunk came toward the room. Jackie dove into the closet. The door opened and a weary, stilt-wearing Ivy stepped inside. Or that's what Jackie assumed for Ivy was now close to ten feet tall and wearing one of the ankle-binding dresses of the Purelanders. The vision broke her heart.

She waited for Ivy to shut the door then slipped from her hiding place.

Ivy recoiled, holding herself steady on the doorframe. "What are you doing here?" she whispered. She ran her fingers self-consciously through her hair.

"I've come to rescue you."

Ivy laughed a numb laugh. "There's no rescuing me, my friend. My father has just signed the papers to hand me off to the Widower Thompson, a cruel man with bad breath and flaking skin."

"Then come with me down the beanstalk!"

Ivy sank down on the bed. "You're kidding, right?"

"No! I know it sounds crazy, but—"

"Ivy!" her mother called. "Are you almost ready?"

"Yes, Mother."

Jackie hoisted herself unto the bed and knelt beside Ivy. "Didn't our kiss mean anything to you?"

Ivy's eyes pooled with tears. She blinked them back. "You have no idea..."

"So come with me."

"Ivy!" her mother yelled again. "Widower Thompson is growing impatient. And so am I!"

"Please," Jackie said, "I can't promise I'll always make you happy—but I know I can do better than this." She waited, aware that she was asking a lot. But she couldn't—wouldn't—doom Ivy to a life of unhappiness. Not if she could help it. She took a breath and played her last card, "I'm not going back without you."

Ivy met Jackie's gaze with such intensity if felt to Jackie as if her innards were being ripped from her belly. "You would forsake this wonderful world you speak of just to save me?"

Jackie nodded.

Ivy looked around her room once then began lifting the heavy gold dress to wrestle off the hideous, metal stilts. "Okay. Take me to this magic beanstalk of yours, to this magic world."

Heart crashing in her chest, Jackie helped Ivy release the clasps, helped her wrestle off the gold dress and put on a short tunic. "Is there anything you want to bring? You won't be able to return."

Ivy thought for a moment then said, "Nothing. Let's just get out of here."

"Ivy!" the giantess yelled.

Once on the road they ran side-by-side matching one another stride for stride. It was getting dark and the streets were mostly empty of people. They hugged the shadows, Jackie praying that the beanstalk would be strong enough to hold them, worried what would happen if it weren't. At the outskirts of the city, an ear-shattering siren began to blare.

"They've found us out," Ivy said, breathlessly. "If they catch us we'll be stoned."

Jackie grabbed her hand and picked up the pace. She was having trouble telling how much further they had to go—if they were even on the right road.

"Hey!" she heard a voice yell out from the shadows. "Where do you think you're going?"

Jackie breathed a sigh of relief. It was the shepherd. "Some-place better than this!"

"Lucky you!" he shouted.

A huge flying machine sputtered up behind them. "Turn back now!" an amplified voice commanded. In the distance dogs began to bark.

Jackie spotted the hole in the road and came to a halt. The tip of the beanstalk was drooping a good six feet away from the road.

"We're going to have to jump," she said.

Ivy leaned over and peered down the hole. Her eyes grew wide. "There really is a beanstalk."

"Yes. And if we don't jump now, our chance will be gone."

Ivy's eyes locked in on Jackie's. "I don't know a thing about you…" was all she said. But it was enough. The two of them leapt, hand-in-hand, onto the top leaf of the beanstalk. It was brittle and dry, and Jackie worried it would disintegrate. But it held, the stalk bending gracefully downward and showering them in a downpour of confetti-like leaf flakes until finally placing them gently into the weedy patch in front of Jackie's studio where they stood, gasping for breath, in the moonlight.

After a few rigid moments, Ivy released her vice-like grip on Jackie's hand and did a slow three-sixty. "Holy Cats! You weren't kidding. Everything is my size!"

"I told you."

"I know, but...look at that house. That tree. That...that..." She took Jackie's face in her hands "...that you!"

Ivy's touch lit Jackie up like a comet, the very air around her changing from dark and brooding to pure effervescence. Or, as the Utonians would later put it: "turned her from a bulb to a flower." The kiss that followed was long and lingering and bursting with promises of happily-ever-after.

Two elderly gentlemen on their evening constitutional stopped to take in the spectacle of the giant beanstalk dropping the two young women to the earth. Standing in the shadows, hand-in-hand, watching them kiss, the one said to the other: "That Marta, she sure knows how to cast a spell." His companion then kissed him on the cheek and together they continued strolling down the magical, moonlit street of Utonia.

RHINESTONE MAGIC
J.R. GREENWELL

Eddie's right foot felt almost completely numb as he pressed it against the accelerator. Moving slowly down the lane, he spotted his old neighbor, Ida Simpson, on her riding mower as he drove by her house. For a moment, Eddie thought he'd mistaken the identity of the woman with heavy makeup sporting a teased-up hairdo accessorized with very large rhinestone earrings and wearing a strapless hot-pink bikini, a bit tight and out of character for a lady in her late sixties, especially for someone like Ida. When she suddenly smiled, displaying a huge set of toothless gums, Eddie realized that the woman was definitely Ida Simpson. Notorious for going out in public without her dentures, there she sat, John Wayne style, straddling a John Deere while displaying her strange makeover without a tooth in her head. Eddie reluctantly waved hello, knowing that Ida probably didn't recognize him in the Miata.

A few minutes earlier, Eddie had wiped the nervous sweat from his brow with the back of his hand as he cautiously negotiated the shoulders of the two-lane highway in route to his parent's home. Riding as a passenger on the switchbacks on the mountainous North Carolina roads as a kid always made him nauseous, and even now as an adult behind the wheel, Eddie felt one curve away from an upchuck. Luckily, the occasional muscle cramps in his calves and the numbness in his feet helped delay the thoughts of throwing up. With the windows down and his knees hugging the front of the dashboard, the cool June morning air whipped through the rented Miata as he finally maneuvered the last leg of the winding road. The sporty black car was way too small for Eddie's two-hundred and thirty pound, six-three frame, and what made the ride worse was that the seat had been pushed forward to fit the previous driver, and Eddie had no idea how to adjust it. Despite the discomfort of sitting in a fetal position snuggled up to the wheel for the entire trip, he was determined to make an impact by driving up to his parent's house in the impressive looking car instead of returning home in his beatup1997 Honda.

Just past Ida's property, Eddie could see the red brick ranch house in the distance nestled on the edge of the forest of pines and hardwoods not too far from the other dwellings in the rural Southern Baptist community. He slowed down, creeping to a complete stop, staring at his old neighbors' houses along the lane that had been so much a part of his life. He'd made this trek many times in the past two years only to lose the gumption to face his parents as the idea of confrontation made him wince, and with each trip he found himself turning around and heading back to his home in Charlotte. He wanted reconciliation with his parents, but this time was different. There was more at stake. There would be no turning back without their blessing.

Within minutes Eddie drove up the long gravel driveway for what seemed an eternity as he felt one small stone at a time make contact with the tires beneath him. He stopped his car at the edge of the walkway where a concrete gnome, once painted red and green, but now seasoned and aged with time, seemed to welcome him. Taking a deep breath, he turned off the engine and carefully opened the door. He rolled out of the car as his bloodless feet touched the ground, his knees stiff and still bent. After slowly rising off the ground and brushing off the bits of gravel stuck to his pants, he stood up straight, stretching his arms into the air, then quietly shut the car door behind him as if he were worried about startling someone in the house.

As Eddie walked by the gnome and up the walkway, the sound of the Forester Sisters singing a gospel song filled the air, and the aroma of freshly baked cookies found its way through the screen door. He knocked on the slightly warped and unpainted wooden frame. There was no response. He knocked again. Still, no answer. The driveway was empty, so perhaps his parents weren't at home.

Just as the Forester Sisters broke into another song, he decided to go to the backyard thinking someone might be there. He cringed as he walked through the uncut grass, disturbed that the morning dew was probably ruining his new loafers, but he was also thrilled that the blood flow had returned to his toes once again.

Rounding the side of the building, Eddie caught sight of the gazebo he'd helped his father build about ten years earlier. Underneath the roof of the domed structure he saw his mother sitting in a chair with a shovel in her hand, staring off into the edge of the yard.

"Mom?" Eddie asked, not sure if the woman was really his mother. Her gray hair was pulled back exposing her high cheekbones that appeared to be painfully red. Perhaps a bad sunburn or too much blush, he thought. Her eyes were smudged with dark eye shadow giving her face a raccoon-like appearance. She had on a pink and green floral muumuu, unlike the gray and black dresses she normally wore. But what surprised Eddie the most about his mother was that she was wearing rhinestone earrings. Very large and gaudy rhinestone earrings. Eerily, it was as if she and Ida had a makeover by the same person.

"Eddie?" Martha responded apprehensively. "I thought I heard a car pull up." There was a sense of joy in her voice that quickly turned to disdain, evident by the shift in her body language. She set the shovel on the gazebo floor and sat back up, crossing her arms in a defensive posture. "Wasn't expecting you, of all people. What are you doing here?"

"Just passing through the neighborhood and I thought I'd drop in," Eddie answered like a child seeking forgiveness as he slowly took a small step toward his mother, afraid at any minute she might chase him off the property.

"Without calling first?"

Eddie stood still. His feet felt wet, but he didn't look down. "Well, I knew if I called you might not let me come by."

"Probably wouldn't. But now you're here. Might as well come on over and get out of that wet grass before it ruins your shoes."

Eddie was delighted to have the chance to be near his mother. Despite their differences, he still longed to be in her presence.

After stepping onto the gazebo, he reached down to offer her a hug, but she didn't respond to his gesture.

Martha crossed her legs, exposing her large ankles and calloused bare feet. "So, how long do you plan to stay? I mean, after all, it's been two years since I've seen you. What happened to your hair?"

"It's just styled differently."

"I don't think I like it," she quipped back.

"Yeah, well. You didn't like it before either," Eddie replied. It was obvious that only after a few short minutes he could see his mother had changed her physical appearance, but her cantankerous attitude was no different than before. If anything, she was probably meaner than ever, he thought to himself. "I just plan to stay a few minutes. I didn't want to impose, and actually, I just decided to stop by a couple of minutes ago."

"So what do you want?" she asked, staring directly into her son's eyes. Eddie had never seen his mother wear makeup, and the smoky-gray eye shadow only intensified the spite in her crystal blue eyes. "You must want something," she said firmly, her brows furling up and down.

"I just wanted to say hello and to see how you're doing. I don't want anything. I mean, it's been a long time."

"No need to want anything. You made your choice. My only child and you ain't been here in over two years, and now you just pop in unannounced, and…"

"Yeah, two years," Eddie mumbled as he pulled a folding chair away from the railing, and after opening it, he sat down next to his mother. "I see the gazebo is still here," he said trying to make small talk. "And the backyard's looking good. The trees are filling out, and I see you still grow those, uh…"

"Lilies. Daylilies, Asiatic lilies, hybrid lilies…" Martha rattled off, undeterred by Eddie's determination to have a congenial conversation.

"Yeah, those."

Sensing she might have acted too tersely, Martha reached down and picked up a potted plant out of a wrinkled-up plastic Wal-Mart bag that had been positioned next to her chair. "Just got this one from Ida Simpson's yard," she said. Not sure where to put it just yet."

"Maybe with the others?" Eddie suggested.

"Maybe." There was a pause as both mother and son nodded their heads, scanning the backyard, searching for the next topic to break the awkward silence.

"Just saw Ida when I drove in," Eddie calmly stated.

"Wearing that damn bikini, I bet," Martha added.

"Yeah," Eddie concurred. "I don't ever remember her dressing or looking like that."

"Well, I guess you could say a lot of us have changed since you've been gone."

Eddie's eyes lit up with curiosity as he spotted his old tennis racquet. "Hey, isn't that mine?" he asked. "So, what are you doing with my old racquet out here?"

"Yes, it's yours, and I play with it," Martha said as she leaned over and grabbed the racquet. "And you can't have it back."

"Wow, you're playing tennis?" Eddie was excited that perhaps his mother had taken up some physical activity to help curb her obesity. It was obvious that he took after his mother's side of the family. Tall and big-boned were the traits he inherited from his mother's relatives, unlike the Mitchells who were short and somewhat weakly. Eddie never understood the attraction his parents had for one another. They just looked funny together.

"I didn't say I played tennis. I said I played with the racquet."

"Should I ask how?"

Martha stood up, her knees cracking as she straightened her legs. She walked a few steps and took a deep sigh. "Eddie, when I'm not working on my chores at the church, this is where I spend most of my time these days, just me, the yard, and my gazebo, and those damn bees. That constant buzzing drives me crazy. Hear it?" She crouched down, cupping her hand to her ear. "I tried knocking them down with a fly swatter, but they're too smart and fast for that, so one day when I was going through your closet, I saw your tennis racquet in the corner, and then I had a bright idea. And now I swat the bees with it."

"Why?" Eddie asked.

"They're carpenter bees. They drill holes in the gazebo."

"Can't you just spray them?"

"That's too easy."

Eddie slid forward, sitting on the edge of his chair. His mother was acting odd, and she looked odd. But then again, she's always been odd, he told himself. She ordered Eddie to sit still and he complied.

"See that bee over there hovering?" she asked in a gentler voice as to not disturb the bee just outside the gazebo. Eddie grinned while thinking that the bee had to be amused with his mother's antics. Perhaps the bee didn't hear his mother, but there was no way that the curious insect couldn't see her awkward stance. "Don't move," Martha ordered. Eddie obeyed as he watched his mother creep off the gazebo and onto the lawn, stalking the bee hovering under the eave with the same stealth aggression of an overweight jaguar. With one fell swoop, Martha swatted the bee with the racquet, knocking it to the ground.

"Wow, you killed it!" Eddie exclaimed with a bit of restraint as he rose from his chair.

With the kind of pride that comes with a successful hunt, Martha defiantly responded by saying, "Hell no, I didn't kill it. I just want the little sucker to know who owns what around here, that's all. He'll be up in a minute or two, wanting more of this," she said as she held the racquet up in the air as a symbol of strength and superiority.

"How do you know it's a he?"

"They got bigger eyes than the female," she answered, leaning down and staring at her stunned prey.

Eddie cleared his throat, and with a more serious tone, he said, "Mom, I want to tell you something, something big."

Ignoring Eddie's statement, Martha continued with her anatomy lesson on the male carpenter bee. "The male bee doesn't have a stinger."

"Seriously, Mom. I want to talk to you about something."

Martha stood up, and with her hands on her hips and a condescending glare in her eyes that Eddie remembered from his childhood that was only enhanced by the heavy eye shadow, she said, "I see. You couldn't just drop in after two years and just say hello. Now you gotta make some big announcement, just like you did when you let me and your daddy know you was gay."

"Mom, I'm a grown man. I didn't want to keep it a secret any longer."

"We all have secrets. Seems like everybody in town knew about yours. Everybody but me and your daddy. Every time I went to play bingo, them old women would walk by, say hello, tell me how good my hair looked, and then they'd ask me how my gay son in Charlotte was doing."

"Sounds like they were okay with it."

"Hardly. They usually finished the conversation by saying they would pray for me."

"Sorry, I didn't mean to shame you."

"Well...you did. Course, I guess a few extra prayers never hurt no one."

"Mom, I want you to know that Larry and I, well, we're getting married."

"Lord, Jesus!" Martha screamed as she held one hand still clutching the racquet over her heart, the other against the gazebo post.

"In New York," Eddie added.

"Oh, my word!" his mother wailed as her head fell back. "I didn't see this coming! Lord, forgive me for my sins!"

"Mom, don't get upset. I just want your blessing," Eddie pleaded. "Just your blessing."

Martha took a deep breath, and just as quickly as though she had an on-and-off switch for her emotions, she bent down and said, "That bee still hasn't moved! I think I killed him. Usually, they lay stunned for a few minutes and then they get back up. I hope I didn't hit it too hard. You know the male doesn't have a stinger. I guess I already told you that. He just hovers around waiting for the female to come by and then he releases this pheromone scent that attracts her, and then they mate. Course, you wouldn't know much about that, you know, mating."

"I just want your blessing, that's all," Eddie said softly.

"Oh, the bingo ladies will have a field day with this one, won't they? They probably already know about it. I'm sure they've already started praying for me."

Eddie watched his mother step back onto the gazebo floor and sit in her chair. He quietly followed her and once again sat next to her. A few minutes of silence followed. "So how's Dad?"

Martha was still for a moment. "Same, I guess. I think he's lost his mind."

"What do you mean?"

Martha covered her eyes from the sun peeking through the trees. "See that big foundation over there made out of cinder blocks? Your daddy invested twelve-hundred dollars in that contraption. Twelve-hundred dollars that we didn't have to spare. Hope you don't want any money, 'cause I don't have any to give."

"I'm not wanting any money," Eddie reassured his mother. "So what's that thing supposed to be? It looks like cinder blocks just stacked together."

"Worms," Martha said, a scowl coming across her face.

"Worms?"

"Yeah, worms. He was going to raise worms."

"Like a worm farm?" Eddie chuckled at the thought of his father harvesting slimy little creatures for profit.

"It ain't funny, but yeah, like that. A worm farm. Some people sell the worms for fishing, but he was gonna make a lot of money on worm poop. 'Helps the soil, like a fertilizer,' so he said."

"So what happened?"

Martha paused, then scratched her neck. "Well, he loaded it up with worms and garbage and everything was going fine until winter came. A deep freeze killed every last one of 'em. I know all things come to an end, but if you ask me, the reason all them worms died was because he didn't read the manual on how to take care of the little poopers when it got cold."

"Sounds like an ill-advised business adventure."

"It gets worse," Martha said. She began to rock her body back and forth, and then she stopped abruptly. "So in the spring he planted the bed full of strawberry plants. They were beautiful, and we had a good crop of the biggest berries you ever saw, probably from all that worm poop. And in one night, slugs ate most of them even after I warned him. He either didn't read the instructions on how to kill the slugs or he just forgot to put protection down to keep those slimy critters away." She hesitated as she fought the tears welling up in her eyes, then smiled ironically. "But we got enough to make some jam. About twelve jars of strawberry jam. Twelve damn jars of strawberry jam is what we got."

Eddie was careful not to interrupt, but he wanted to console his mother. Trying to be positive, he said, "Well, at least you got something out of it."

Once again, Martha glared at her son with that you're going to hell look. "Eddie," she said, gritting her teeth, "do the math in your head. It cost us twelve-hundred dollars to set up that patch. Now divide that by twelve. Those twelve jars of jam cost us a hundred dollars each," she said raising her voice. "No kind of jam is worth that kind of money. I was so sick about it I couldn't even eat any of it. Gave every one of 'em to the bingo ladies." Martha shook her head in disgust. "I'll probably plant daylilies in that darn thing. Nothing much kills them, you know."

Again, Eddie was at a loss for words, and even less careful about how to segue in to the next topic. "And where is Dad? I thought he'd be here."

Martha grinned and looked up as though she were searching for the right words. "Oh, he's made friends with the music director at the church, a young man they hired from Charlotte. Your daddy's over there at his apartment all the time. Guess he finds Nicky a whole lot more fun to be around than being with me. But that's okay. Nicky's a likable fellow. Quite charming, as a matter of fact. And he and your daddy get along just fine. He's mocha, you know."

"Mocha?"

"Yes, mocha. Since Nicky's been here, he's been educating us about the right kind of terminology to use, especially about race and other cultures."

"So, Nicky is black?" Eddie asked.

"We don't use that word, or colored, or African-American any more. We don't even use the N-word either. In fact, I'm not even supposed to use the term, the N-word. But to answer your question, Nicky is mocha."

"So Dad's friends with a black man? I can't believe it."

Martha giggled. "Yeah, I guess you could say that, but please use the right words around him. Yeah, your daddy's changed, at least in some ways, but not in others."

"What do you mean?"

"Well, he keeps making really strange decisions as if he didn't learn from his mistakes from before. His new investment is in raising cocker spaniels. He said Nicky talked him into it, but I don't believe that for a minute. Who in the hell buys cocker spaniels these days? Lord, they've been inbred so much they're nothing more than furry little prissy pissers." Martha walked over to the grass, bending over to observe the bee she had earlier knocked to the ground. "This one's been out for a long time. Hope I didn't hit it too hard. Come on little bee. Move your wings," she said as she nudged it with her racquet.

"Can't say when I last heard of anyone who owned a cocker spaniel," Eddie said softly.

"Hell, even I know that beagles would bring in more money than those four-legged lap yelpers. And don't ask me how much he invested in that project. He wouldn't even tell me." Martha's body froze stiff as she caught sight of another carpenter bee. "Stay still!" she whispered to her son. She stood in a motionless position for a good two minutes luring the bee closer to her, when suddenly without any warning she began swatting the racquet erratically at the insect, eventually knocking it to the ground.

Eddie had only been home for a very short while, but he'd been there long enough to know that his family was very different than before. The change was quite remarkable. His racist and bigoted father now had a black friend, and his mother, though still a bit cynical, was more eccentric than ever, wore brightly colored clothes and god-awful makeup, and conducted daily raids on carpenter bees.

"So what's with the rhinestone earrings? I've never seen you wear anything like them before."

"Cause you ain't been around to see me wear them!" Martha snapped back, still standing over her bees on the ground. "Your daddy gave them to me last year for our anniversary. I thought we'd go out to dinner that night, but he came home with these instead. Said Nicky helped pick them out for me."

Eddie felt intrigued with the new man in his parents' lives as his mother told him about how Nicky came to the small community, and how he single handedly took over the church events. Once a month Nicky hosted a Tupperware party on Saturday afternoon, and he sold Avon products out of the church every Wednesday night right after choir practice. Thursday nights were Movie Classic nights, and of course, bingo was held on the regular Monday evenings as before, but Nicky added a few special games to add excitement to the somewhat mundane event. It seemed to Eddie that this stranger was a whirlwind of fresh air in a somewhat slow-paced western Carolina town.

"So, is Dad coming home soon?" Eddie asked as Martha appeared to complete her list of Nicky's accomplishments.

"You mean in the next few minutes? I know you've stayed too long already. I can tell. You never could sit very long in one place. And no, he's spending the evening over at Nicky's. Seems they have to work on planning some fishing trip or something." Martha paused for a moment. "Eddie, I saw that *Brokeback Mountain* movie. You don't think he's gonna take his fishing gear and not really go fishing, if you know what I mean."

"You're kidding. You saw *Brokeback Mountain*?"

"Nicky showed it on movie night. Does that surprise you?"

"No, well…actually, yes. But about Dad not going fishing, of course not, not Dad."

"It was just a thought. Just a thought. I felt Nicky might be gay when I first met him in church, you know with his well-manicured fingernails and his perfectly shaped eyebrows, but apparently he isn't. Word has it that a woman's been seen going in and out of his apartment on a regular basis, mostly on Friday nights. Thelma Goddard said she saw the woman herself and that she looked like a hooker or a stripper 'cause she was wearing so much makeup and she had on long eyelashes, and she had her hair teased up real high. Said the woman looked like she could be Nicky's sister. But then you know Thelma can't see without her glasses, and she never wears them. You remember her, don't you?"

"Vaguely. Didn't she work at the bank?"

"Yeah, that's her. That Thelma never could count money correctly either." Martha inhaled the morning air, then slowly let it back out. "Eddie, I think it's the fog."

"The fog?"

"Yeah. The blue fog. Remember how your grandmother used to talk about the fog? Well, I think it came. It had to be the fog," Martha said with a puzzled look in her eyes.

Eddie recalled the many Sunday nights as a boy at his grandmother's house when after dinner, the family would sit on the porch, and facing the late evening sun she'd tell the tales of the blue fog. Whether folklore or Cherokee myth, his grandmother would speak of the fog with respect and reverence in her voice. According to her account, in late fall or early spring, if the blue fog rolled down from the mountain into the valley just as the temperature reached the freezing point, the fog would be so dense that even the best hunter or trapper would lose his way. The fog carried with it supernatural powers, sometimes good, sometimes evil, but always a spirit of change. Of course, Eddie never saw a real blue fog, and if he had, he didn't remember it. But he now listened to his mother, sounding so much like her mother before her, talk about the fog and how the changes in the Carolina community may have been the result of the frozen mist engulfing the valley and all who lived there.

"The fog came in March. I remember it well. I was worried about the lilies popping their heads up, and then the weatherman said there was a chance of a freeze, but he didn't say nothing about the fog. But anyway, that very next day, Nicky shows up at church with the newspaper ad for a new choir director. The pastor hired him on the spot. Things have been different ever since."

Not quite as superstitious as his mother, Eddie muttered, "Could be coincidental."

Martha shook her head in disagreement then shifted her attention to the bees. Seemed that each time she didn't want to talk or hear about something that disturbed her, she focused on her prey. "Got two down on the ground and, hey look. That first one is coming around. Look at him walk and flutter those wings. He's a bit wet from the dew. He's mad as hell. Look at him trying to get his little brain back together. He's real mad now. Watch him make that circle and then, like magic, there he goes, flying away," she said, her eyes following the soaring bee. "But he'll be back. Happens like that every time. I used to just kill them right off, and then I decided to play their game and watch them get angry with me. It gives me something to do, and they keep coming back, getting in my face when I work in the yard, making that annoying buzzing sound. I used to just kill them, but then I started to read about them, understanding them, you know, that they have a right to live and do what the good Lord put them here to do. Don't know why they keep coming back, but they usually do."

"I would think that if you keep on swatting them down like that then eventually they wouldn't come back. You know, they'd stay away from you."

"Is that supposed to be some kind of what they call a metaphor or something like that?"

"If you think it is, then maybe it is. Mom, I've gotta go. I'm sorry, I shouldn't have just dropped in like I did."

"You're not going to wait and watch this other one come around, or maybe help me plant my lily?" Martha asked with an air of desperation, apparent that she wanted Eddie to stay for a while longer.

The sound of a car door being slammed shut came from the front of the house. Both Martha and Eddie looked at each other. Perhaps it was Eddie's father.

"Martha! Martha, are you home?"

"It's Nicky," Martha announced. "Holy shit, I forgot about the cookies. He was supposed to come by to pick them up."

Nicky quickly appeared from the side of the house. "There you are, sweet lady!" he yelled as he sashayed toward the gazebo. It was obvious to Eddie that from the moment Nicky appeared that he was one of the gayest men he'd ever seen. But not only that, he also sensed he knew him, only he couldn't quite remember from where. The man's hands fluttered in the air with each step, his clothes were tight-fitting and fashionably coordinated with a small sparkling rhinestone broach pinned to his collar, and, yes, just as his mother had stated, his eyebrows were perfectly shaped.

"He always calls me that," Martha mumbled under her breath. A smile came over her face as her new friend approached.

"I hope I'm not interrupting," Nicky said as he stepped onto the gazebo, reaching out his hand for Eddie to shake. "I'm Nicky."

"This is Eddie, my gay son from Charlotte," Martha stated as the two men shook hands.

"Ah, yes," the choir director said, his eyes widening, his hand still clutched to Eddie's. "The gay son from Charlotte. And a big one you are as well."

"Yeah, I guess that one would be me," Eddie replied as if his mother had other gay sons in other cities. He pulled his hand away from Nicky's grip.

"Well, it's a pleasure to meet you. I've heard so much about you from your parents, and how proud they are of you."

"Proud?" Eddie asked, a bit shocked, in a tone that questioned the sincerity of the statement.

"Oh, yes. All the time," Nicky added, his hands now placed on his hips as though he were posing. He turned to Martha. "Well, I won't interrupt your visit. I just came by to pick up those wonderful cookies you promised for the church bake sale. I know you've baked 'em, 'cause I can smell 'em," he said as he gyrated his slim body in sync with his words.

"Lord, yes they're done. They've been cooling off, and then Eddie came, and I got to talking and..." She blushed, then politely shifted her muumuu in place. "It won't take me but a minute to get them bagged up. Yeah, just give me a minute. You two stay right here and chat and I'll be right back."

Martha quickly waddled through the yard to the backdoor and disappeared into the kitchen.

"Gosh, I feel like I know you from somewhere," Eddie said, breaking the short bit of silence.

"Well, I used to live in Charlotte," Nicky confessed.

"So what brought you here?"

"I was looking for opportunity, you know, to get more involved with the church, and I saw an ad in the paper, and I thought what the heck? So I drove over and applied, and voila, I got the job. Of course, I've had to make some adjustments, but I love it here, and Charlotte's not that far away. I go back there every Friday night."

"Oh my God, that's where I know you from," Eddie exclaimed.

"Why, what do you mean?" Nicky asked as though some big secret was about to be revealed.

"You're Mocha, aren't you?" Eddie stated with the excitement of a rooky detective on a big case, and without giving the time to have his question answered, he added, "And you perform at Scorpios on Friday nights, don't you?"

Nicky paused, then said, "Yes, that would be me. So, I suppose you'll be telling the world about this, won't you?"

"Are you kidding? I think it's great. I don't know what you're doing around here, but I've only been back for a short time, and all I've heard from Mom is 'Nicky this and Nicky that', and well, there are the bees of course, but primarily, you're all she's talked about. A lot of changes have been happening. I'm assuming for the good."

"I'm hoping so," Nicky said, still a bit apprehensive about the revelation.

Eddie leaned over, getting quite close to Nicky, and whispered, "My partner thinks you're the greatest. He loves your Patty Labelle performances."

Nicky straightened his back and lifted his head as he felt a wave of comfort come over his body. "That's too funny, you know, this coincidence and all."

Without any warning, Eddie blurted out, "Nicky, are you having an affair with my father?"

"What?" Nicky howled, a bit taken aback with the bold accusation.

"My mother might be thinking you're having an affair with my father because of the fishing trips that you guys take, and how he hangs out with you so much." Eddie suddenly found himself boxed uncomfortably in a corner.

"Eddie," Nicky said somberly. "Your father can't read."

"He can't read? Of course, he can read."

"No, he can't. When I first came to the church, he was showing me plans for the parking lot expansion, and I asked him to read the summary report to me. He put me off, and I just sensed that something wasn't right. I challenged him, and he admitted he couldn't read it because he didn't have his glasses with him. I offered him my readers, and don't you whisper to a soul that I wear them, and that's when he told me that he couldn't read. Not sure why he chose to tell me, but he just came out and confessed right then and there."

"So that explains the directions about protecting the worms, and not killing the slugs…and how he never wanted to read with me," Eddie said.

"Yeah, it explains a lot. So, your dad and me, well, we have reading classes every weekend and whenever we can get together. There's nothing going on between us. I mean seriously, he's not gay and he doesn't care for black people."

"But you're mocha," Eddie interrupted with a laugh.

"You've heard? Well, yes, I am," Nicky responded with a gay chuckle of his own. "Next time you visit I'll explain that whole mocha thing to you."

"But what's with the rhinestone earrings? I mean, with Mom, I kind of get it, but you'll have to agree with me that they look ridiculous on Ida."

"When she's got her teeth in, she looks pretty presentable," Nicky said sarcastically. "Eddie, it's about how people feel about themselves. With the Avon products, the flattery, the sense of belonging, and yes, the glamour of the rhinestone earrings, these women feel there's at least a spark of attractiveness still left in their aging bodies."

"But Ida Simpson?" Eddie questioned.

"Oh honey, you haven't seen Thelma Goddard lately, have you? She makes Ida look like a young movie star. Thelma wears more makeup than anyone in town, and it's a bit creepy how she looks like Betty Davis in *Whatever Happened to Baby Jane?*. Now that's scary," Nicky added.

"Don't know if you've heard, but Mom thinks you're here because of the blue fog."

Nicky, leaned back and smiled flirtatiously. "Maybe I am. But I like to think it's the rhinestone magic."

"Rhinestone magic?"

"Yeah, there's something about the sparkle. It's magical. But really, Eddie, these people just confuse what's in the head with what's in the heart. They just need to see things from a different perspective."

"Yeah, I guess."

"Here, I want you to have this," Nicky said as he grasped his collar and unpinned his broach.

"Oh, I can't take that," Eddie responded.

"I won't take 'no' for an answer, and anyway, I have plenty more," he said as he held the silver-stoned piece with one hand, slipping his other hand between two buttons to the inside of Eddie's shirt, fastening it in place. "There. Now you're one of us."

Eddie reluctantly agreed, "Yeah, I guess I am. But what does that really mean?"

"You'll know in time," Nicky said as he nodded his head. "You'll know."

"But when will I know?"

Nicky smiled. "No one ever knows when. Just know that it will happen, some day, some time."

The creaking sound of the screen door opening and closing ended the conversation between the two men. "Here they are, all packaged and ready to sell," Martha hollered as she approached the gazebo. She stopped in front of the couple. "Eddie, did Nicky give you that broach?"

"Yes, he did," Eddie replied, a bit embarrassed to being wearing jewelry, especially a piece so gaudy.

"Looks just like the one your daddy wears," Martha said as she examined the broach closely.

"Dad wears rhinestones?"

"Everyone around here does," Nicky answered. "I must go now. Eddie, it was nice to meet you," he said as they shook hands.

"You too," Eddie replied, acting as though the two were mere acquaintances who had just met.

Martha handed the large paper grocery bag full of wrapped cookies to Nicky. Both she and Eddie watched as he walked to his car. Before turning the corner, Nicky yelled, "See you in church on Sunday, sweet lady!"

"And wearing my earrings!" Martha quipped back as Nicky disappeared around the side of the house. She and her son listened as Nicky backed down the driveway onto the main road.

"Nice man, that Nicky," Martha said quietly.

"Mom, I need to go. Tell Dad I said hello."

"Yeah, I'll do that. I'll tell him."

"Bye now," Eddie said, an awkwardness in his voice. He wasn't sure if he should just walk away, reach for a hug or even stay a bit longer. He turned and slowly left the frame of the gazebo.

"Eddie, wait. How about Sunday dinner next week?"

"You're inviting me?" Eddie asked.

"I guess I am. Say around four?"

Eddie paused. "Sure. I'd like that."

"And bring Harry if you want."

"His name is Larry, and yes, I want to."

"That's right. Larry," Martha said softly. "I'll try to remember that."

The two stared at each other, just for a moment, when Eddie said, "So, I guess you're giving us your blessing, you know, for the wedding."

"Let's just start with dinner. I'd like to meet this friend of yours first."

"That's fair," Eddie said as he nodded his head in agreement. "But he's more than just a friend."

"Give me time, Eddie. Just a little time."

"I can do that. Think Dad will be here for dinner?"

Martha's brow furled up. "Who knows, but probably not. I'm sure he and Nicky will be going fishing like they usually do every weekend. Maybe I'll invite Nicky, that way your daddy will be here too."

"That would be nice."

"Eddie, I have a piece of advice for you. Just know that marriage ain't what it's cracked up to be. It's not all that great, but it ain't all that bad either. Just remember that." Martha picked up her racquet from the ground, and in finding the comfort she needed in escaping from reality, she began to coax the carpenter bee still lying on the ground. "Come on bee, start moving them wings."

"I will. I'll remember that. See you on Sunday," Eddie said walking to his car knowing that his mother was now oblivious to his comment or presence.

"Come on now," Martha demanded of the bee. "I can't hang out here all day," she scolded. "I've got some digging to do. Get up, and start spreading them pheromones. That's right, get mad now. Come on, come on and fly, you little sucker." She watched the bee awaken and take flight, soaring out of the reach of her domain. Suddenly, she heard the sound of Eddie's car engine starting. Her body went limp. "That's right, fly away," she said with sadness. "But don't forget to come back. Don't ever forget to come back."

Driving toward the switchbacks at the base of the mountains, Eddie grimaced in anticipation of the carsickness that lay ahead of him. The visit went better than anticipated, he thought aloud, and his face beamed in awe thinking about the changes that had taken place in his old neighborhood. It was as if his parents and neighbors were living in their own weird and eerie version of the *Andy Griffith Show*, but directed by Rod Serling. It was a good thing. Complicated, odd, but good.

Eddie passed the last house on the left where Ida Simpson sat on her porch with a glass of iced tea in her hand, her John Deere idle in the front yard. She smiled, showing off her famous over-sized gums and waved as Eddie drove by, a gleam in her eyes, and a sparkle of glitz from the rhinestone earrings that dangled from her ears. *She just didn't look right*, Eddie thought to himself as he waved back. Then, just as he headed down the lane, he thought how pretty she looked in pink. Suddenly, there was a jolt and the bucket seat jerked back a few inches leaving Eddie the legroom he needed to be comfortable. *Coincidence?* he asked himself as he shook his head, perplexed by what had just happened. He ran his fingers over the broach pinned to his shirt. *Perhaps there was truth to the rhinestone magic after all*, he thought. He felt a pleasant tingle in his feet as he pressed harder against the accelerator.

"No way," he said out loud. "No way."

The Red Coat
George E. Jordan

1971. New Orleans.

The light was turning into the gray of evening while John McNeal left the motor running in his car and walked to the outside mailbox of the post office. It was a cool evening but the December wind had not yet whipped the leaves of the banana plants making them look like tattered gowns for gypsies—the first sign of winter in New Orleans.

John had arrived in October, happy that his company had transferred him from Kentucky. Here, although almost Christmas, he could still drive around with the top down on his car. John paused to watch workman unload a shipment of Christmas trees in a vacant lot. Some of the trees had ice clinging to the ropes that held their branches closed. He shivered at the thought of how cold it must be in Kentucky.

Returning to his car, he noticed a frail figure looking into the open window. He started to drive away but something about the person fascinated him. She had a boyish appearance with short bobbed hair, not at all like the long unruly hair styles the hippies and flower children had recently made so popular. This lady looked elegant, way out of the league of the women John usually met. He couldn't tell her age and for a moment he wasn't certain if she was a young man or woman. At 40, he was having trouble getting used to the younger generation's androgynous appearance. He was, however, enjoying their sexual freedom.

In her casual blazer and neatly pressed slacks, he was pleased to see someone so put together and lovely. As a friend had joked about some of his hippie conquests: "You have no idea what you've brought home 'till you get it in the bath tub and cleaned up a bit." At first he thought she was admiring the car's black leather interior and polished wooden dashboard. But then he realized it was his coat she was eyeing. He usually kept his red corduroy coat with the fur-trimmed collar in the seat next to him. If the evenings turned cold, he slipped on the coat instead of bothering to raise the top of the car. He sat for a moment observing her.

"I wasn't going to take it," she said, blushing at his look, "I was only admiring it." The voice reminded him of an old Lauren Bacall movie, low and sensual with a quality that commanded attention and respect.

He had heard about the old aristocratic Creole families, an outsider like himself would never be privileged to meet. Often when he drove past the shuttered townhouses in the French Quarter or walked past the columned mansions in the Garden District of the city, he dreamed about the slow manner of 19th century life that might exist behind the walls.

"Oh I know that you were not going to take it," he said and smiled. "It isn't yet cold enough for a coat that heavy, besides, it would never fit you." He wanted to make her feel at ease.

Again she blushed. "It truly is a beautiful coat," she said allowing a tiny smile to creep across her lips. "It looks like one a modern-day Papa Noël would wear." She looked him full in the face and flashed a sincere smile without blushing.

John laughed. He knew about Papa Noël, but he was unaware the New Orleans creoles still used this French name for Santa Claus. He had often been compared to Santa Claus, since he was large in stature, not fat, but burly. He had a short beard which was beginning to show signs of gray. He sincerely liked people and his eyes had a way of sparkling that made strangers feel at ease. He was fully aware that when he wore the red coat with its fur-trimmed collar, he might pass for a contemporary version of Santa Clause—Papa Noël.

"Thank you. I have always had the greatest admiration for the man," he replied.

The woman smiled again. John kept looking at her trying to decide her age and perhaps her sex. She wore little make-up and she had a quality he had hoped to find in all Southerners. Yet, she was rather thinly clad for the evening coolness. For a moment he thought perhaps she really was planning to take the coat. But she seemed to be a true lady and nothing in her appearance or manner revealed a need for money. She had, John thought, a look of quiet security, whether male or female.

"It's starting to turn cooler. Could I possibly have the honor of driving you to your home?" John felt awkward about the way he phrased his question. He would have never said this to anyone he didn't know in Kentucky or even anyone he had met in the bars on Bourbon Street, "May I have the honor of driving you home?" He considered himself a gentleman, but even a gentleman today was not that genteel. Something made him feel this person should be treated in the old style.

"Would you mind terribly?" She said, "It is getting cold and I came out without my wrap. The sun was so lovely this afternoon; I stayed much later than expected."

John was startled that this lovely stranger would consider getting into the car with another stranger. She opened the door and slipped into the seat next to him. He watched her long slender hands gracefully fold his corduroy coat and place it over her lap.

"Do you always get into cars with strange men?" John stammered showing his surprise.

"No—never."

"Then why are you in the car with me?"

"Because you look gentle, and I suspect very kind."

Her statement was so matter-of-fact that John was at a loss for words. He wondered if this was the way Southern ladies seduced their men. Something about her made him feel like a little boy. He imagined himself falling all over his big feet trying to be overly formal with this person. The color quickly returned to his face, making his eyes twinkle.

"And where may I drive you?"

"Go along the edge of the French Quarter, down Rampart Street to Esplanade. It isn't far by car." She stroked the fur collar on his coat like it was a kitten.

John was totally fascinated by her soft accent. He tried to think of something to ask so she would say more. But she began speaking again on her own.

"I saw you looking at the evergreen trees by the post office. Do you have a family to go to for Christmas?"

"No, just me."

"I'm very sorry. Everyone should have a family for Christmas. Your voice tells me you are not from here?"

"I'm from Kentucky. I have been here since October. I like it very much, especially the weather."

"We'll have our share of cold weather, probably in February just before Mardi Gras. The dampness here makes it more noticeable. But the sun continues to shine and the patios and gardens remain green. It is a lovely city, isn't it?"

"The loveliest I have ever seen."

"Really? And have you seen many cities?"

"Hundreds of them. You see, since I have no family the company I work for sends me all over the world. I like to travel, so I'm willing to go.

"Were you thinking of buying a tree for Christmas?" she asked.

"No. Christmas trees are no fun when you are alone. Don't get me wrong, I don't get lonely, it's that I think you should have someone special at Christmas before going to the trouble of a tree."

"Nonsense. I have one almost completely trimmed waiting for someone to help me add the final touches. There are always those special ornaments which require two, instead of one, to put them in their place."

This was not necessarily said like a hint, but John recognized it as a possible chance to get to know her better.

"By the way, my name is John McNeal."

"I know. I noticed it on the letters lying on the dashboard of your car. You may turn in here," she pointed, "the old carriageway is very narrow, but I think your car will fit nicely. Now I must invite you in so that you can see that I really was not intending to steal your lovely coat."

John fought to keep his excitement from showing. He slowly eased his car through the thick foliage that lined the old carriageway along the side of the house. The windows were shuttered and the jungle of tropical plants was so thick that only the tops of the porch columns could be seen from the street. John could feel the dampness on the giant elephant ear plants as they parted to let his car push its way deeper into the driveway.

"I must apologize," she said, "I don't keep a car and I allow the plants to grow large to keep out intruders. The tourists are terrible to open gates and gape through their cameras at these old houses. If they had to maintain one, perhaps they would change their minds."

When John stepped out of the car and held the door for his new-found friend, he was shocked at the depth of the house. It was four or five times deeper than the width which partially showed from the street. He glanced down the long carriageway through which he had just driven. Already the leaves had rearranged themselves in their lush greenness, appearing undisturbed. He was thrilled at the thought of being invited into one of these Creole mansions.

"My name is Desiree." She extended her hand with a smile. "Forgive me for not introducing myself before, but I am unaccustomed to meeting strangers. Most people know who I am so I never have to remind myself." Was there a slight coy flirtation in her voice when she spoke? John's eyes twinkled at the thought of this lovely creature leading him through the jungle to a brick wall with an iron gate.

"Desiree is a beautiful woman's name," John said.

"Oh?" she replied, "In French speaking countries it can also be a man's name, like Michel and Renee, Americans always think those are girls' names. The spelling of the name reveals the gender."

"I didn't know that. What does Desiree mean?"

"The desired one."

"And how do you spell your name? I'm sorry, that was rude of me the way I worded it."

"No, I don't mind. I can spell it for you, but will you know the difference? Do you speak French? With such a name I can be anything I want to be. I am a human being, a person. Why do I have to be placed into a category? In this case, gender. Why can't people like one another as people? Must we seduce everyone we meet? I don't think so. Just think of me as Desiree."

"The desired one," John smiled, totally confused.

"If you like," she returned the smile. "Does it matter?" She glanced at John's red coat. "Oh, your lovely coat," she said, "you mustn't leave it in the car. Boys often roam the streets looking for things to take. Please bring it in."

John started to protest, saying that he always left it in the car, but that silly schoolboy feeling came over him and he obeyed without a word. He loved the way the moisture embraced his body as he walked toward Desiree through the giant caladium plants growing throughout the patio.

She looked up at John's towering frame. "Watch your head. I'm afraid this gate was meant for the first creoles who lived here, not for a towering Norseman like yourself."

"When was it built?" he asked, carefully stepping through the gate.

"I think about 1810, but several rooms were added later. I keep much of it closed. No point in rambling around the place by myself. I do enjoy this patio. It's very private and there are lovely fruit trees in the rear."

Again, John was shocked that this person would bring a stranger to a house so secluded, it would be impossible for anyone to hear a scream for help. Watching her, he thought she might be in her late 30's, but perhaps it was only in the way she dressed. She might be younger. But what if she turns out to be an elegant young he? John had teased and flirted with the drag queens on Rampart Street. Some were so convincing that he often wondered what they would be like in bed. But he had never met anyone as lovely as Desiree.

"I hope you don't mind entering from the rear of the house. The front door hasn't been opened in years."

"This is a pretty grand rear entrance."

"It is, isn't it," she said. "I'm afraid some of my ancestors were terribly pretentious. It could use a new coat of paint but I don't want to pull down all of those lovely vines.

"Come along," she said standing on the steps, smiling at him. "It will be dark in a moment. I have to keep the shutters closed for safety. It is a shame, but it keeps out the dirt and noise from the street."

They entered a hall that was wider than most living rooms John had seen. The last rays of daylight, casting long shadows through the beveled glass windows of the front door revealed the extreme length of the hall. He caught a glimpse of a partially trimmed tree in the shadows.

"These vast halls were used for dances and parties during the 19th century. In here," she turned as she opened one of the doors. "I know that since you are in one of these decadent old places you probably think I shall bore you with a glass of sherry or tea, but a man your size probably prefers scotch or bourbon. I prefer bourbon, myself." She smiled over her shoulder while she led John into one of the side rooms.

He began to wonder if this was going to be a seduction in a grand New Orleans mansion. "I prefer scotch," he answered.

"Fine," she said, turning on the lamps in the room. "My father drank scotch. Scotch in the winter and gin in the summer. Everyone thinks all southerners drink bourbon, but I think I'm the only one in my family who ever liked it."

John expected the room to look like the outside of the house, neglected and crying for help. He half expected her to light candles or oil lamps instead of flicking on light switches. He was amazed. The room had a loved and cared-for look that generations had contributed.

"Please make yourself comfortable," Desiree said. "I'll get the ice. Do you take water or soda?"

"Just a little water, I like it strong."

"Good." She disappeared behind a Chinese screen at the end of the room.

John laid his red coat over the arm of an antique chair and sat on the more substantial looking sofa. A large crystal chandelier hung overhead and the light cast colors across the faces of portraits looking at him from the walls. He nervously rubbed his shoes across the thick oriental carpet. He was certain one of the ancestors on the walls was going to throw him out of the house before he received his scotch.

"She won't hurt you." John heard Desiree's voice from behind the screen. "As a matter of fact, she probably would have been frightened of you, you are so tall."

"How did you know what I was thinking?" John laughed, looking again at the portrait of one rather stern woman.

"I gathered from your silence that grandmother had caught your glance and was holding on," Desiree answered, entering the room carrying a silver tray of ice, water, decanters and two glasses. "When an artist is really good, I think he captures the soul of the sitter who then lives forever in the portrait."

John watched as she sat the tray on the table. He was impressed. Any one he knew would have gone to the kitchen, dumped the booze into the glasses, taken the ice from the freezer and carried them in hand to the room where he sat. When he picked up his glass, he was more impressed. It was heavy. He liked the way the design pressed into his hand when he squeezed it. Like Desiree, the glass had a feeling of lasting quality—a feeling of something that could be broken, but before it happened, it would leave a major imprint in the palm of your hand.

"When I invited you in for a drink, it didn't occur to me that I might be keeping you from something important," said Desiree while snuggling into an easy chair.

"I'm delighted that you came to my rescue," John replied.

"Your rescue?" she asked, peaking at him from over the rim of the sparkling glass.

"Of course. If you had not happened along, I would have ended up in some Bourbon Street bar quietly escaping the sound of Christmas carols. I had no one lined up for tonight," he blushed when he realized how he phrased his sentence, "I mean, I was planning to spend the evening alone."

"That's all right," she assured him.

He sipped his drink while he looked at her. *This is the joy of being 40 years old,* he thought. *Women are intrigued by me, from 18 through 80. I am still young enough to fascinate the young ones but old enough that the old ones don't feel foolish being seen with me. I wish I could stay this age forever. But how old is Desiree?* he wondered. *Is she really just being nice, or am I supposed to try something? I always thought I was an excellent make-out artist and I have never been afraid of elegant ladies, but this one has me baffled. Guess I had better leave it up to her. Besides, I'm enjoying being here too much.*

She watched John carefully while he studied her. "You have no one?"

"Just me," he said.

She paused for a moment, smiling innocently like a small child trying to make up her mind, and replied, "Then no one knows where you are. I could slit your throat and steal your pretty coat."

John was startled by her comment and laughed nervously. She laughed as she moved across the room to refill their drinks.

"Whatever I may be, I could never be a thief," she said in an attempt to put him at ease. "You see, I have everything I need here. I do like you, John McNeal. You have a marvelous beard, twinkling eyes—you shall be my new Papa Noël."

John relaxed and watched her. She looked like a child admiring a new toy when she spoke to him. She was so unlike any one he knew. At this moment, he didn't care about her age or whether she was a woman or a man. He stretched his long legs in front of him and sipped his drink. The scotch felt good. It was a very fine scotch and it gave the room an extra glow. Desiree was so perfect in all of it.

"Then you will have dinner with me," he announced.

"It's very early; we can eat here later tonight. I hate eating out in New Orleans, so many tourists. Besides, I am an excellent cook. But on one condition."

"Anything at all," John's excitement showed in his tone.

"Good," she gave him a full smile, "you will be my Papa Noël and help me finish trimming the tree."

"You're kidding."

"No, I should love to trim the tree with you. Will you do it for me—for us?"

He studied her fine features. Her lips were slightly full, but not seductive. More refined like in a classical painting. "All right, but only if you swear you are a fine cook."

"Wonderful! I know we'll make an occasion of it. Come along." She pulled him from the security of the sofa into the dark hall. "Stand right here. Don't move."

She positioned him in the middle of the floor. He felt like a child again, perhaps getting ready to count to a hundred and play hide-and-seek in this marvelous house. He could hear her behind the massive stairwell near the front door.

"Are you ready?" she waited a moment and said "Here goes." and flipped a light switch.

Overhead were six crystal chandeliers that lit up filling the hall with glittering light. Between the closed doors were mirrors framed in enormous golden branches held by cherubs, reflecting the sparkling light from the back of the hall to the glass door at the entrance.

"See? I told you some of my ancestors were terribly pretentious," laughed Desiree as she came from behind the stairwell.

The Christmas tree was glowing with lights and ornaments. But the room—John could hardly believe it. He had seen such grandeur in hotel lobbies and convention centers, but never in a private home. A great feeling of comfort and belonging came over him when he saw their reflection in one of the mirrors with the chandeliers reflecting golden light all around them.

"Isn't it a majestic tree?" Desiree purred and slipped her arm through John's. "It is truly worthy of us both."

Yes, John thought in silence, *it truly is worthy of us both*. He felt wonderful. *So this is what Christmas is like in a grand mansion with a true aristocrat*. He liked the feeling. He wondered if he was falling in love—or was it the scotch or the Christmas tree.

She pressed against his arm. "Now for the special part. I have boxes of ornaments that have been in the family for generations. Follow me to the very soul of the house."

Together they climbed the winding stairway to the top floor and continued up a smaller stairway to the attic.

"I adore attics," Desiree said looking deeply into John's eyes. "When I was a child, I played up here for hours, hiding from the servants. Be careful, the stairs are narrow and steep, watch your head on the door—you are so tall.

"You stay here," whispered Desiree, "I know where everything is."

The attic sprawled over the entire front of the house. Bizarre patterns of light created by the street lamps outside danced across the floor. He waited quietly in the dim light and watched while she carried several boxes to the center of the room.

"This one is very special, we must be extra careful with it. Here, hold out your arms. I'll place these three flat ones and this lovely glass one on top. Now do be careful. I'll take the other two."

He glanced into the box. Peering through the dust at him were tiny figures, dozens of them, each in its own little compartment. He studied the detail of their dress and features. These delicate dolls made especially for Desiree's tree looked so real. John followed her down the narrow attic steps. He felt as special as her lovely ornaments.

"Are they wax or glass?" John asked. He had seen pictures of the perfect glass and wax figures fashioned in the 19th century for royalty in Europe. Surely, Desiree's family would have had no less.

"Perhaps," she said as she lead the way down the great stairway. "Aren't they lovely? Some of them are very old and probably a bit worn, especially their costumes. The cloth is real, you know. I wonder if some should be replaced. Especially the angels, it seems there just aren't any angels left in the world." She tossed her head and for a moment he was certain she was flirting with him.

John liked it. He liked her. He liked everything around him. "I think you placed magic in my scotch," he said.

"Whatever for?" she laughed.

"Plain old scotch never gave me this kind of enchantment before. You—this place—the Christmas tree."

"Enchantment or illusion? I think everything is an illusion. Perhaps at the moment of death we are shown which is truly real and which is an illusion. Perhaps it is your red coat that has given us a moment of magic out of the bacon-and-eggs reality of our everyday lives. Here, give me the precious beauties for the tree. I'll fix you a scotch. This time with lots of ice."

Desiree placed a few of the smaller antique chairs around the tree. On a table sat the silver tray with their drinks.

"I can't sit on one of those," he laughed. "I'm too heavy."

"Don't be silly, Papa Noël. My grandfather, though short, weighed much more. These are very sturdy chairs. Now sit and drink your scotch while I go and change. A lady should always look her best when assisting Papa Noël. I won't be but a moment."

John obeyed her command, sipped his drink and watched while she glided gracefully up the stairs. He tried to make himself comfortable on one of the antique chairs. It was sturdy as she had said it would be, but his legs were much too long. He stood up and admired the luxury around him. It was almost impossible to believe that he, John McNeal, an ordinary guy from Kentucky could be in such fabulous surroundings helping a real aristocrat trim a Christmas tree. And what a tree; what a lady. He poured another tumbler of scotch and studied his reflection in one of the massive mirrors. He extended his arm toward his reflection and was about to drink a toast to himself when a vision in white appeared alongside of him.

"I told you I would be only a moment. Now you can drink a toast to both of us. A Christmas toast." Desiree slowly and deeply curtsied in front of him.

John watched her natural gracefulness in the mirror. He had only seen that kind of grace in movies. Her gown was the color of ivory with yards of material that swept the floor. Somewhere in his mind he remembered the description he had once read of a southern lady: The rustle of satin and the fragrance of lemon. Looking at her at this very moment, how could she be anything but a real woman?

"To Desiree," he said lifting his glass to her reflection, "May you have the Merriest of Christmases forever and ever."

"Regardless of the spelling?" she teased.

"Regardless of the speling," he replied.

"Thank you, my kind Papa Noël." She took the heavy glass from his hand and glided toward the decanter on the table. "Only a slight more scotch for you until we finish the tree. Oh, perhaps a little sip here and there." She placed one of the boxes on the table.

"You must be especially careful with my precious little people," she said when she opened the glass cover of the dusty box. "They are so delicate. See? Here is a little soldier, a dancer, almost every profession is in the box. They are very fragile and some are very old." She held a tiny ballerina up to the light so John could admire the detail. "These we will hang rather low so we can admire their beauty. I can't decide which one I like the best."

John watched her every move while she carefully tied each tiny figure to the branches of the great tree. He was afraid to touch them, they were much too delicate for his large hands.

"There now," she said as she backed away from the tree. "Each and every one is in place. Isn't it a lovely sight? Come, time to refresh our drinks and turn on the music."

"The music?"

"You'll see." Desiree walked to the end of the room and placed a large brass disc into a rosewood box. Turning the handle on the side, she opened the lid. "Now listen."

The music box filled the house with a tinkling waltz. He sipped his drink and watched while Desiree danced with her reflection in the mirrors, slowly moving toward him down the long wide hall.

"Do you like my pretty gown?" she flirted.

"It's gorgeous—you're gorgeous."

"Thank you. I was afraid it had yellowed, but it is still in perfect condition. My great-grandmother wore it the year she was Queen of Carnival. We all descend from royalty in New Orleans, one way or another. I wear it every year when we trim the tree."

We. John liked the sound of we.

"Now come dance with me." She held out her hands to him. "It's a very simple waltz, you can do it—one, two, three—see? It's quite easy. Wonderful! Look, everyone, see how lovely John dances!"

To John the music seemed never ending and he hoped it would not. They danced up and down the great hall and around the sparkling tree all the while watching their reflection in the mirrors.

"But it's not complete," she smiled, "you must put on your lovely coat. Then I'll really be dancing with Papa Noël."

John quickly walked into the next room and returned wearing his red coat with the fur collar.

"Perfect," she cooed handing him another full glass of scotch. She leaned toward him on her toes and kissed him on the lips. It was so sudden, he didn't have time to hold her and return the kiss. She danced away from him toward the center of the hall.

"Look, everyone, I'm dancing with Papa Noël. Isn't he splendid?" She kept her eyes on his gaze, smiling the entire time, waltzing toward his outstretched arms.

This time he held her closer, not moving his feet, but allowing his body to sway in time to the music. She was light and delicate to the touch. In her white gown, she reminded him of one of the ornaments on the tree. *How truly desirable this person is*, he thought.

I could squeeze and crush her with one hand, she is so fragile, he thought as she leaned close to him. He felt high, but this high was much lighter and more beautiful than any he had experienced.

Again her lips touched his, only this time she held them there like a butterfly gathering nectar from a flower. He closed his eyes and lifted her body off the floor and held her as he danced her around the tree.

"You're wonderful," she smiled, "but I shall have to make you a red hat to match your coat. You will be the youngest Papa Noël I have ever had."

He didn't speak. He wanted to dance with her in his arms forever.

The lights reflecting in the mirrors along the hall began to blur. Her face shone like a golden light on his. Still they danced. He was warm but not from the weight of the coat or the dancing.

"Look, I'm getting closer to you," she teased.

He opened his eyes. It seemed as if she was closer to his face. He did not have to look down or hold her up in the air to kiss her lips. "It's the scotch," he murmured. "We shall dance until I am sober again. We shall dance forever and forever." He closed his eyes and rested his massive bearded head on her shoulder. Perhaps he was stooping too much, but he was so comfortable and holding her in his arms was so lovely.

They continued to dance. She began to lead, holding him gently and slowly moving around and around the room. Several times he opened his eyes to reassure himself that this was all real. The tree seemed to grow bigger and Desiree became less tiny.

Damn the scotch, he thought, *the happiest moment of my life and I had to drink too much. Still she didn't seem to mind.* They were dancing, lightly—ever so lightly. She was as happy as he, he could tell by the reassuring smiles when he opened his eyes and looked up into her face. *Up,* he thought, *how could he be looking up? No matter. Everything is so beautiful and feels so good.*

John could hear the music getting louder and louder. He could feel his feet still moving with her frail strong arms guiding him around the room, but instead of the warm flesh of her neck, he was aware that his head was resting in the folds of her white gown.

Is she seducing me? he thought. *My God, what are we doing?*

He looked up. Desire was still holding him, smiling sweetly down at him and swaying to the sounds of the music box.

"Keep dancing," she said in her lovely alto voice, "we are almost there."

Too confused and drunk to think, he obeyed her regal command. Perhaps he was having some sort of bizarre sexual experience with her and he was too drunk to understand it. But he obeyed and continued to dance, the liquor creeping over him like a warm delicate blanket.

The room and everything around him became black for what seemed like a moment. He rubbed his eyes and reached out for Desiree, but she was not there. The floor seemed soft as if a deep carpet had been placed under his feet. The music began to hurt his ears.

"Desiree!" he cried out.

"I'm here," she whispered, "See? Keep dancing."

His feet continued to move across the white cushioned carpet. He stopped rubbing his eyes. He stopped dancing. Desiree was looking into his face, smiling.

"What's happened?" he tried to scream, but the music overpowered the sound of his cries. He looked down. He could see only darkness.

Desiree's face was like a giant head on a billboard. The tiny wrinkles in her flesh were like deep crevices; her smiling mouth was like an ugly cavern. She held him up in front of her face. He could see his reflection in her eyes. He was dancing in the palm of her hand. He screamed again, but there was no sound.

"Look my precious little ones. I promised you we would have a new Papa Noël this year. Now the tree is complete," she said while she pinned a hook in his red coat with the fur collar, and placed him on the tree with the other ornaments.

Contributor Bios

Eric Andrews-Katz lives and writes in Seattle. His 'Agent Buck 98' mystery series includes *The Jesus Injection* and the (upcoming) sequel *Balls & Chain* from Bold Strokes Books. Other works are included in the anthologies: *So Fey, Best Date Ever, Charmed Lives, Zombiality, Gay City: Vols: 2, 3, & 4* (also co-edited), and many years of writing with the *Seattle Gay News*.

Rich Barnett lives in Rehoboth Beach, DE, and writes the popular "Camp Stories" column in *Letters from Camp Rehoboth*, a monthly LGBT magazine. In 2012, he published *The Discreet Charms of a Bourgeois Beach Town*, a humorous and slightly satiric portrait of Rehoboth Beach. His story "Crimes Against Nature" was published in *No Place Like Here: An Anthology of Southern Delaware Poetry and Prose*. It won first prize in the 2011 Delaware Press Association Communications Contest.

Sally Bellerose is author of *The Girls Club,* Bywater Books, winner of many awards including an NEA Fellowship. Her current project *Fishwives* features old women behaving badly. The title story won first place in the 2012 Saints and Sinners fiction contest, and an excerpt appeared in BLOOM Literary Magazine. Bellerose writes about class, sex, illness, absurdity, and lately, growing old. In her work, she loves to mess with rhythm, rhyme, and awkward emotion.

Born and raised in Chicago, **N.S. Beranek** received a Bachelor of Arts degree in Technical Theater and Design from Southern Illinois University at Carbondale in 1989 and from 1990 until

2009 was the Assistant Propmaster for Stage One: The Louisville Children's Theatre. Previous work includes "Thou Shalt Not Lie" in *Saints + Sinners 2013: New Fiction from the Festival* (Bold Strokes Books) and "There's No Question It's Love" in *Best Gay Romance 2014* (Cleis Press).

JEWELLE GOMEZ is a writer and activist and the author of the double Lambda Award-winning novel, *The Gilda Stories* which celebrates its 20th year in print in 2011. Among her other publications are three collections of poetry, a book of personal and political essays entitled *Forty-three Septembers*, and a collection of short fiction, *Don't Explain*. She is the recipient of a literature fellowship from the National Endowment for the Arts; two California Arts Council fellowships and an Individual Artist Commission from the San Francisco Arts Commission. Her new projects include a comic novel about black activists of the 1960s as they face middle age entitled *Televised*. Her new play, written in collaboration with Harry Waters Jr. is called *Waiting for Giovanni*. A dream play exploring the inner life of author James Baldwin, it had its world premiere at the New Conservatory Theatre Center in the Fall of 2011.

J.R. GREENWELL, from Louisville, KY, draws inspiration from larger-than-life characters by utilizing dry humor in often dark situations. He has been honored as a Saints and Sinners Short Fiction Contest finalist in 2011, 2012, 2013, and 2014. In 2011, he completed his memoir, *Teased Hair and the Quest for Tiaras*, and in 2013, his debut collection of short fiction, *Who the Hell is Rachel Wells?*, was published by Chelsea Station Editions.

WILLIAM HAWKINS lives in Baton Rouge but isn't married to the idea. He writes every day and is successful every other day.

ROBERT HYERS has been published in several magazines including *The Summerset Review* and *3:AM Magazine*. This is his second time as a finalist for the Saints and Sinners Short Fiction Contest. He has taught writing at a few different places, and was recently the Visiting Fiction Writer at River Pretty Writing Retreat.

George E. Jordan, art historian, was born in Kentucky, and lived in New Orleans for 20 years before moving to Connecticut in 1988. A free-lance writer and authority on Louisiana art, he wrote the art column for the Times Picayune in the 1970s. He has authored two books, and numerous articles for museum and art publications. Writing about gay life before the AIDS epidemic has been a parallel pursuit.

Jeff Lindemann is a graduate of Stephen F. Austin University located in the heart of East Texas, the regional setting for his short stories. He currently teaches composition and literature at Houston Community College. After a long career of teaching stories, he now writes them in a style he calls East Texas gothic. He has been published in the *Saints + Sinners: New Fiction from the Festival* in 2011, 2012, and 2013.

Jerry Rabushka is a playwright, novelist, songwriter, and musician. He won the 2012 Saints & Sinners Short Fiction Contest with *Wasted Courage* and the 2010 Saints & Sinners Playwriting Contest with *Brushup Ten*. His novel, *Star Bryan,* is published by Rebel Satori Press. He has many plays published by Brooklyn Publishers and Heuer Publishing, which have been produced nationwide. He is bandleader and composer for The Ragged Blade Band. He lives in St. Louis, MO, with his partner Isaac Cherry.

James Russell writes, blogs, and teaches in New Jersey, where he lives with his husband, who is an inspired and inspiring editor. His first novel, *Jesse Rules*, is about a closeted catholic schoolboy's fall from grace. He hopes to revive the short story collection and is in the process of building a collection around "Voodoo John" about obsession, heartbreak, and, to a lesser degree, love.

ABOUT THE EDITORS

AMIE M. EVANS has published over 56 short stories and essays as well as one novella. She is a creative-nonfiction and literary erotica writer. Evans is the co-editor of five volumes of *Saints + Sinners: New Fiction from the Festival* with Paul J. Willis and the anthology *Queer and Catholic* with Trebor Healey. She also writes gay male erotica under a pen name. Evans is on the board of directors of Saints and Sinners Literary Festival. She is a student in the Fashion Design Program at MassArt and has worked at Harvard University for 16 years. She is currently working on a memoir about food, religion and mothers as well as a satirical novel about saving lesbian sex.

PAUL J. WILLIS has over 20 years of experience in non-profit management. He earned a B.S. degree in Psychology and an M.S. degree in Communication. He started his administrative work in 1992 as the co-director for the Holos Foundation in Minneapolis. The Foundation operated an alternative high school program for at-risk youth. Willis has been the executive director for the Tennessee Williams/New Orleans Literary Festival since 2004. He is the founder of the Saints and Sinners Literary Festival (established in 2003), and has edited various anthologies including the award-winning *Love Bourbon Street* with his partner Greg Herren.

Saints and Sinners Literary Festival

The first Saints and Sinners Literary Festival took place in May of 2003. The event started as a new initiative designed as an innovative way to reach the community with information about HIV/AIDS. It was also formed to bring the LGBT community together to celebrate the literary arts. Literature has long nurtured hope and inspiration, and has provided an avenue of understanding. A steady stream of LGBT novels, short stories, poems, plays, and non-fiction works has served to awaken lesbians, gay men, bisexuals, and transgendered persons to the existence of others like them; to trace the outlines of a shared culture; and to bring the outside world into the emotional passages of LGBT life.

After the Stonewall Riots in New York City, gay and lesbian literature finally came 'out of the closet'. In time, noted authors such as Dorothy Allison, Michael Cunningham, and Mark Doty (all past Saints' participants) were receiving mainstream award recognition for their works. But there are still few opportunities for media attention of gay-themed books, and decreasing publishing options. This Festival helps to ensure that written work from the LGBT community will continue to have an outlet, and that people will have access to books that will help dispel stereotypes, alleviate isolation, and provide resources for personal wellness.

The event has since evolved into a collaborative effort between the Tennessee Williams/New Orleans Literary Festival and the NO/AIDS Task Force. The Saints and Sinners Literary Festival works to achieve the following goals:

1. To create an environment for productive networking to ensure increased knowledge and dissemination of LGBT literature;

2. To provide an atmosphere for discussion, brainstorming, and the emergence of new ideas;

3. To recognize and honor writers, editors, and publishers who broke new ground and made it possible for LGBT books to reach an audience; and

4. To provide a forum for authors, editors, and publishers to talk about their work for the benefit of emerging writers, and for the enjoyment of readers of LGBT literature.

Saints and Sinners is an annual celebration that takes place in the heart of the French Quarter of New Orleans in the month of May. The Festival includes writing workshops, readings, panel discussions, literary walking tours, and a variety of special events. We also aim to inspire the written word through our short fiction contest. Each year we induct individuals to our Saints and Sinners Hall of Fame. The Hall of Fame is intended to recognize people for their dedication to LGBT literature. Selected members have shown their passion for our literary community through various avenues including writing, promotion, publishing, editing, teaching, book-selling, and volunteerism.

Past year's inductees into the Saints and Sinners Literary Hall of Fame include: Dorothy Allison, Ann Bannon, Lucy Jane Bledsoe, Maureen Brady, Patrick Califia, Bernard Cooper, Jameson Currier, Mark Doty, Jim Duggins, Amie M. Evans, Otis Fennell, Michael Thomas Ford, Katherine V. Forrest, Nancy Garden, Jewelle Gomez, Jim Grimsley, Tara Hardy, Ellen Hart, Kenneth Holditch, Andrew Holleran, G. Winston James, Michele Karlsberg, Joan Larkin, Lee Lynch, Jeff Mann, William J. Mann, Marianne K. Martin, Stephen McCauley, Val McDermid, Tim Miller, Michael Nava, Achy Obejas, Felice Picano, Radclyffe, J.M. Redmann, David Rosen, Steven Saylor, Carol Seajay, Kelly Smith, Cecilia Tan, Patricia Nell Warren, Jess Wells, and Paul J. Willis.

For more information about the Saints and Sinners Literary Festival including sponsorship opportunities and our Archangel Membership Program, visit: www.sasfest.org. Be sure to sign up for our e-newsletter for updates for future programs. We hope you will join other writers and bibliophiles for a weekend of literary revelry not to be missed!

"Saints and Sinners is hands down one of the best places to go to revive a writer's spirit. Imagine a gathering in which you can lean into conversations with some of the best writers and editors and agents in the country, all of them speaking frankly and passionately about the books, stories and people they love and hate and want most to record in some indelible way. Imagine a community that tells you truthfully what is happening with writing and publishing in the world you most want to reach. Imagine the flirting, the arguing, the teasing and praising and exchanging of not just vital information, but the whole spirit of queer arts and creating. Then imagine it all taking place on the sultry streets of New Orleans' French Quarter. That's Saints and Sinners—the best wellspring of inspiration and enthusiasm you are going to find. Go there."

—Dorothy Allison, National Book Award finalist
for *Bastard Out of Carolina*, and author
of the critically acclaimed novel *Cavedweller*.